Lithic Technologies in
Sedentary Societies

LITHIC TECHNOLOGIES
in Sedentary Societies

EDITED BY
Rachel A. Horowitz
and **Grant S. McCall**

UNIVERSITY PRESS OF COLORADO
Louisville

© 2019 by University Press of Colorado

Published by University Press of Colorado
245 Century Circle, Suite 202
Louisville, Colorado 80027

All rights reserved
Printed in the United States of America

 The University Press of Colorado is a proud member of the Association of University Presses.

The University Press of Colorado is a cooperative publishing enterprise supported, in part, by Adams State University, Colorado State University, Fort Lewis College, Metropolitan State University of Denver, Regis University, University of Colorado, University of Northern Colorado, Utah State University, and Western State Colorado University.

∞ This paper meets the requirements of the ANSI/NISO Z39.48-1992 (Permanence of Paper).

ISBN: 978-1-60732-890-2 (cloth)
ISBN: 978-1-60732-892-6 (ebook)
DOI: https://doi.org/10.5876/9781607328926

Library of Congress Cataloging-in-Publication Data

Names: Horowitz, Rachel A., editor. | McCall, Grant S., editor.
Title: Lithic technologies in sedentary societies / edited by Rachel A. Horowitz and Grant S. McCall.
Description: Louisville : University Press of Colorado, [2018] | Includes bibliographical references and index.
Identifiers: LCCN 2019000678| ISBN 9781607328902 (cloth) | ISBN 9781607328926 (ebook)
Subjects: LCSH: Stone implements—Analysis. | Tools, Prehistoric—Analysis. | Prehistoric peoples—Antiquities. | Economics, Prehistoric. | Excavations (Archaeology)
Classification: LCC CC79.5.S76 L57754 2018 | DDC 930.1/2—dc23
LC record available at https://lccn.loc.gov/2019000678

Cover photographs by Francesca Manclossi.

Contents

List of Figures   vii
List of Tables   xiii
Acknowledgments   xv

1 Lithics in Sedentary Societies: Themes, Methods, and Directions
   Rachel A. Horowitz and Grant S. McCall   3

2 Urban Lithics: The Role of Stone Tools in the Indus Civilization and at Harappa
   Mary A. Davis   36

3 The Importance of Being Ad Hoc: Patterns and Implications of Expedient Lithic Production in the Bronze Age in Israel
   Francesca Manclossi and Steven A Rosen   69

4 Leaving No Stone Unturned: Expedient Lithic Production among Preclassic Households of San Estevan, Belize, and K'o and Hamontún, Guatemala
   Jason S.R. Paling   89

5 The Economic Organization of the Extraction and Production of Utilitarian Chert Tools in the Mopan Valley, Belize
   Rachel A. Horowitz   139

6   Chert at Chalcatzingo: Implications of Knapping Strategies and Technological Organization for Formative Economics
    Grant S. McCall, Rachel A. Horowitz, and Dan M. Healan   164

7   Unraveling Sociopolitical Organization Using Lithic Data: A Case Study from an Agricultural Society in the American Southwest
    Fumiyasu Arakawa   184

8   Using Portable X-Ray Fluorescence (pXRF) to Source Burlington Chert from the Carson Site, 22CO505, Coahoma County, Mississippi
    Jayur Madhusudan Mehta, Grant S. McCall, Theodore Marks, and James Enloe   208

9   Stone Age Economics: Efficiency, Blades, Specialization, and Obsolescence
    John C. Whittaker   229

    List of Contributors   245
    Index   249

Figures

2.1.	Map of Indus region with location of sites and raw materials mentioned in the text	40
2.2.	Rohri Hills landscape	42
2.3.	Artifact scatters likely dating to the Paleolithic and Harappan periods	42
2.4.	Harappan period quarry sites	43
2.5.	Production areas in Rohri Hills region	44
2.6.	Sample of lithics including artifacts associated with primary and secondary production at Harappa	46
2.7.	Example of precore from Harappan Museum Collection	46
2.8.	Raw material by time period at Harappa	50
2.9.	Example of complete blade from Harappan Museum Collection	51
2.10.	Examples of blade segments and raw materials from HARP sample	52
2.11.	Map of the site of Harappa with proposed neighborhoods	53
3.1.	Frequencies of the ad hoc industry according to the techno-typological classes produced in various steps of the reduction sequence	71
3.2.	Frequencies of different types of texture of raw material used for the ad hoc industry	73
3.3.	Ad hoc core dimensions	74

3.4.	Technological analysis of ad hoc cores showing isolated removals and series of contiguous removals	75
3.5.	Ad hoc core permutations	76
3.6.	Technological analysis of ad hoc cores	77
3.7.	Technological analysis of ad hoc cores	79
3.8.	Retouched and unretouched flake dimensions	80
3.9.	Proportion of cortex on flakes	81
3.10.	Scar patterns plotted against flakes and flake tools	82
3.11.	Typical ad hoc blanks and tools	83
4.1.	Northern Belize Chert-bearing Zone and chert- and chalcedony-bearing soils in northern Belize	91
4.2.	Map of Maya area, showing the location of San Estevan and Holmul region	92
4.3.	Thin oval biface from San Estevan	107
4.4.	General Utility Biface from Hamontún	107
4.5.	Polished bifacial celt distal fragment from San Estevan	107
4.6.	Eccentric from San Estevan	107
4.7.	Informal biface from San Estevan	107
4.8.	Chert blade from San Estevan	107
4.9.	Proximal, medial, and distal fragments of macroblades from San Estevan	108
4.10.	Stemmed macroblade	108
4.11.	Notch from K'o	108
4.12.	Spur notched perforator	108
4.13.	Burin spall perforators from San Estevan	108
4.14.	Denticulates from San Estevan	108
4.15.	Polyhedral cores	109
4.16.	Spherical hammerstone from Hamontún	109

5.1.	Map showing the location of research	141
5.2.	Map of Callar Creek Quarry illustrating the layout of the quarry, production, and household areas	144
5.3.	Map of San Lorenzo, SL-28, illustrating the layout of the quarry, production, and household areas	145
5.4.	Map of Succotz, TA2-001, illustrating the layout of the quarry, production, and household areas	146
5.5.	Photograph of the quarry cut from Callar Creek Quarry	147
5.6.	Photographs of typical cores and flakes from Callar Creek Quarry	149
5.7.	Image of the sherd with the Buenavista device fragment	153
5.8.	Drawing of the Buenavista device	153
6.1.	Location of Chalcatzingo in Morelos, Mexico	166
6.2.	Sample of representative flakes from Chalcatzingo chert assemblage	170
6.3.	Representative sample of cores from Chalcatzingo chert assemblage	170
6.4.	Sample of retouched tools from Chalcatzingo chert assemblage	171
6.5.	Histogram showing longest linear dimensions of whole cores	172
6.6.	Histogram showing masses of whole cores	173
6.7.	Histogram showing lengths of whole flakes	174
6.8.	Histogram showing masses of whole flakes	175
6.9.	Bar chart showing frequencies of striking platform facet patterns	175
6.10.	Histogram showing striking platform widths	176
6.11.	Closed system lithic raw material acquisition dynamics at Chalcatzingo	180

7.1.	Study area of the central Mesa Verde region	187
7.2.	The Tewa world	189
7.3.	Map showing the reconnaissance in the upper portions of Yellow Jacket Canyon	191
7.4.	Map showing all three pueblos and outcrops/quarries of KDB SS	193
7.5.	Interaction and exchange systems for obsidian connecting the central Mesa Verde region to other portions of the Southwest	197
7.6.	Possible destination areas by the ancestral Pueblo people in the central Mesa Verde region	198
7.7.	Frequency of obsidian artifacts in total chipped stone assemblages, by time period	199
7.8.	Proportion of obsidian points and non-local bowl sherds through time	200
8.1.	Locations of Burlington chert outcrops in northern Arkansas and south-central Missouri	210
8.2.	Location of the Carson site relative to Burlington chert resources	212
8.3.	Microlithic Burlington chert drills from Structure 1 at Carson	215
8.4.	Archaeological features inside the Carson site excavation	217
8.5.	Carson samples, Arkansas Ozark material, and Crescent Quarry material	220
9.1.	Underside of a typical old threshing sledge (*duven*) in Kastamonu, Turkey	232
9.2.	Closer view of the flint blades inset into the underside of the threshing sledge	233
9.3.	Waste cores from blade making, Çakmak, Turkey	234
9.4.	Retired knapper Nihat Yilmaz demonstrates flaking, Harmancik, Turkey	235

9.5. Flintlock mechanism 236
9.6. British gunflint blades segmented to produce characteristic waste bits and finished rectangular gunflints 237

Tables

2.1.	Indus Tradition chronology	38
2.2.	Chronology for the site of Harappa	39
2.3.	Count and percentage of Harappan (HARP) lithic sample by major artifact type	47
2.4.	Frequency of cortex in Harappan (HARP) sample	47
2.5.	Quantitative measures of blade tools from Harappan (HARP) sample	47
2.6.	Ratios of blade segments at Indus sites	54
2.7.	Spatial distribution of raw material by neighborhood	55
2.8.	Invasiveness of edge modification	57
2.9.	Edge damage class	57
4.1.	Technological descriptions of Preclassic lithic tools	103
4.2.	Frequency of each tool type across each site and period	112
4.3.	Percentage of tool classes across each site and period	117
4.4.	Frequency of non-cortical versus cortical lithic debitage across each site and period	122
4.5.	Utilized flakes	123
5.1.	Frequency of core types at Callar Creek Quarry	148

5.2.	Table showing lithic density (by excavation area/volume) for households from the upper Belize River valley	155
6.1.	Count by tool type of items from the Chalcatzingo assemblage	169
6.2.	Descriptive statistics for length and mass of materials	174
7.1.	Summary of the stb (standard slope estimates) from the Basketmaker III to late Pueblo III periods	195
8.1.	Counts of archaeological samples and geological samples used in the study	216
8.2.	Results of the discriminant function analysis	218
8.3.	Wilks's Lambda from the discriminant function analysis	219

Acknowledgments

This volume began as a session at the 2015 SAAs in San Francisco, California. Several of the original participants in this session could not contribute to this volume (Jason Barrett and Zach Hruby, Theresa Raczek, Caroline Schmidt and Ryan Parish, Nick Kardoulis, and Jason Nesbitt), but we appreciate their participation in the session and the exchange of ideas that occurred during this gathering. We have added several other authors to expand our geographic and temporal coverage as well, and we thank these contributors for their participation.

Many thanks to Jessica d'Arbonne, formerly at University Press of Colorado, for her assistance and her patience as we prepared the volume. Thanks also to Charlotte Steinhardt for taking over preparation of the volume.

RAH would like to thank Marcello Canuto, Jason Nesbitt, Caroline Parris, Erin Patterson, Jason Yaeger, Bernadette Cap, and Lisa Fontes for discussions that led to ideas present in this volume. Thanks also to Carol, Joel, and Sarah Horowitz for their support.

Lithic Technologies in Sedentary Societies

1

Lithics in Sedentary Societies

Themes, Methods, and Directions

RACHEL A. HOROWITZ AND
GRANT S. MCCALL

Archaeologists studying sedentary, hierarchical societies have offered vivid accounts of many striking forms of material culture: monuments requiring complex engineering and massive investments of labor; crafts requiring enormous skill and specialized networks of production and distribution; prestige goods marking the wealth, status, and power of elites; and other manifestations of social complexity too numerous to list. Similarly, archaeologists studying stone tools have documented an endlessly diverse range of complex core reduction and tool manufacture practices: thinned bifacial projectile points, the Levallois technique, prismatic blade production, obsidian and chert eccentrics, and countless others. In certain instances, stone tool production in sedentary societies itself took the form of a specialized craft—for example, the production of obsidian blades in Mesoamerica or Neolithic daggers in Scandinavia—and it has thus been studied by the nexus of those concerned with both sedentary societies and stone tools. Unfortunately, however, the vast majority of lithic production in sedentary societies (which tended to be informal and expedient) has received very little attention.

This volume presents case studies of lithics in sedentary societies around the world. The chapters generally reflect the traditional directions of lithic studies in sedentary societies and emphasize the important information lithics can provide about anthropological questions of interest to scholars of sedentary societies.

DOI: 10.5876/9781607328926.c001

This chapter reviews some of the general trends in global analyses of lithic technology and draws on the chapters in this volume to discuss directions for future research and the relevance of lithic studies to broader anthropological questions. This chapter is organized around four general themes: (1) what lithics can and cannot tell us about sedentary societies, (2) why we should study informal/expedient lithic technologies, (3) how studies of specialized stone tool production fit into the archaeology of both lithics and sedentary societies, and (4) how we build a better approach to the archaeology of stone tools in contexts in which they have generally been ignored up to this point.

Our answers to these questions point to some broader theoretical issues in terms of our reconstruction and modeling of prehistoric economic systems. On the one hand, we find fault with the overwhelming—sometimes seemingly exclusive—focus on production. Our conceptions of production in sedentary societies have articulated well with the latter-day preference for theories based on agency and practice. Yet as this book will show, there are many instances in which unspecialized forms of economic activity profoundly reflect important dynamics of both everyday life and the broader organization of prehistoric economies. Conversely, when stone tools are the result of craft specialization, there are many aspects of their manufacture that may shed light on prehistoric social and economic systems that go beyond a simple sequence of production, the acquisition of a craftsperson's skill, or the elite control of economic commodities. The chapters in this book shed light on these problems and explore some ways forward.

LITHICS IN SEDENTARY SOCIETIES

One axiom about the archaeology of stone tools is that as the most durable form of artifact in the archaeological record, lithics virtually last forever. As such, they are often the *only* remaining manifestation of the activities of our hunter-gatherer ancestors. Thankfully, mobile forager societies often did us the favor of producing handsome and complex lithic technologies, and the field of archaeology has done (relatively) well in relating this inherently unfamiliar form of artifactual patterning with the life ways of long-dead hunter-gatherers, especially in terms of subsistence and mobility. Put simply, hunter-gatherer archaeologists have paid so much attention to stone tools because we have not had many other options.

In contrast, more recent sedentary societies have usually left behind a bewildering diversity of durable garbage, and archaeologists of sedentary societies have therefore tended to focus on more familiar or more striking phenomena or both. (*Never mind that pile of broken rocks; let's go explore that pyramid.*) In addition, relative to other forms of material culture, such as ceramics, lithics aren't even terribly chronologically or culture-historically diagnostic. Thus, for eminently understandable reasons, archaeologists of sedentary societies have tended to prioritize research on monuments, burials, tombs, palaces, jewelry, and ceramics and not studies of lithic technology. Sometimes certain specialized forms of lithic manufacture have been dazzling enough to warrant investigation alongside these other trappings of complexity, though such instances are comparatively rare. Furthermore, the outcomes of such research have tended to be understood with reference to the power of elites, which is, after all, probably reflected better by other forms of material remains, such as those listed above.

Another axiom of lithic analysis is that stone tool technology is reductive; that is, the process of producing and recycling stone tools involves taking large rocks and systematically breaking them to produce smaller rocks. This process of systematically detaching pieces from lithic objects (e.g., reducing cores, thinning bifaces, retouching blanks, and the like) results in an inferable sequence of technical procedures, or a *chaîne opératoire*, spanning the initial acquisition of lithic raw materials to the ultimate deposition of lithics into the stasis of the archaeological record. In some cases, entire sequences of technical operations took place at a single location, and thus such sites may include evidence concerning the complete life history of the stone tools present at them. In other cases, different stages of the operational sequences involved in stone tool reduction took place at different locations, reflecting mobility or the exchange of lithics as an economic commodity or some combination of the two. Reconstructing the operational sequences involved in stone tool production, as well as the spatial distribution of the various stages of these sequences of reduction, provides an invaluable window on the economic activities and decisions faced by prehistoric peoples involved in the production, exchange, and consumption of lithic technology.

On this point, we come to an important truth about the nature of lithic technology in the lives of past peoples in sedentary or complex societies or both: stone tools were probably not that important relative to other forms of technology and other economic concerns. Disasters happened when crops failed, when water sources dried up, when deadly diseases struck, or when enemy neighbors attacked. In contrast, it was perhaps a modest inconvenience when tool stone became scarce, when working edges became dull, when bifaces broke, or when the blades ran out. Unlike other aspects of economic production, lithic technology was seldom a life-or-death issue for prehistoric peoples (excepting perhaps the rare craft specialists whose livelihoods depended on stone tool production).

This does not mean, however, that archaeological stone tools cannot provide profoundly important information about the lives of prehistoric peoples. Stone tools may not have been as important as all of the other economic commodities exchanged through the trade networks linking polities in various complex societies. Yet by virtue of their durability, their reductive transformation from the quarry to point of consumption and discard, and the spatial variation in the diagnostic waste associated with different stages of reduction, stone tools may be crucial sources of information about the organization of exchange networks over space and time. All the perishable goods that flowed through those exchange networks—goods on which people's lives often literally depended—may be long gone, leaving behind little or no trace. But the archaeological record of the stone tools that flowed through those exchange networks remains, layered with sequential information concerning the activities of the people who produced them, exchanged them, used them, and threw them away.

Likewise, for farmers, assuring the availability of appropriate lithic technology was likely a rather ephemeral issue relative to the planting, tending, harvesting, and processing of food crops—economic activities on which the lives of family members directly depended. Sometimes, of course, stone tools were specialized components of composite tools that were fairly important in agricultural activities, such as sickle blades or the *tribula* of threshing sledges. Such forms of agricultural lithic technology have indeed received significant attention from archaeologists (e.g., Anderson et al. 2004; Kardulias 2008; Whittaker 1996, 2003, 2014a, 2014b, 2014c; Whittaker et al. 2009, this volume; Yerkes 2000), and rightly so. More often than not, however, stone tools were used to manufacture and maintain the components of other tools and weapons (McCall 2012). And since there is almost always *some* usable stone around *somewhere*, assuring the presence of appropriate lithic technology usually boiled down to a set of tactics for minimizing inconvenience in finding stone and reducing cores.

Yet while the vital economic activities of farmers usually left little or no trace in the archaeological record, the stone tools associated with these agricultural economic tasks are permanently present, often in cyclopean quantities. Once again, we can make inferences about the sequences of technical activities involved in the manufacture and use of stone tools in such contexts. These operational sequences were articulated with the broader organization of economic activities in which agricultural peoples were involved, and the structure of economic activities within agricultural systems conditioned the activities involved in the production of stone tools. We can learn indispensable things about the organization of agricultural economies by investigating how, when, and where people (1) acquired tool stone, (2) reduced cores and produced tools, (3) used tools in different ways over the course of their use-lives, and (4) discarded spent tools in the context of other refuse. Therefore, while the expedient flaking of some chert core in the residential compound of some ancient Mesoamerican farmstead may not be very interesting in its own right (see McCall et al., this volume), the articulation of knapping activities over space and time with the life-and-death economic activities of those farmers can provide uniquely important information about the life ways of long-dead peoples. Lithic technology, in a sense, *mapped onto* the economic activities of agricultural peoples that we would like to know more about.

Finally, there is a third axiom about lithic technology: it is globally and temporally ubiquitous in prehistory. Prior to the spread of metallurgy, stone tools had been produced by virtually every prehistoric society on every inhabited continent, from Plio-Pleistocene australopiths in the Rift Valley of sub-Saharan Africa to the sixteenth-century Aztecs of central Mexico. In fact, many resourceful peoples in complex societies continued to produce stone tools long after the advent of metal counterparts (see Davis, Manclossi and Rosen, and Whittaker, this volume), in part because of the widespread (although uneven) distribution of suitable lithic raw material sources. And a reasonable number of modern peoples continue to produce stone tools today (see McCall 2012 for discussion).

One implication of all this is that the archaeological record of stone tools is immense, diverse, and associated with nearly all past peoples. The other implication is that we can surely profit from studying variability in lithic technology over the vast diversity of contexts in which it may be found. We have accomplished this, at least to some extent, in our examinations of prehistoric hunter-gatherer technological systems, where we have demonstrated that stone tool technologies tend to vary in relation to mobility, settlement systems, and subsistence strategies. Yet our understanding of the lithic technologies of sedentary societies remains relatively poor, and in these cases the conventional hunter-gatherer organizational currencies of mobility/settlement and subsistence do not make sense. Obviously, a better empirical understanding of these cases is needed, as is a better theoretical toolkit for making sense of lithic variability as we continue to document it.

Chapters in this book build on a certain set of theoretical innovations in the study of the lithic technological systems present among sedentary agricultural societies. Specifically, the chapters examine the ways lithics may provide information about economic activity, political organization, resource and production management, and the relationship between societal and technological change. Lithics are perhaps most commonly studied in sedentary societies as a way of understanding the segmentation and organization of past economic systems (Druart 2010; McDonald 1991; Parry and Kelly 1987; Rosen 2010; Sorensen 2010; Teltser 1991; Torrence 1984, 1986; Horowitz, McCall et al., and Paling, this volume). Lithic distribution patterns have sometimes been used as indicators of various types of economic activities, vectors of resource distribution, and the relevant involvement of different individuals in economic activity (i.e., market exchange; Garraty 2009; Hirth 1998, 2010; Minc 2006, 2009; Santone 1993; Speal 2009; Stark and Garraty 2010).

These sorts of theoretical approaches to the study of lithic technology have been particularly prevalent in the archaeology of Mesoamerica, as exemplified by the three Mesoamerican chapters in the volume (Horowitz, McCall et al., and Paling). All three chapters focus on the importance of formal and informal tools in various aspects of Mesoamerican economies, pointing out in all cases that household residents participated in many aspects of lithic production, particularly of informal tools. These chapters illustrate the variability of lithic production across Mesoamerica, in particular the presence of both formal and informal tool technologies, a phenomenon discussed further below and by Manclossi and Rosen, and McCall et al. (this volume).

Our understanding of prehistoric economic strategies, variability among economic activities, and the actors involved in lithic economies affects our understandings of economic variables as sources of power for individuals of varying socioeconomic and political statuses, hence facilitating information on political organization and sources of power (see Schroeder 2005). In this volume, Arakawa provides an example of such studies from the southwestern United States. He uses lithics as a marker of sociopolitical organization, particularly for examining territoriality and the movement of populations. Similarly, Mehta and colleagues (this volume) address the role of political influence from other areas on the obtention of chert materials in the Lower Mississippi Valley, particularly the Carson site. The use of lithics to address economic and sociopolitical organization enhances our abilities to examine these systems in the past, particularly highlighting the ways different materials may illustrate variability in such systems, or throughout their use-life (see Appadurai 1986).

Another direction in the study of stone tool technology is the organization of resource procurement, particularly in terms of the management of lithic raw material sources. Within sedentary societies, extensive variability exists in the ways raw material sources were managed. In many Egyptian, Greco-Roman, and Inka contexts, quarry areas for building materials and tool construction, and the resultant products, were under some degree of imperial control (Cantarutti 2013; Degryse et al. 2009; Harrell and Storemyr 2009; Jennings et al. 2013; Kelany et al. 2009; Lollet et al. 2008; McCallum 2009; Ogburn 2011, 2013; Peacock and Maxfield 2007; Teather 2011; Torrence 1984; Tripcevich and Contreras 2011, 2013; Weisberber 1983). Evidence for such control takes the form of (1) organized work areas, including storage facilities (Cantarutti 2013; Harrell and Storemyr 2009; Storemyr et al. 2010); (2) transportation routes (Harrell and Storemyr 2009; Heldal 2009; Kelany et al. 2009; Ogburn 2013; Storemyr et al. 2010); (3) the scale and organization of production (Heldal 2009; Salazar et al. 2013); (4) widespread distribution of finished products (McCallum 2009); (5) organized villages for workers (Harrell and Storemyr 2009; Peacock and Maxfield 2007); and (6) state-sponsored ritual in and around work areas (Vaughn et al. 2013). Less evidence, however, exists in other areas of the world for such strict top-down management (i.e., Cobb 1988, 2000; Horowitz 2015, 2017, 2018; King 2000; Horowitz, this volume). This is an indication that there is variability in the management of lithic resources in sedentary societies and that this variability may shed light on the nature of prehistoric social, economic, and political systems.

The manufacture techniques involved in lithic production are perhaps the most widely studied aspect of stone tool technologies in sedentary societies, as they have often been linked to broader features of economic organization in prehistoric societies (Chinchilla Mazariegos 2011; de Leon 2008; Dolores Soto 2005; Gaxiola Gonzalez 2005; Gaxiola Gonzalez and Guevara 1989; Healan 1989, 2002, 2003; Hirth 2011; Kerley 1989; Lewis 1995; Parry 2002). Such studies focus on the location of production, continuity/regularity of production, and management of production activities by non-craft producers. The temporality of production (full-time versus part-time specialization, intermittent production, multicrafting) is an arena of great debate among scholars, both in how one determines production amounts and also concerning the importance of such production activities for understanding the involvement of various actors in different aspects of production (see Costin 1991, 1996, 2000, 2004; Costin and Hagstrum 1995; Hirth 2009 for more details). Determining the relationship between craft producers and other individuals can be complicated (see Carballo 2013; Hirth 2009, 2011), although establishing such relationships can provide information about the economic implications of production activities.

Perhaps one of the most important emerging avenues of discussion/elaboration in studying lithics in sedentary societies involves technological change and what it can tell us about change in other aspects of society. While major social and economic transitions may not always be reflected in lithic technological systems (e.g., McCall and Horowitz 2014), major periods of technological change can often signal profound shifts in prehistoric socioeconomic systems. As Marx (1971 [1859]: 109) commented in *Das Kapital*, "The hand-mill gives you society with the feudal lord; the steam-mill society with the industrial capitalist." On the one hand, we doubt that the obsidian prismatic blade gives you Mesoamerican civilization or any other equivalent sentiment for other times and places. On the other hand, we are confident that major changes in prehistoric social, economic, and political systems were indeed reflected in archaeological patterning associated with the production, distribution, and consumption of lithic technological resources.

Chapters in this book address two areas of particular interest to technological change in sedentary societies: the advent of metallurgy and the changes to technology that occur with cultural contact. In many cases, after the introduction of metal, stone tools were no longer utilized. In others, lithic use continued for longer periods of time. In some cases, tools that continued to be produced from stone were those for which the functional characteristics of raw materials were superior to metal or when lithics were used for ritual purposes (Bamforth 1993; Bronowicki and Masojc 2010; Cobb 2003a, 2003b; Cobb and Pope 1998; Cobb and Ruggiero 2003; Flexner and Morgan 2013; Frieman 2010; Johnson 1997, 2003; Karimali 2010; McCall 2012; Odell 2001, 2003; Raczek 2010; van Gijn 2010; Davis, this volume; Manclossi and Rosen, this volume). The longest-lasting of these examples is gunflints, made in Europe and the Americas from the early 1500s to the late 1800s (Kenmotsu 1990; Kent 1983; Watt and Horowitz 2017; White 1975; Whittaker 2001; Woodall et al. 1997).

Other examples in sedentary societies include blades for sickle production in the Near East (Whittaker 1996, 2003, this volume; Whittaker et al. 2009; Yerkes 2000) and other types of tools in the circum-Mediterranean world (Eriksen 2010; Kardulias 2008, 2009; Milevski 2013; Rosen 1996). Blade production for use as parts of sickles and threshing sleds continued after the advent of metal; Canaanean blade technology in the Near East began in the Early Bronze Age (Rosen 1983, 1997), in conjunction with the advent of metallurgy (Anderson et al. 2004; Rosen 1996, 1997; Rosen et al. 2014). In some areas of the Mediterranean, the Balkans, and the Black Sea, the threshing industry, using stone blades, continued as late as the 1950s in Cyprus and the 1980s in some areas of western Turkey, probably as an extension of the techniques that began in the Bronze Age (Anderson et al. 2004; Kardulias 2008; Whittaker 1996, 2003, 2014a, 2014b, 2014c, this volume; Whittaker et al. 2009; Yerkes 2000). The persistence of specialized lithic technology beyond the introduction of metal tools adds complexity to our understanding of how technologies change and what this can tell us about the ways technological change reflects—or does not reflect—broader patterns of sociopolitical organization. In this case, the continuity of some lithic production traditions in conjunction with the production of new tool types of different materials highlights the importance of raw material properties for specific tasks and the continuity of tools that are best for such tasks.

In other cases, lithic technology persisted past the appearance of metal for other economic reasons. Lithics often offer a cheap and effective alternative to metal tools in situations in which the latter may be difficult or expensive to acquire. In this volume, Manclossi and Rosen describe the persistence of expedient lithic technologies into the Near Eastern Bronze Age. In this case, and others like it in the early metal ages, stone tools weren't necessarily more functionally effective than their metal counterparts, but they were much cheaper and ubiquitously available. Resourceful peoples around the world and into the modern day have repeatedly returned to basic practices of stone tool production in situations where metal is hard to find, expensive, or otherwise impractical.

Another widespread example of this phenomenon involves the knapping of new materials, especially bottle glass (Johnson 1997; Raczek 2010; Shott and Weedman 2007; Weedman 2000, 2002, 2006; see also McCall 2012). Glass knapping is particularly interesting because it often occurs alongside the use of metal tools and as a continuation of older practices of stone knapping. In Ethiopia, modern hideworkers produce and use glass scrapers, which may have functional advantages over putative metal counterparts and which are cheaper than scrapers made on chert or obsidian, since lithic raw material sources are often tightly controlled by local clans and stone is often sold in markets at considerable cost (Weedman 2000, 2002, 2006). Here, glass knapping provides a more effective solution to the technical problems than does metal and is a cheap alternative to knapped stone.

The utilization of knapped glass has also been documented among the Highland and Lacandon Maya (Clark 1989, 1991; Deal and Hayden 1987; Hayden and Deal 1989; Maler 1902; Tozzer 1907; see also Weigand 1989). Under one set of circumstances, expediently knapped glass, which is often salvaged from garbage deposits, provides a cheap and easy solution in the manufacture and maintenance of wood, bone, and leather components of other tools. In other situations, glass has replaced obsidian in the manufacture of tools for rituals, such as blood-letting ceremonies. Obsidian is generally hard to come by in the modern Maya world, but glass is not. Thus glass as an obsidian replacement facilitates the continuation of an ancient set of ritual practices using a modern raw material. In general, the production of glass tools informs us about how technological change co-occurs with changing social and political interactions and the impact of colonial contact on material culture (e.g., Chatfield 2013; Harrison-Buck et al. 2013; Tolmie 2013).

While variation among the lithic technologies of sedentary societies is immense, the chapters in this book focus on a central distinction between the production of *informal tools*, which are often expedient and take the form of utilized flakes produced from locally occurring raw material sources, and the production of *formal tools*, which are often complex in their design, require considerable skill on the part of the craftspeople who produce them, and are often distributed widely from their sources through extensive networks of exchange. We recognize that this distinction likely retains some of the baggage of the culture-historical focus of the early field of archaeology, as well as the typological tunnel vision of early approaches to lithic analysis. But we have to start somewhere, and learning about the sources of this distinction, as well as the nature of variation within these two categories, can be seen as a first step in using lithic technology to understand the social, economic, and political systems of sedentary agricultural societies.

INFORMAL TOOLS, OR THE COMPLEXITY OF THE INFORMAL

As Nelson (1991) and Andrefsky (2005) define them, *informal tools* are unstandardized, require minimal effort in construction, and are produced with immediately available raw materials and with little concern for the final tool form. *Formal tools* require more effort, planning, and skill in their manufacture and are more costly in terms of production effort and raw material quality, but they hold added value in terms of their design, such as increased versatility, maintainability, or effectiveness relative to some specific function. As an overlapping concept, Binford (1976) defines *expediency* as the ad hoc production of a tool from immediately available materials for the resolution of some immediate technical problem, followed by the immediate discard of the tool once its use has been completed. Binford contrasts expediency with *curation*, which refers to the retention of a tool for some period of time in anticipation of a future need.

The field of archaeology has not fully recovered from the confusion surrounding these concepts (e.g., Shott 1996). We stress that expediency and curation are not merely contrasting strategic options available to individuals in making decisions about their technology and that informal tools may sometimes be curated and formal tools may sometimes be used expediently. Furthermore, the distinction between informal and formal tools offers a simple vocabulary for talking about the basic formal qualities of stone tools in the archaeological record and the manufacture processes through which they were produced. Expediency and curation are a vocabulary for talking about the technological strategies employed by past peoples, about which we strive to make inferences based on the things we find in the archaeological record.

Some time ago, archaeologists studying sedentary agricultural societies and the lithic technologies they produced had to come to grips with the fact that many—perhaps most—of these lithic technologies are dominated by the production of informal tools, which provides evidence for largely expedient lithic technological systems. Much of our way of thinking about this situation stems from the influential paper by Parry and Kelly (1987), which argues that sedentism results in the stockpiling of lithic raw materials within residential units, meaning that people no longer needed to conserve these materials by producing complex formal tools (e.g., bifaces, blades), as did most mobile hunter-gatherers. Thus sedentary peoples tended to utilize unretouched flakes produced expediently from cores made on raw materials stored at residential units.

Parry and Kelly's (1987) generalization about the lithic technology associated with sedentary societies has been remarkably durable, even in the light of three decades of subsequent research. Likewise, their theoretical explanation of this empirical generalization has remained fairly popular because of its clear intuitive appeal. While the Parry and Kelly paper has propelled the field forward in thinking about the sources of variability in the lithic technologies of prehistoric societies, some cracks in the foundation of this model have become apparent. For one thing, as we discuss in more detail below, there are many cases in which the facts defy the Parry and Kelly generalization (see also Cobb and Webb 1994; Hofman 1987; McNerney 1987). We approach this issue in the next section, which deals with specialized lithic technologies.

For another thing, there are some problems with the Parry and Kelly (1987) theoretical explanation of the prevalence of expedient/informal lithic technologies in sedentary societies. Specifically, in both archaeological and ethnographic cases of stone tool production, the evidence for lithic raw material abundance and stockpiling at residential centers is scarce. In this volume, McCall and colleagues examine a dimension of this problem at the site of Chalcatzingo. Here, prehistoric knappers collected locally available chert and knapped it using informal/expedient knapping strategies—all in keeping with the Parry and Kelly model. In contrast, in many cases the Chalcatzingo chert knappers reduced cores to almost ridiculous extremes, including through the use of bipolar percussion. Clearly, knappers at Chalcatzingo were concerned with economizing raw material in the reduction of chert cores. However, they achieved this goal through the exhaustive use of informal strategies of core reduction rather than adoption of more formal methods of core reduction for the purposes of raw material economy, such as bifacial thinning or prismatic blade production. Furthermore, there is no evidence for stockpiling in this case or in many others like it.

Similarly, Manclossi and Rosen (this volume) find continuity in the informal, or ad hoc, lithic industries associated with metal technologies in the Near East, and they attribute more formal lithic technologies to the rise of specialization in lithic production. Increased specialization led to a decrease in lithic production skill by other knappers, hence increasing the importance of these informal but common tools created by individuals as needed. The causes of informal tool technologies illustrate the importance of the detailed examination of those technologies, as such technologies inform us about the organizational dynamics of past societies. Once again, Manclossi and Rosen show that the Parry and Kelly (1987) model only partially tells the story of informal lithic technologies in the later prehistory of the Near East. Studies such as these help demonstrate the vital importance of understanding informal stone tool industries in sedentary societies and of doing so in a way that focuses on the isolation of strategic variability over space and time. Doing so will allow us to get beyond the Parry and Kelly (1987) model—successful though it has been—to build a better framework for making inferences about the economic and social contingencies that shaped the lives of individuals in past sedentary farming societies.

Building an analytical framework for making sense of variability among informal stone tool industries in sedentary societies may also allow us to improve upon a preoccupation with craft production both as the basis of individual economic activity and as the source of identity at its many scales. A great deal of archaeological theory in the twenty-first century, especially that dealing with complex societies, has been based on concepts of agency and practice (Bourdieu 1977; Dobres and Robb 2000; Giddens 1979). For example, in examining the production of obsidian eccentrics at the Classic Maya site of Piedras Negras, Hruby (2007) argues that the highly complex and ritually structured knapping practices involved in producing this extreme form of prestige good were themselves key mechanisms in the embodiment of both individual and collective identity.

Agency and practice theory puts a premium on the study of craft production involving products with distinctive formal characteristics and complex sequences of production activities, usually those involving great skill on the part of the craftsperson. In lithic technology terms, Hruby's (2007) study of Maya eccentrics fits the bill perfectly. Yet expedient and informal technologies, such as those endemic to large numbers of sedentary societies, hold little appeal for those interested in agency and practice. To put it bluntly, it is hard to argue that a prehistoric farmer who expediently removed a sequence of flakes from some core lying around the farm somehow embodied her identity in doing so when it was the geometry of the core and perhaps the immediate contingencies associated with the need for a sharp flake that shaped the gestures involved in knapping.

In thinking about a modern equivalent, it would be like arguing that one could embody one's identity or individual agency in how one goes about repairing a hole in a screen door with a strip of duct tape. Even if some people derive aspects of their identity from their use of duct tape (many of them archaeologists, no doubt), this is not the principal dynamic reflected in the technical gestures associated with the duct tape repair—and the issue obviously becomes much trickier in the archaeological record, where we have access to evidence about what people did with technology and not how such practices may or may not have fit into their identity. Even if some aspect of expedient flaking was part of the identity of certain past individuals, what we see archaeologically is the immediate technical response to the problems posed by (1) the requirements of the task at hand and (2) the characteristics of the available technological raw materials.

It may simply be the case that some activities are meaningful in terms of agency and practice but that others are not; that there is a French way to make a *croissant* but not a French way to hammer in a nail. Yet the difficulty that agency and practice theories have in dealing with expedient technologies highlights a potential analytical critique: how do we know when someone in the past did something a particular way in order to manifest some aspect of their identity and not simply because it was the easiest way of responding to the technical contingencies that happened to be facing them at that moment? Answering this question would require us to know something that we, as archaeologists, are fundamentally incapable of knowing: what was on the minds of people in the past. We return to this theme again in the next section, which deals with formal stone tool traditions.

In any case, for now we have established that expedient/informal core reduction does not relate very well to current theoretical foci of agency and practice—or, for that matter, to materiality, monumentality, temporality, memory, and so on. So why should we bother studying this phenomenon at all? As we stated earlier, while the gestures involved in expedient core reduction themselves are not that interesting, they are carried out and distributed over space and time in ways that reflect economic activities that are of utmost interest. As the chapters in this volume will demonstrate, there are many ways in which the various stages of the expedient core reduction process are integrated within the broader economic activities of prehistoric farmers. Here are a few points of particular interest discussed in this book:

1. The integration of lithic raw material collection into other economic activities, such as the tending of farm fields, the extraction of other kinds of raw material resources from the landscape, and interaction/exchange with other populations and settlements
2. The technological goals reflected in the specific strategies of expedient core reduction, the production of utilizable flakes, and the selection of particular flakes for use in performing certain tasks
3. The raw material economic decisions reflected by the use of certain core reduction strategies, the length of core reduction sequences, and the degrees of core exhaustion
4. The technical contingencies reflected by the recycling and repurposing of utilized flakes through different retouch tactics
5. The location and timing of knapping activities as reflected by the context of discarded lithic materials and the other artifacts and features with which they are associated.

Naturally, this is only the beginning of a list of things we should study about the informal stone tool traditions of sedentary societies, but it is a place to start. More generally, we need to develop a better analytical framework for relating the characteristics of informal lithic industries in sedentary societies with the salient economic dynamics they are capable of reflecting. This is no easy task, and it will require profound creativity when it comes to thinking through how lithic manufacture as a spatially and temporally distributed reductive process related to other economic activities in ways that are archaeologically visible. We hope this volume makes a contribution in this pursuit, if for no other reason because it demonstrates that the Parry and Kelly (1987) model does not explain it all and that studying informal lithic traditions in sedentary societies has a legitimate place in the field of archaeology alongside studies of other, more complex forms of craft production.

SPECIALIZED TOOL FORMS

Specialized tools have formed the core (if you will excuse the pun) of lithic studies in sedentary societies, and for good reason. For one thing, specialized tool forms tend to be more culture-historically diagnostic and significant, at least in contrast to expedient flake production, which tends to be ubiquitously lacking in typologically distinctive formal features. In addition, specialized tool forms relate more clearly to political-economic issues that are of theoretical interest to archaeologists, such as craft specialization, trade, elite control of economic resources, sociopolitical inequality, and similar factors.

Two prime examples of specialized tool production, resulting from formal core technology, are obsidian prismatic blades found throughout Mesoamerica and sickle blades in the Near East and elsewhere in the Old World. These specialized implements are functionally distinct from informal lithic technologies, which were often used alongside them contemporaneously. In addition, specialized tools were produced and distributed in unique ways, often involving both the restricted control of lithic raw material sources and the production activities of highly skilled and specialized craftspeople. In places like Mesoamerica and the Near East, the production of these specialized tool forms articulates with the operation of broader economic systems in important and illustrative ways. It is no wonder that they have garnered so much previous attention.

Mesoamerican obsidian prismatic blade production in particular has been discussed at great length elsewhere (see Gaxiola Gonzalez and Clark 1989; Hester 1978; Hirth 2003, 2006; Hirth and Andrews 2002; Levine and Carballo 2014 for summaries of this research). The production of such materials involves preparation and production of highly structured formal cores, which were then distributed outside the areas of raw material accessibility (a relatively restricted volcanic area of highland Guatemala and Mexico). Prismatic blades were produced by craft specialists and distributed through a variety of mechanisms, including elite management and itinerant craftspeople. The study of obsidian prismatic blade production has shed light on the political-economic systems of prehistoric societies from nearly every region and time period of Mesoamerica, from the Formative villages of the Olmecs to the Spanish contact-period cities of the Aztecs.

Morphologically similar tools were used for agricultural activities in the Near East; sickles produced on blades became more formal over time, with early examples in the Late Natufian period (12,800–10,200 BP; Belfer-Cohen and Goring-Morris 1996) giving rise to the highly formalized Naviform blade core technology in the Pre-Pottery Neolithic B (PPNB; 9500–7900

BP; Bar-Yosef et al. 1991; Goodale et al. 2002, 2010; Nishiaki 2000) and continuing into the Bronze Age (see Davis, this volume). Naviform blade cores are boat-shaped and standardized in shape and size, use percussion technology for blade production (Quintero and Wilke 1995), and are generally produced on high-quality, exotic raw materials (Quintero 1996). By the Pottery Neolithic (PN; 7500–6000 BP), the formality of cores decreased, with an emphasis on the production of similar tools through blank retouch as opposed to similarities in the blanks themselves (Finlayson et al. 2003; Gopher et al. 2001). This blade technology exists through the introduction of metal tools, referred to by this time as Canaanean blades, which are extremely standardized (Anderson and Chabot 2001; Anderson et al. 2004; Milveski 2013; Rosen 1996, 1997), although those found at Harrapa are less standardized (Davis, this volume).

In both Mesoamerica and the Near East, the formality of cores contrasts with Parry and Kelly's (1987) expectations for the informality of core technology in sedentary societies. In both cases, blades were used for composite technologies (Anderson and Chabot 2001; Bleed 1986; Nelson 1991; Shott 1989). Ethnographic studies illustrate that haft construction is frequently the most expensive part of component tools (Gould 1980; Rule and Evans 1985; Weedman 2002, 2006), which explains the preference for replacing the components rather than the haft. In both Mesoamerica and the Near East, blades are preferentially produced on high-quality raw materials, mostly non-local, which results in specialized production areas close to sources and intensive utilization of cores and tools outside source areas (Anderson et al. 2004; Davis, this volume; Quintero and Wilke 1995; Rosen 2013; Willke 1996; Wilke and Quintero 1994).

The production and exchange of these specialized tool forms in sedentary societies was predicated on the exchange systems and craft specialization present in these societies. We might ask, for example, why are there cases such as the production of obsidian blades in Mesoamerica and sickle blades in the Near East that so thoroughly defy the Parry and Kelly (1987) generalization about lithics in sedentary societies? We would argue that the presence of extensive networks of exchange was, in a sense, the tail that wagged the dog of specialized stone tool production. Such exchange networks arose in the context of the distribution of a wide range of consumable goods and durable craft products. Once in place, these exchange networks created economic opportunities for those who controlled major sources of high-quality lithic raw materials and the craftspeople who were involved in specialized stone tool production at workshops located near these sources. Without suitable networks of exchange, the exploitation of such high-quality lithic raw material sources would have remained a local phenomenon, and the Parry and Kelly (1987) pattern of expedient knapping would most likely have been borne out.

For example, in this volume McCall and coauthors document the expedient knapping of chert at Chalcatzingo, which occurred alongside the highly specialized production of obsidian prismatic blades in elite-controlled craft workshops (see also Grove 2014). Were it not for the presence of the exchange networks through which the many goods from Chalcatzingo flowed into the Olmec world, there would have been no demand for obsidian prismatic blades, no need for control/exploitation of the obsidian quarries in the region, and no need for specialized workshops to produce blades. Thus the prevalent pattern of expedient chert core reduction would have been the norm, obsidian would have been rare, and blade production (for the most part) would not have occurred.

It is also the case that the limited locations of specialized stone tool production identified archaeologically in sedentary societies indicate that relatively few producers were responsible for the production of prepared cores. Most sites with Canaanean blades show no evidence of local production, indicating that the finished products arrived from elsewhere through trade (Anderson and Chabot 2001; Milevski 2013; Rosen 2013). This is also true throughout much of the Maya lowlands, which received blades through trade with settlements in the volcanic highlands that had access to obsidian sources. In addition, at both Near Eastern sites with Canaanean blades and lowland Maya sites with obsidian prismatic blades, there is also a great deal of expedient/informal stone tool production using locally available lithic raw materials. Thus the production of these formalized tools co-occurs with a more informal lithic tool technology, produced locally or, in the Canaanean case, with bronze tools.

The organizational properties of lithic technologies in sedentary societies permit the coexistence of informal stone tools, which were produced expediently using local raw materials, and formal technologies, which rely on specialized producers and long-distance trade. While this phenomenon has been noted previously, it has generally been treated as little more than a curiosity. The contrasting dynamics suggested by the coexistence of specialized and informal stone tools, however, have profound implications for our understanding of prehistoric economic systems, as well as clear directions for future research.

First, we suggest that the production of specialized stone tools is most interesting when viewed through the lens of what it can tell us about the economic networks and systems that fostered their production. At every stage in the process of specialized stone tool production—from raw material acquisition to the core reduction activities of specialist knappers to the transmission of finished products to the recycling and discard of these products at the location of their consumption—the effects of the political-economic systems and exchange networks in which the various actors were involved can be detected in the technological decisions that were made. Therefore, we would argue that there is great value in studying the organization of specialized stone tool production in relation to the political, in studying the economic systems that brought specialized stone tool production activities into existence.

Second, we feel there are problems associated with the use of agency and practice theory frameworks in examining specialized stone tool production. On a philosophical level, we might ask if prehistoric craftspeople made specialized stone tool products using such systematically consistent techniques because (1) they were ideologically committed, constrained, or both by social, political, or ritual norms and institutions; (2) they manifested some aspect of their identity by doing things that way; or (3) it was the most economically efficient set of methods given the generally invariant conditions of production faced by craftspeople in workshops. It could be none of the above, all of the above, or some combination—but more critically, how would we know?

The interchangeable and simultaneous use of specialized and informal stone tool products also points out the complexity in approaching the ideational underpinnings of any particular pattern of technological behavior. Can practice be an appropriate way of looking at specialized stone tool production when informal/expedient lithic technological systems, which are much harder to deal with using this framework, operated concurrently and co-locationally? If so, why are we so sure of the social significance of one form of technological activity but not the other? And finally, given the primacy of economic networks of exchange in structuring patterns of specialized stone tool manufacture, it is worth questioning how much agency individuals actually had in the face of the necessity for efficiency fostered by commodification of specialized lithic products in the context of trade.

In general, we would argue that examining lithic production without relating it to the specific economic and social conditions under which it occurred leads to the construction of speculative scenarios about knapping behavior in prehistory. When viewed in context as technical responses to the constellation of opportunities and constraints imposed by the operation of economic systems, however we choose to view those, lithic production can provide key clues about the nature of exchange networks, the control of economic commodities, and political systems that guided the activities of extractors, craft producers, traders, and consumers. When viewed in isolation, archaeological accounts of lithic production often lead to bald speculation about why knappers did things in certain ways and what knapping activities meant to prehistoric peoples. Once again, as purely ideational phenomena, such quests for motivation and meaning are doomed to ambiguity and conjecture about the past.

GAPS AND FUTURE DIRECTIONS

Unfathomable volumes of knapping debris are associated with the archaeological records of sedentary societies, and we now know a good deal about the basic characteristics of many of these lithic industries. Yet with the exception of a few famous studies mostly having to do with the role of specialized stone tool production in certain sedentary societies, research on lithics in sedentary societies has unfortunately yielded sadly little concrete information about human prehistory and our theoretical explanation of it. There are still large gaps in our understanding of the importance of lithics, particularly some of the subtitles inherent in the ways they were produced, exchanged, and consumed.

This book illustrates some of the lacunae in our knowledge of lithics in sedentary societies, as well as some analytical, theoretical, and culture-historical points of emphasis that may be useful in resolving them. In terms of analytical methods, one lesson from the chapters in this volume concerns the value of studying whole lithic assemblages rather than focusing on specific tool types or specialized production contexts in isolation. Although the specialized tool types, such as those discussed above, are important in understanding past societies, recognizing variability in lithic production both within and between contexts has much to tell us about the role of lithics in the past. Part of this approach involves the recognition that neither specialized nor informal stone tool production was a monolithic or an invariant phenomenon. Both forms of stone tool production varied over time within particular contexts and (more obviously) between different contexts. The formation of systematic comparisons between the stone tool assemblages associated with different units of the space-time systematics we study as archaeologists is poised to provide novel insights about prehistory. In addition, an examination of the many cases in which specialized and informal stone tool production coexisted contemporaneously may speak to the nature of the broader economic systems in which stone tool production occurred.

Detailed analyses of assemblage-level data, as proposed by McCall and coauthors in this volume, provides additional information about reduction processes and the ways those processes interacted with broader social and political systems in ways invisible when only parts of assemblages are addressed. Manclossi and Rosen, in this volume, use detailed core analyses to address differences in informal core and tool technologies, a method that has potential for widespread application in other regions. Other chapters in this volume focus on workshop-level lithic production (Whittaker; Davis) or household-level production (Arakawa; Horowitz; Manclossi and Rosen; McCall et al.; Mehta et al.; Paling). The combination of these types of analyses—that is, comparisons of both formal and informal technology and production areas—provides a more holistic understanding of the production types and techniques employed within sedentary societies.

Other gaps that exist in our studies of lithic technology of sedentary societies are geographic and culture-historical in nature. Although our volume focuses on global perspectives on lithic technologies, some world areas are much more heavily represented than others. This is at least in part a result of the absence of scholars studying lithics in certain world regions. Chapters in this volume examine cases in West Asia, North America, and Mesoamerica. Most striking perhaps is the relative dearth of lithic analysis in much of South America in sedentary societies. Although the study of hunter-gatherers in the region is quite robust, lithics in later societies have received scant attention.

Colloquially, many scholars (including both lithicists focusing on mobile societies and non-lithicist scholars of complex societies) discount the significance of lithics in places like South America and Mesoamerica as "poor quality" or "uninteresting," mostly because of the high frequency of informal tools. As the chapters in this volume show, the very informality of certain lithic assemblages itself and its contrast with specialized forms of stone tool production provide wide ranges of important information on past organizational dynamics. Such preconceptions about informal lithic industries in sedentary societies limit the ways in which both lithic production and economic organization are studied.

We hope this book, if nothing else, makes the case for the value of studying the various lithic industries to be found in the archaeological record of sedentary societies—regardless of whether you agree with our analytical and theoretical perspectives on them. While we have made a good start by addressing a variety of broad anthropological themes from lithic technology around the globe, much more work remains to be done to increase our understanding of the ways studies of lithics can complicate our understandings of the archaeological record and the organization of past societies.

REFERENCES

Anderson, Patricia C., and Jacques Chabot. 2001. "Functional Analysis of Glossed Blades from Northern Mesopotamia in the Early Bronze Age (3000–2500 BC): The Case of Tell 'Atij." *Série archéométrie* 1: 257–276.

Anderson, Patricia C., Jacques Chabot, and Annelou van Gijn. 2004. "The Functional Riddle of 'Glossy' Canaanean Blades and the Near Eastern Threshing Sledge." *Journal of Mediterranean Archaeology* 17 (1): 87–130.

Andrefsky, William, Jr. 2005. *Lithics: Macroscopic Approaches to Analysis*. 2nd ed. Cambridge: Cambridge University Press.

Appadurai, Arjun. 1986. "Introduction: Commodities and the Politics of Value." In *The Social Life of Things: Commodities in Cultural Perspectives*, ed. Arjun Appadurai, 3–63. Cambridge: Cambridge University Press.

Bamforth, Douglas B. 1993. "Stone Tools, Steel Tools: Contact Period Household Technology at Helo." In *Ethnohistory and Archaeology: Approaches to Postcontact Change in the Americas*, ed. J. Daniel Rogers and Samuel M. Wilson, 49–72. New York: Springer.

Bar-Yosef, Ofer, Avi Gopher, Eitan Tchernov, and Mordechai E. Kislev. 1991. "Netiv Hagdud: An Early Neolithic Village Site in the Jordan Valley." *Journal of Field Archaeology* 18 (4): 405–424.

Belfer-Cohen, Anna, and Nigel Goring-Morris. 1996. "The Late Epipaleolithic as the Precursor of the Neolithic: The Lithic Evidence." In *Neolithic Chipped Stone Industries of the Fertile Crescent, and Their Contemporaries in Adjacent Regions: Proceedings of the Second Workshop on PPN Chipped Lithic Industries*, ed. Stefan Karol Kozlowski and Hans Georg K. Gebel, 217–225. Studies in Early Near Eastern Production, Subsistence, and Environment 3. Berlin: Ex Oriente.

Binford, Lewis R. 1976. "Forty-Seven Trips: A Case Study in the Character of Some Formation Processes." In *Contributions to Anthropology, the Interior Peoples of Northern Alaska*, ed. Edwin S. Hall Jr., 299–351. Ottawa: National Museum of Canada.

Bleed, Peter. 1986. "The Optimal Design of Hunting Weapons: Maintainability or Reliability." *American Antiquity* 51: 737–747.

Bourdieu, Pierre. 1977. *Outline of a Theory of Practice*. Cambridge: Cambridge University Press.

Bronowicki, Jaroslaw, and Miroslaw Masojc. 2010. "Lusatian Flint Industries in Silesia, Southwest Poland." In *Lithic Technology in Metal Using Societies—Proceedings of a UISPP Workshop, Lisbon, September 2006*, ed. Bert Valentin Eriksen, 107–127. Hojbjerg, Denmark: Jutland Archaeological Society.

Cantarutti, Gabriel E. 2013. "Mining under Inca Rule in North Central Chile: The Los Infieles Mining Complex." In *Mining and Quarrying in the Ancient Andes:*

Sociopolitical, Economic, and Symbolic Dimensions, ed. Nicholas Tripcevich and Kevin J. Vaughn, 185–211. New York: Springer.

Carballo, David M. 2013. "The Social Organization of Craft Production and Interregional Exchange at Teotihuacan." In *Merchants, Markets, and Exchange in the Pre-Columbian World*, ed. Kenneth G. Hirth and Joanne Pillsbury, 113–140. Washington, DC: Dumbarton Oaks Research Library and Collection.

Card, Jeb J. 2013a. "Introduction." In *The Archaeology of Hybrid Material Culture*, ed. Jeb J. Card, 1–21. Center for Archaeological Investigation, Occasional Paper 39. Carbondale: Southern Illinois University.

Card, Jeb J. 2013b. "Italianate Pipil Potters: Mesoamerican Transformation of Renaissance Material Culture in Early Spanish Colonial El Salvador." In *The Archaeology of Hybrid Material Culture*, ed. Jeb J. Card, 100–130. Center for Archaeological Investigation, Occasional Paper 39. Carbondale: Southern Illinois University.

Chatfield, Melissa. 2013. "Worshipping with Hybrid Objects: Assessing Culture Contact through Use and Context." In *The Archaeology of Hybrid Material Culture*, ed. Jeb J. Card, 131–161. Center for Archaeological Investigation, Occasional Paper 39. Carbondale: Southern Illinois University.

Chinchilla Mazariegos, Oswaldo. 2011. "The Obsidian Workshop of El Baul Cotzumalhuapu." In *The Technology of Maya Civilization: Political Economy and Beyond in Lithic Studies*, ed. Zachary X. Hruby, Geoffrey E. Braswell, and Oswaldo Chinchilla Mazariegos, 102–118. Sheffield, UK: Equinox.

Clark, John E. 1989. "La tecnica de talla de los lacandones de Chiapas." In *La obsidiana en Mesoamerica*, ed. Margarita Gaxiola Gonzalez and John E. Clark, 443–448. Mexico City: Instituto Nacional de Antropología e Historia.

Clark, John E. 1991. "Flintknapping and Debitage Disposal among the Lacandon Maya of Chiapas." In *The Ethnoarchaeology of Refuse Disposal*, ed. Edward Staski and Livingston D. Sutro, 63–88. Phoenix: Arizona University Press.

Cobb, Charles. 1988. "Mill Creek Chert Biface Production: Mississippian Political Economy in Illinois." PhD dissertation, Southern Illinois University, Carbondale.

Cobb, Charles. 2000. *From Quarry to Cornfield: The Political Economy of Mississippian Hoe Production*. Tuscaloosa: University of Alabama Press.

Cobb, Charles. 2003a. "Introduction: Framing Stone Tool Traditions after Contact." In *Stone Tool Traditions in the Contact Era*, ed. Charles Cobb, 1–12. Tuscaloosa: University of Alabama Press.

Cobb, Charles, ed. 2003b. *Stone Tool Traditions in the Contact Era*. Tuscaloosa: University of Alabama Press.

Cobb, Charles, and Melody Pope. 1998. "Sixteenth Century Flintknapping Kits from the King Site, Georgia." *Journal of Field Archaeology* 25: 1–18.

Cobb, Charles, and Dino A. Ruggiero. 2003. "Lithic Technology and the Spanish Entrada at the King Site in Northwest Georgia." In *Stone Tool Traditions in the Contact Era*, ed. Charles Cobb, 13–28. Tuscaloosa: University of Alabama Press.

Cobb, Charles, and Paul A. Webb. 1994. "A Source Area Perspective on Expedient and Formal Core Technologies." *North American Archaeology* 15 (3): 197–219.

Costin, Cathy L. 1991. "Craft Specialization: Issues in Defining, Documenting, and Explaining the Organization of Production." *Archaeological Method and Theory* 3: 1–56.

Costin, Cathy L. 1996. "Craft Production and Mobilization Strategies in the Inka Empire." In *Craft Specialization and Social Evolution: In Memory of V. Gordon Childe*, ed. Bernard Wailes, 211–225. University Museum of Archaeology and Anthropology, Monograph 93. Philadelphia: University of Pennsylvania.

Costin, Cathy L. 2000. "The Use of Ethnoarchaeology for the Archaeological Study of Ceramic Production." *Journal of Archaeological Method and Theory* 7 (4): 377–403.

Costin, Cathy L. 2004. "Craft Economies of Ancient Andean States." In *Archaeological Perspectives on Political Economy*, ed. Gary M. Feinman and Linda M. Nichols, 189–221. Salt Lake City: University of Utah Press.

Costin, Cathy L., and Melissa B. Hagstrum. 1995. "Standardization, Labor Investment, Skill, and the Organization of Ceramic Production in Late Prehispanic Highland Peru." *American Antiquity* 60 (4): 619–639.

De Leon, Jason P. 2008. "The Lithic Industries of San Lorenzo Tenochtitlan: An Economic and Technological Study of Olmec Obsidian." PhD dissertation, Pennsylvania State University, State College.

Deal, Michael, and Brian Hayden. 1987. "The Persistence of Pre-Columbian Lithic Technology in the Form of Glassworking." In *Lithic Studies among the Contemporary Highland Maya*, ed. Brian Hayden, 235–331. Tucson: University of Arizona Press.

Degryse, Patrick, Ebru Torun, Markku Corremans, Tom Heldal, Elizabeth G. Bloxam, and Marc Waelkens. 2009. "Preservation and Promotion of the Sagalassos Quarry and Town Landscape, Turkey." In *Quarry Scapes: Ancient Stone Quarry Landscapes in the Eastern Mediterranean*, ed. Nizar Abu-Jaber, Elizabeth G. Bloxam, Patrick Degryse, and Tom Heldal, 99–104. Geological Survey of Norway Special Publication 12. Trondheim, Norway: Geological Survey of Norway.

Dobres, Marcia-Ann, and John E. Robb, eds. 2000. *Agency in Archaeology*. New York: Routledge.

Dolores Soto de Arechalaleta, Dolores. 2005. "Teuchitlan: Un sitio con especializacion en el trabajo: La manufactura de herramientas de obsidiana." In *Reflexciones sobre la industria lítica*, ed. Leticia Gonzalez Arratia and Lorena Mirambell, 135–180. Mexico City: Instituto Nacional de Antropología e Historia Colección Científica.

Druart, Chloe. 2010. "Production and Function of Stone Arrowheads in the Mycenean Civilization: A Technomorphological and Functional Approach." In *Lithic Technology in Metal Using Societies—Proceedings of a UISPP Workshop, Lisbon, September 2006*, ed. Bert Valentin Eriksen, 143–155. Hojbjerg, Denmark: Jutland Archaeological Society.

Eriksen, Berit. 2010. "Flint Working in the Danish Bronze Age: The Decline and Fall of a Master Craft." In *Lithic Technology in Metal Using Societies—Proceedings of a UISPP Workshop, Lisbon, September 2006*, ed. Bert Valentin Eriksen, 81–93. Hojbjerg, Denmark: Jutland Archaeological Society.

Finlayson, Bill, Ian Kuijt, Trina Arpin, Meredith Chesson, Samantha Dennis, Nathan Goodale, Seiji Kadowaki, Lisa Maher, Sam Smith, Mark Schurr, and J. McKay. 2003. "Dhra' Excavation Report, 2002 Interim Report." *Levant* 35: 1–38.

Flexner, James L., and Colleen L. Morgan. 2013. "The Industrious Exiles: An Analysis of Flaked Glass Tools from the Leprosarium at Kalawao Molokaii." In *The Archaeology of Hybrid Material Culture*, ed. Jeb J. Card, 295–317. Center for Archaeological Investigation, Occasional Paper 39. Carbondale: Southern Illinois University.

Frieman, Catherine. 2010. "Imitation, Identity, and Communication: The Presence and Problems of Skeumorphs in the Metal Ages." In *Lithic Technology in Metal Using Societies—Proceedings of a UISPP Workshop, Lisbon, September 2006*, ed. Bert Valentin Eriksen, 33–44. Hojbjerg, Denmark: Jutland Archaeological Society.

Garraty, Christopher P. 2009. "Evaluating the Distributional Approach to Inferring Marketplace Exchange: A Test Case from the Mexican Gulf Lowlands." *Latin American Antiquity* 20 (1): 157–174.

Gaxiola Gonzalez, Margarita. 2005. "Rancho la Canada: Una unidad de producción de instrumentos de obsidiana en Huapalcalco, Hidalgo." In *Reflexciones sobre la industria lítica*, ed. Leticia Gonzalez Arratia and Lorena Mirambell, 181–203. Mexico City: Instituto Nacional de Antropología e Historia Colección científica.

Gaxiola Gonzalez, Margarita, and John E. Clark, eds. 1989. *La obsidiana en Mesoamérica*. Mexico City: Instituto Nacional de Antropología e Historia.

Gaxiola Gonzalez, Margarita, and Jorge Guevara. 1989. "Un conjunto habitacional en Huapalcalco, Hidalgo, especializado en la talla de obsidiana." In *La obsidiana en Mesoamérica*, ed. Margarita Gaxiola Gonzalez and John E. Clark, 227–242. Mexico City: Instituto Nacional de Antropología e Historia.

Giddens, Anthony. 1979. *Central Problems in Social Theory: Action, Structure, and Contradictions in Social Analysis*. Berkeley: University of California Press.

Goodale, Nathan, Ian Kuijt, and Bill Finlayson. 2002. "Results from the 2001 Excavations at Dhra', Jordan: Chipped Stone Technology, Typology, and Intraassemblage Variability." *Paleorient* 28 (1): 125–140.

Goodale, Nathan, Heather Otis, William Andrefsky Jr., Ian Kuijt, Bill Finlayson, and Ken Bart. 2010. "Sickle Blade Life-History and the Transition to Agriculture: An Early Neolithic Case Study from Southwest Asia." *Journal of Archaeological Science* 37 (6): 1192–1201.

Gopher, Avi, Ran Barkai, and Amnon Asaf. 2001. "Trends in Sickle Blades Production in the Neolithic of the Hula Valley, Israel." In *Beyond Tools: Redefining the PPN Lithic Assemblages of the Levant*. Proceedings of the Third Workshop of PPN Chipped Lithic Industry, ed. Isabella Caneva, Cristina Lemorini, Daniela Zampetti, and Paola Biagi, 411–425. Berlin: Ex Oriente.

Gould, Richard A. 1980. *Living Archaeology*. Cambridge: Cambridge University Press.

Grove, David C. 2014. *Discovering the Olmecs: An Unconventional History*. Austin: University of Texas Press.

Harrell, James A., and Per Storemyr. 2009. "Ancient Egyptian Quarries: An Illustrated Overview." In *Quarry Scapes: Ancient Stone Quarry Landscapes in the Eastern Mediterranean*, ed. Nizar Abu-Jaber, Elizabeth G. Bloxam, Patrick Degryse, and Tom Heldal, 7–50. Geological Survey of Norway Special Publication 12. Trondheim, Norway: Geological Survey of Norway.

Harrison-Buck, Eleanor, Ellen Spensley Moriarty, and Patricia A. McAnany. 2013. "Classic Maya Ceramic Hybridity in the Sibun Valley of Belize." In *The Archaeology of Hybrid Material Culture*, ed. Jeb J. Card, 185–206. Center for Archaeological Investigation, Occasional Paper 39. Carbondale: Southern Illinois University.

Hayden, Brian, and Michael Deal. 1989. "Vitreous Material Used by the Contemporary Maya." In *La obsidiana en Mesoamerica*, ed. Margarita Gaxiola Gonzalez and John E. Clark, 435–441. Mexico City: Instituto nacional de antropolología e historia.

Healan, Dan M. 1989. "Informe Preliminar de las excavaciones en la zona de talleres de Tula, Hidalgo." In *La obsidiana en Mesoamerica*, ed. Margarita Gaxiola Gonzalez and John E. Clark, 219–225. Mexico City: Instituto Nacional deAntropología e Historia.

Healan, Dan M. 2002. "Producer versus Consumer: Prismatic Core-Blade Technology at Epiclassic/Early Postclassic Tula and Ucareo." In *Pathways to Prismatic Blades: A Study in Mesoamerican Obsidian Core-Blade Technology*, ed. Kenneth G. Hirth and Bradford Andrews, 27–35. Los Angeles: Cotsen Institute of Archaeology, University of California.

Healan, Dan M. 2003. "From the Quarry Pit to the Trash Pit: Comparative Core-Blade Technology at Tula, Hidalgo, and the Ucareo Obsidian Source Region." In *Mesoamerican Lithic Technology: Experimentation and Interpretation*, ed. Kenneth G. Hirth, 153–169. Salt Lake City: University of Utah Press.

Heldal, Tom. 2009. "Constructing a Quarry Landscape from Empirical Data: General Perspectives and a Case Study at the Aswan West Bank, Egypt." In *Quarry*

Scapes: Ancient Stone Quarry Landscapes in the Eastern Mediterranean, ed. Nizar Abu-Jaber, Elizabeth G. Bloxam, Patrick Degryse, and Tom Heldal, 125–153. Geological Survey of Norway Special Publication 12. Trondheim, Norway: Geological Survey of Norway.

Hester, Thomas R., ed. 1978. *Archaeological Studies of Mesoamerican Obsidian*. Socorro, New Mexico: Ballena.

Hirth, Kenneth G. 1998. "The Distributional Approach: A New Way to Identify Marketplace Exchange in the Archaeological Record." *Current Anthropology* 39 (4): 451–476.

Hirth, Kenneth G. 2003. *Mesoamerican Lithic Technology: Experimentation and Interpretation*. Salt Lake City: University of Utah Press.

Hirth, Kenneth G., ed. 2006. *Obsidian Craft Production in Ancient Central Mexico*. Salt Lake City: University of Utah Press

Hirth, Kenneth G. 2009. "Craft Production, Household Diversification, and Domestic Economy in Prehispanic Mesoamerica." *Archaeological Papers of the American Anthropological Association* 19 (1): 13–32.

Hirth, Kenneth G. 2010. "Finding the Mark in the Marketplace: The Organization, Development, and Archaeological Identification of Market Systems." In *Archaeological Approaches to Market Exchange in Ancient Societies*, ed. Christopher P. Garraty and Barbara L. Stark, 227–247. Boulder: University Press of Colorado.

Hirth, Kenneth G. 2011. "The Organization of Domestic Obsidian Craft Production." In *Producción artesanal y especializacion en Mesoamerica: Áreas de actividad y procesos productivos*, ed. Linda R. Manzanilla and Kenneth G. Hirth, 177–203. Mexico City: Instituto Nacional de Antropología e Historia.

Hirth, Kenneth G., and Bradford Andrews, eds. 2002. *Pathways to Prismatic Blades: A Study in Mesoamerican Obsidian Core Blade Technology*. Los Angeles: Cotsen Institute of Archaeology, University of California.

Hofman, Jack L. 1987. "Hopewell Blades from Twenhafel: Distinguishing Local and Foreign Core Technology." In *The Organization of Core Technology*, ed. Jay K. Johnson and Carol A. Morrow, 87–110. Boulder: Westview.

Horowitz, Rachel A. 2015. "Production at the Source: Lithic Extraction and Production at Callar Creek Quarry, Belize." In *Research Reports in Belizean Archaeology: Papers of the 2014 Belize Archaeology Symposium*, vol. 12, ed. John Morris, Melissa Badillo, Sylvia Batty, and George Thompson, 45–54. Belmopan, Belize: Institute of Archaeology.

Horowitz, Rachel A. 2017. "Understanding Ancient Maya Economic Variability: Lithic Technological Organization in the Mopan Valley, Belize." PhD dissertation, Tulane University, New Orleans, LA.

Horowitz, Rachel A. 2018. "Uneven Lithic Landscapes: Raw Material Procurement and Economic Organization among the Late/Terminal Classic Maya in Western Belize." *Journal of Archaeological Sciences: Reports* 19: 949–957.

Hruby, Zachary X. 2007 "Ritualized Chipped-Stone Production at Piedras Negras, Guatemala." *Archaeological Papers of the American Anthropological Association* 17 (1): 68–87.

Jennings, Justin, Felix Palacios, Nicholas Tripcevich, and Willy Yepez Alvarez. 2013. "The Huarhua Rock Salt Mine: Archaeological Implications of Modern Extraction Practices." In *Mining and Quarrying in the Ancient Andes: Sociopolitical, Economic, and Symbolic Dimensions*, ed. Nicholas Tripcevich and Kevin J. Vaughn, 123–136. New York: Springer.

Johnson, Jay K. 1997. "Stone Tools, Politics, and the Eighteenth Century Chickasaw in Northeast Mississippi." *American Antiquity* 62: 223–235.

Johnson, Jay K. 2003. "Chickasaw Lithic Technology: A Reassessment." In *Stone Tool Traditions in the Contact Era*, ed. Charles Cobb, 51–58. Tuscaloosa: University of Alabama Press.

Kardulias, P. Nick. 2008. "Interpreting the Past through the Present: The Ethnographic, Ethnoarchaeological, and Experimental Study of Agriculture." In *Archaeology and History in Roman, Medieval, and Post-Medieval Greece: Studies on Method and Meaning in Honor of Timothy E. Gregory*, ed. William R. Caraher and R. Scott Moore, 109–126. London: Ashgate.

Kardulias, P. Nick. 2009. "Flaked Stone from Isthmia." *Hesperia: The Journal of the American School of Classical Studies at Athens* 78 (3): 307–346.

Karimali, Evangelia. 2010. "Lithic and Metal Tools in the Bronze Age Aegean: A Parallel Relationship." In *Lithic Technology in Metal Using Societies—Proceedings of a UISPP Workshop, Lisbon, September 2006*, ed. Bert Valentin Eriksen, 157–167. Hojbjerg, Denmark: Jutland Archaeological Society.

Kelany, Adel, Mohamed Negem, Adel Tohami, and Tom Heldal. 2009. "Granite Quarry Survey in the Aswan Region, Egypt: Shedding New Light on Ancient Quarrying." In *Quarry Scapes: Ancient Stone Quarry Landscapes in the Eastern Mediterranean*, ed. Nizar Abu-Jaber, Elizabeth G. Bloxam, Patrick Degryse, and Tom Heldal, 87–98. Geological Survey of Norway Special Publication 12. Trondheim, Norway: Geological Survey of Norway.

Kerley, Janet M. 1989. "Preliminary Report on a Technological Analysis of Obsidian Artifacts from an Early Postclassic Workshop in Tula, Hidalgo." In *La obsidiana en Mesoamerica*, ed. Margarita Gaxiola Gonzalez and John E. Clark, 165–174. Mexico City: Instituto Nacional de Antropología e Historia.

Kenmotsu, Nancy. 1990. "Gunflints: A Study." *Historical Archaeology* 24 (2): 92–124.

Kent, Barry C. 1983. "More on Gunflints." *Historical Archaeology* 17 (2): 27–40.

King, Eleanor M. 2000. "The Organization of Late Classic Lithic Production at the Prehistoric Maya Site of Colha, Belize: A Study in Complexity and Heterarchy." PhD dissertation, University of Pennsylvania, Philadelphia.

Levine, Marc N., and David M. Carballo, eds. 2014. *Obsidian Reflections: Symbolic Dimensions of Obsidian in Mesoamerica*. Boulder: University Press of Colorado.

Lewis, Brandon S. 1995. "The Role of Specialized Production in the Development of Socioeconomic Complexity: A Test Case from the Late Classic Maya." PhD dissertation, University of California, Los Angeles.

Lollet, Helene, Anne Hauzeur, and Jacek Lech. 2008. "The Prehistoric Flint Mining Complex at Spiennes (Belgium) on the Occasion of Its Discovery 140 Years Ago." In *Flint Mining in Prehistoric Europe: Interpreting the Archaeological Records*, ed. Pierre Allard, Francoise Bostyn, Francois Gillghy, and Jacek Lech, 41–77. BAR International Series 1891. Oxford: Archaeopress.

Marx, Karl. 1971 [1859]. *Capital: A Critique of Political Economy*. Moscow: Progress Publishers.

Maler, Teobert. 1902. *Researches in the Central Portion of the Usumatsinta Valley: Report of the Explorations for the Museum 1898–1900*. Memoirs of the Peabody Museum of American Archaeology and Ethnology, vol. 12 (1). Cambridge: Harvard University.

McCall, Grant S. 2012. "Ethnoarchaeology and the Organization of Lithic Technology." *Journal of Archaeological Research* 20: 157–203.

McCall, Grant S., and Rachel A. Horowitz. 2014. "Comparing Forager and Pastoralist Technological Organization in the Central Namib Desert, Western Namibia." In *Works in Stone: Contemporary Perspectives on Lithic Analysis*, ed. Michael J. Shott, 63–77. Salt Lake City: University of Utah Press.

McCallum, Myles. 2009. "The Supply of Stone to the City of Rome: A Case Study of the Transport of Ancient Building Stone and Millstone from the Santa Trinita Quarry (Orvieto)." In *Trade and Exchange: Archaeological Studies from History and Prehistory*, ed. Carolyn D. Dillian and Carolyn L. White, 75–94. New York: Springer.

McDonald, Mary M.A. 1991. "Technological Organization and Sedentism in the Epipaleolithic of Dakhleh Oasis, Egypt." *African Archaeological Review* 9: 81–109.

McNerney, Michael J. 1987. "Crab Orchard Core Technology at the Consol Site, Jackson County, Illinois." In *The Organization of Core Technology*, ed. Jay K. Johnson and Carol A. Morrow, 63–85. Boulder: Westview.

Milevski, Ianir. 2013. "The Exchange of Flint Tools in the Southern Levant during the Early Bronze Age." *Lithic Technology* 38 (3): 202–219.

Minc, Leah D. 2006. "Monitoring Regional Market Systems in Prehistory: Models, Methods, and Metrics." *Journal of Anthropological Archaeology* 25 (1): 82–116.

Minc, Leah D. 2009. "Style and Substance: Evidence for Regionalism within the Aztec Market System." *Latin American Antiquity* 20 (2): 343–374.

Nelson, Margaret C. 1991. "The Study of Technological Organization." In *Archaeological Method and Theory*, vol. 3, ed. Michael B. Schiffer, 57–100. Tucson: University of Arizona Press.

Nishiaki, Yoshihiro. 2000. *Lithic Technology of Neolithic Syria*. BAR International Series 840. Oxford: Archaeopress.

Odell, George H. 2001. "The Use of Metal at a Wichita Contact Settlement." *Southeastern Archaeology* 20 (2): 173–186.

Odell, George H. 2003. "Wichita Tools on First Contact with the French." In *Stone Tool Traditions in the Contact Era*, ed. Charles Cobb, 29–50. Tuscaloosa: University of Alabama Press.

Ogburn, Dennis E. 2011. "Obsidian in Southern Ecuador: The Carboncillo Source." *Latin American Antiquity* 22 (1): 97–120.

Ogburn, Dennis E. 2013. "Variation in Inca Building Stone Quarry Operations in Peru and Ecuador." In *Mining and Quarrying in the Ancient Andes: Sociopolitical, Economic, and Symbolic Dimensions*, ed. Nicholas Tripcevich and Kevin J. Vaughn, 45–64. New York: Springer.

Parry, William J. 2002. "Aztec Blade Production Strategies in the Eastern Basin of Mexico." In *Pathways to Prismatic Blades: A Study in Mesoamerican Obsidian Core Blade Technology*, ed. Kenneth Hirth and Bradford Andrews, 36–45. Los Angeles: Cotsen Institute of Archaeology, University of California.

Parry, William J., and Robert L. Kelly. 1987. "Expedient Core Technology and Sedentism." In *The Organization of Core Technology*, ed. Jay K. Johnson and Carol A. Morrow, 285–304. Boulder: Westview.

Peacock, David, and Valerie Maxfield. 2007. *The Roman Imperial Quarries: Survey and Excavation at Mons Porphyrites 1994–1998*, vol. 2: *The Excavations*. London: Egypt Exploration Society.

Quintero, Leslie A. 1996. "Flint Mining in the Pre-Pottery Neolithic: Preliminary Report on the Exploitation of Flint at Neolithic 'Ain Ghazal in Highland Jordan." In *Neolithic Chipped Stone Industries of the Fertile Crescent, and Their Contemporaries in Adjacent Regions: Proceedings of the Second Workshop on PPN Chipped Lithic Industries*, ed. Stefan Karol Kozlowski and Hans Georg K. Gebel, 233–242. Studies in Early Near Eastern Production, Subsistence, and Environment 3. Berlin: Ex Oriente.

Quintero, Leslie A., and Philip J. Wilke. 1995. "Evolution and Economic Significance of Naviform Core Blade Technology in the Southern Levant." *Paleoriente* 21 (1): 17–33.

Raczek, Teresa P. 2010. "In the Context of Copper: Indian Lithics in the 3rd Millennium BC." In *Lithic Technology in Metal Using Societies—Proceedings of a UISPP Workshop, Lisbon, September 2006*, ed. Bert Valentin Eriksen, 231–245. Hojbjerg, Denmark: Jutland Archaeological Society.

Rosen, Steven A. 1983. "The Canaanean Blade and the Early Bronze Age." *Israel Exploration Journal* 33 (1–2): 15–29.

Rosen, Steven A. 1996. "The Decline and Fall of Flint." In *Stone Tools: Theoretical Insights into Human Prehistory*, ed. George H. Odell, 139–158. New York: Plenum.

Rosen, Steven A. 1997. *Lithics after the Stone Age: A Handbook of Stone Tools from the Levant*. Walnut Creek, CA: Altamira.

Rosen, Steven A. 2010. "The Desert and the Sown: A Lithic Perspective." In *Lithic Technology in Metal Using Societies—Proceedings of a UISPP Workshop, Lisbon, September 2006*, ed. Bert Valentin Eriksen, 203–219. Hojbjerg, Denmark: Jutland Archaeological Society.

Rosen, Steven A. 2013. "Arrowheads, Axes, Ad Hoc, and Sickles: An Introduction to Aspects of Lithic Variability across the Near East in the Bronze and Iron Ages." *Lithic Technology* 38 (3): 141–149.

Rosen, Steven A, Aaron Shugar, and Jacob Vardi. 2014. "Function and Value in Sickle Segment Analysis: Odellian Perspectives." In *Works in Stone: Contemporary Perspectives on Lithic Analysis*, ed. Michael J. Shott, 116–130. Salt Lake City: University of Utah Press.

Rule, Pamela, and Jane Evans. 1985. "The Relation of Morphological Variability to Hafting Technology among Paleoindian Endscrapers at the Shawnee Minisink Site." In *Shawnee Minisink: A Stratigraphic Paleoindian-Archaic Site in the Upper Delaware Valley of Pennsylvania*, ed. Charles W. McNett Jr., 221–259. Orlando: Academic.

Salazar, Diego, Cesar Borie, and Camilia Onate. 2013. "Mining, Commensal Politics, and Ritual under Inca Rule in Atacama, North Chile." In *Mining and Quarrying in the Ancient Andes: Sociopolitical, Economic, and Symbolic Dimensions*, ed. Nicholas Tripcevich and Kevin J. Vaughn, 253–274. New York: Springer.

Santone, Leonore. 1993. "Interregional Exchange: Aspects of the Prehistoric Lithic Economy of Northern Belize." PhD dissertation, University of Texas, Austin.

Schroeder, Ralph. 2005. "Introduction: The IEMP Model and Its Critics." In *An Anatomy of Power: The Social Theory of Michael Mann*, ed. John A. Hall and Ralph Schroeder, 1–16. Cambridge: Cambridge University Press.

Shott, Michael J. 1989. "Technological Organization in Great Lakes Paleoindian Assemblages." In *Eastern Paleoindian Lithic Resource Use*, ed. Christopher J. Ellis and Jonathan C. Lothrop, 221–237. Boulder: Westview.

Shott, Michael J. 1996. "Innovation and Selection in Prehistory: A Case Study from the American Bottom." In *Stone Tools: Theoretical Insights into Human Prehistory*, ed. George H. Odell, 279–314. New York: Plenum.

Shott, Michael J., and Kathryn J. Weedman. 2007. "Measuring Reduction in Stone Tools: An Ethnoarchaeological Study of Gamo Hidescrapers from Ethiopia." *Journal of Archaeological Science* 24: 1016–1035.

Sorensen, Lasse. 2010. "Obsidian from the Final Neolithic Site of Pangali in Western Greece: Development of Exchange Patterns in the Aegean." In *Lithic Technology in Metal Using Societies—Proceedings of a UISPP Workshop, Lisbon, September 2006*, ed. Bert Valentin Eriksen, 183–202. Hojbjerg, Denmark: Jutland Archaeological Society.

Speal, C. Scott. 2009. "The Economic Geography of Chert Lithic Production in the Southern Maya Lowlands: A Comparative Examination of Early-Stage Reduction Debris." *Latin American Antiquity* 20 (1): 91–119.

Stark, Barbara L., and Christopher P. Garraty. 2010. "Detecting Marketplace Exchange in Archaeology: A Methodological Review." In *Archaeological Approaches to Market Exchange in Ancient Societies*, ed. Christopher P. Garraty and Barbara L. Stark, 33–58. Boulder: University Press of Colorado.

Storemyr, Per, Elizabeth Bloxam, Tom Heldal, and Adel Kelany. 2010. "Conservation of Ancient Stone Quarry Landscapes in Egypt." In *Ancient Mines and Quarries: A Trans-Atlantic Perspective*, ed. Margaret Brewer-LaPorta, Adrian Burke, and David Field, 38–55. Oxford: Oxbow Books.

Teather, Anne. 2011. "Interpreting Hidden Chalk Art in Southern British Neolithic Flint Mines." *World Archaeology* 43 (2): 230–251.

Teltser, Patrice A. 1991. "Generalized Core Technology and Tool Use: A Mississippian Example." *Journal of Field Archaeology* 18 (3): 363–375.

Tolmie, Clare. 2013. "The Chatelperronian: Hybridity Culture or Indigenous Innovation?" In *The Archaeology of Hybrid Material Culture*, ed. Jeb J. Card, 279–294. Center for Archaeological Investigation, Occasional Paper 39. Carbondale: Southern Illinois University.

Torrence, Robin. 1984. "Monopoly or Direct Access? Industrial Organization at the Melos Obsidian Quarries." In *Prehistoric Quarries and Lithic Production*, ed. Jonathan E. Ericson and Barbara A. Purdy, 49–64. Cambridge: Cambridge University Press.

Torrence, Robin. 1986. *Production and Exchange of Stone Tools: Prehistoric Obsidian in the Aegean*. Cambridge: Cambridge University Press.

Tozzer, Alfred M. 1907. *A Comparative Study of the Mayas and the Lacandones*. New York: Archaeological Institute of America.

Tripcevich, Nicholas, and Daniel A. Contreras. 2011. "Quarrying Evidence at the Quispisisa Obsidian Source, Ayacucho, Peru." *Latin American Antiquity* 22 (1): 121–136.

Tripcevich, Nicholas, and Daniel A. Contreras. 2013. "Archaeological Approaches to Obsidian Quarries: Investigations at the Quispisisa Source." In *Mining and Quarrying in the Ancient Andes: Sociopolitical, Economic, and Symbolic Dimensions*, ed. Nicholas Tripcevich and Kevin J. Vaughn, 23–44. New York: Springer.

van Gijn, Annelou. 2010. "Not at All Obsolete: The Use of Flint in the Bronze Age Netherlands." In *Lithic Technology in Metal Using Societies—Proceedings of a UISPP Workshop, Lisbon, September 2006*, ed. Bert Valentin Eriksen, 45–60. Hojbjerg, Denmark: Jutland Archaeological Society.

Vaughn, Kevin J., Hendrick van Gijseghem, Verity H. Whalen, Jelmer Eerkens, and Moises Linares Grados. 2013. "The Organization of Mining in Nasca during the Early Intermediate Period: Recent Evidence from Mina Primavera." In *Mining and Quarrying in the Ancient Andes: Sociopolitical, Economic, and Symbolic Dimensions*, ed. Nicholas Tripcevich and Kevin J. Vaughn, 157–182. New York: Springer.

Watt, David J., and Rachel A. Horowitz. 2017. "Analysis of a Gunflint Assemblage from the Natchez Fort Site (16CT18)." *Southeastern Archaeology* 36 (3): 214–225

Weedman, Kathryn J. 2000. "An Ethnoarchaeological Study of Stone Scrapers among the Gamo People of Southern Ethiopia." PhD dissertation, University of Florida, Gainesville.

Weedman, Kathryn J. 2002. "On the Spur of the Moment: Effects of Age and Experience on Hafted Stone Scraper Morphology." *American Antiquity* 67: 731–744.

Weedman, Kathryn J. 2006. "An Ethnoarchaeological Study of Hafting and Stone Tool Diversity among the Gamo of Ethiopia." *Journal of Archaeological Method and Theory* 13: 188–237.

Weigand, Phil C. 1989. "Notes Concerning the Use and Re-Use of Lithic Material among the Huicholes of Jalisco." In *La obsidiana en Mesoamerica*, ed. Margarita Gaxiola Gonzalez and John E. Clark, 465–466. Mexico City: Instituto Nacional de Antropología e Historia.

Weisberber, Gerd 1983. "The Technological Relationship between Flint Mining and Early Copper Mining." In *The Human Uses of Flint and Chert: Proceedings of the Fourth International Flint Symposium Held at Brighton Polytechnic 10–15 April*, ed. G. de G. Sieveking and Mark H. Newcomer, 131–135. Cambridge: Cambridge University Press.

White, Stephen W. 1975. "On the Origins of Gunspalls." *Historical Archaeology* 9: 65–73.

Whittaker, John C. 1996. "Athkiajas: A Cypriot Flintknapper and the Threshing Sledge Industry." *Lithic Technology* 21 (2): 108–120.

Whittaker, John C. 2001. "The Oldest British Industry: Continuity and Obsolescence in a Flintknapper's Set Sample." *Antiquity* 75: 382–390.

Whittaker, John C. 2003. "Threshing Sledges and Threshing Floors in Cyprus." In *Le Traitement des recoltes, un regard sur la diversite, du nelithique au present: XXIIII Rencontres Intrenationales D'Archéologie et D'historie D'antibes*, ed. Patricia C. Anderson, Linda S. Cummings, and Thomas K. Schippers, 375–387. Antibes, France: Editions APDCA.

Whittaker, John C. 2014a. "Threshing Processes and Tools: Exploring Diversity in the Past: An Introduction." In *Explaining and Exploring Diversity in Agricultural Technology*, ed. Annelou van Gijn, John C. Whittaker, and Patricia C. Anderson, 133–135. Oxford: Oxbow Books.

Whittaker, John C. 2014b. "Threshing Floors in Cyprus." In *Explaining and Exploring Diversity in Agricultural Technology*, ed. Annelou van Gijn, John C. Whittaker, and Patricia C. Anderson, 136–137. Oxford: Oxbow Books.

Whittaker, John C. 2014c. "The Manufacture and Use of Threshing Sledges." In *Explaining and Exploring Diversity in Agricultural Technology*, ed. Annelou van Gijn, John C. Whittaker, and Patricia C. Anderson, 141–144. Oxford: Oxbow Books.

Whittaker, John C., Kathryn Kamp, and Emek Yilmaz. 2009. "Cakmak Revisited: Turkish Flintknappers Today." *Lithic Technology* 34: 92–110.

Wilke, Philip J. 1996. "Bullet-Shaped Microblade Cores of the Near Eastern Neolithic: Experimental Replicative Studies." In *Neolithic Chipped Stone Industries of the Fertile Crescent and Their Contemporaries in Adjacent Regions: Proceedings of the Second Workshop on PPN Chipped Lithic Industries*, ed. Stefan Karol Kozlowski and Hans Georg K. Gebel, 289–310. Studies in Early Near Eastern Production, Subsistence, and Environment 3. Berlin: Ex Oriente.

Wilke, Philip J., and Leslie A. Quintero. 1994. "Naviform Core and Blade Technology: Assemblage Character as Determined by Replicative Experiments." In *Neolithic Chipped Stone Industries of the Fertile Crescent*. Proceedings of the first workshop on PPN Chipped Lithic Industries, ed. Hans Georg K. Gebel and Stefan Karol Kozlowski, 33–60. Studies in Early Near Eastern Production, Subsistence, and Environment 1. Berlin: Ex Oriente.

Woodall, J. Ned, Stephen T. Trage, and Roger W. Kirchen. 1997. "Gunflint Production in the Monti Lessini, Italy." *Historical Archaeology* 31 (4): 15–27.

Yerkes, Richard W. 2000. "Ethnoarchaeology in Central Cyprus: Interdisciplinary Studies of Ancient Population and Agriculture by the Athienou Archaeological Project." *Near Eastern Archaeology* 63 (1): 20–34.

2

Urban Lithics

The Role of Stone Tools in the Indus Civilization and at Harappa

Mary A. Davis

Chipped stone tool use during the urban phase of the Indus tradition had a complex system of specialized production and long-distance exchange. It did not witness a decline in the use of lithic tools despite readily available copper and copper alloy tools. The system of production, distribution, and consumption appears to be a unique model compared to the models supported in Mesoamerica (e.g., Andrieu 2014; Aoyama 2001, 2007; De León et al. 2009; Hirth 1998a, 2012; Hirth et al. 2006; Moholy-Nagy and Álvarez-Sandoval 2011; Shafer and Hester 1991) or West Asia (e.g., Chabot and Pelegrin 2012; Edens 1999; Frahm 2014; Hartenberger and Runnels 2001; Hartenberger et al. 2000; Kardulias 2003; Rosen 1997). Here, an overview of the state of chipped stone tool studies across the Indus region is given and integrated with new data from my study of nearly 13,000 tools and other chipped stone artifacts from recent excavations at the site of Harappa, Pakistan (3500–1300 BCE).

I propose a preliminary model for the complete lithic life cycle and the potential reflections of larger political and social networks in the region, which can be further tested and evaluated with more data. The blade-focused production was carried out intensively at or near the source of raw materials, with limited production taking place in workshops at consumer sites such as Harappa. Corporate groups largely transported whole blades or, to a lesser extent, prepared cores to the site. The blade tools were most likely exchanged in a market system and consumed widely, crosscutting many classes and occupations. The tools were segmented by the consumer in a wide variety of activities and not extensively curated or retouched. Like other materials in an urban environment, it is likely that these tools were deposited in proximate refuse areas or abandoned buildings.

BACKGROUND

The Indus Civilization is among the earliest urbanized societies in the world, composed of thousands of known sites of multiple sizes and levels of complexity. These sites share similar material culture and physical organization across a one million square kilometer area (Kenoyer 1998) that straddles the area of modern-day Pakistan and Northwest India. The term *Indus Civilization* is commonly used to describe the urban period of the Indus Tradition, which begins with the Early Food Producing Era (roughly 7000–5500 BCE) (table 2.1). This era is best documented at the Neolithic site Mehrgarh (Jarrige and Meadow 1980; Jarrige et al. 1995), where the origins of long-distance trade of exotic raw material (Barthélemy de Saizieu 2003; Kenoyer 1995) and later craft specialization (Jarrige et al. 1995; Kenoyer 1995; Vidale 1995) are evident. Regional material culture styles emerged as trade networks intensified and expanded. Increased specialization is also evidenced in the Regionalization Era as new technologies developed and old technologies were elaborated upon (Kenoyer 1991b, 1994b, 2011; Shaffer 1992: 442). The Integration Era describes the period of a literate, urbanized landscape with a complex hierarchy of materials and finished goods, commonly produced with sophisticated technologies traded across the region (Belcher 1997; Bhan et al. 1994, 2002; Hoffman and Miller 2014; Kenoyer 1984a, 1984b, 1989, 1991b, 1994a, 2005, 2007; Kenoyer and Miller 2000; Law 2008, 2011; Meadow and Kenoyer 2001; Miller 1999, 2004; Vidale 2000; Vidale and Miller 2001).

We are obliged to explore and discover this landscape solely through archaeology because the limited text from these sites has yet to be deciphered. Recent archaeological work, particularly at the type site of Harappa where the Harappan Archaeological Research Project (HARP) initiated the first modern question-orientated research in 1985 (e.g., Belcher 1991; Clark 2003; Dales and Kenoyer 1991; Kenoyer 1991a; Kenoyer and Meadow 1997; Law 2008; Meadow and Kenoyer 1993; Meadow et al. 1997, 2001; Miller 1996, 1997, 2000), has expanded our understanding of the development and trajectory of the Indus Civilization and has rectified many outdated theories and models (e.g., Kenoyer 2008; Vidale 2005, 2010) established in the first phases of discovery

TABLE 2.1. Indus Tradition chronology (from Kenoyer 2008)

FORAGING ERA	10,000–2000 BCE
Mesolithic and Microlithic	
EARLY FOOD PRODUCING ERA (NEOLITHIC)	7000–5500 BCE
Mehrgarh phase	
REGIONALIZATION ERA (PROTO-URBAN PHASE)	5500–2600 BCE
Early Harappan phases	
Hakra, Ravi, Sheri Khan Tarakai, Balakot, Amri, Kot Diji, Amri, Nal, Sothi, and so on	
INTEGRATION ERA	
Harappan phase (Urban phase)	2600–1900 BCE
LOCALIZATION ERA (POST-URBAN PHASE)	
Late Harappan phases	1900–1300 BCE
Punjab, Jhukar, Rangpur	

and investigation. Indus archaeology is now at a point in which new models and theories are exploring and testing with new evidence. This new evidence suggests that the Indus Valley did not follow extant trajectories and models in archaeology for the development and perpetuation of complex "state"-level societies and urbanism. There is a consistent and striking lack of evidence for aggrandizing and authoritarian rulership. Indeed, there is a lack of overt centralization, despite the relatively extreme complexity. As an alternative, the Indus is now modeled either as a state-like entity that employed corporate strategies or as a corporate state (Kenoyer 1994b, 1997, 2014; Possehl 2002: 57; Wright 2010).

THE SITE OF HARAPPA

The site of Harappa is one the largest urban centers of the Indus Tradition and in the Bronze Age world. It is also one the most extensively and precisely dated and excavated sites in the Indus region. Harappa is situated on the alluvial plain in the Pakistani Punjab. It is a multi-nodal site with four major mounds spread over 150 hectares (Dales and Kenoyer 1991). The village of "Harappatown" currently occupies the "fifth" mound and about a third of the site (Kenoyer 2008). At present, the calibrated radiocarbon dates for Harappa show a continuous occupation of the site for over 2,000 years, 3900–1700 BCE (table 2.2).

Harappa, like a majority of Indus sites, is located in a floodplain without access to mineralogical resources, such as knappable stone (figure 2.1). It was

TABLE 2.2. Chronology for the site of Harappa (from Kenoyer 2008)

Periods 1A and 1B: Early Harappan/Ravi phase	ca. 3900(?)–2800 BCE
Period 2: Early Harappan/Kot Diji phase	ca. 2800–2600 BCE
Period 3A: Harappan phase	ca. 2600–2450 BCE
Period 3B: Harappan phase	ca. 2450–2200 BCE
Period 3C: Harappan phase	ca. 2200–1900 BCE
Period 4: Harappan/Late Harappan Transitional	ca. 1900–1800 BCE(?)
Period 5: Late Harappan phase (Cemetery H)	ca. 1800(?)–1700 BCE

located 500 km upstream from the major source of chert in the Rohri Hills, yet the site consumed a great quantity of material. The emergence of metal in the Indus Tradition did not mark the demise of stone tools. Despite the relative ubiquity of bronze and copper during the Indus Bronze Age in comparison to other, similar archaeological cultures (Hoffman and Cleland 1977; Shaffer 1984), copper and copper alloys still did not eclipse the use of stone tools. In fact, in some crafting traditions, such as shell, the use of stone was "indispensable" (Kenoyer 1984b). The continued importance of chipped stone tools applies in particular to cosmopolitan centers such as Harappa.

At the site of Harappa, the class of chipped stone is second only to ceramics in archaeological occurrence and comprises nearly a third of the site's rock and mineral assemblage (Law 2008). Early excavators devoted little study to Indus lithics, often just noting their existence in passing and collecting a few specimens. Many, but not all, researchers today are focusing increasingly on the chipped stone in the region, particularly at the quarrying and production sites (see below). I add to this growing body of knowledge my attribute analysis of chipped stone artifacts from the HARP excavations, the largest and most in-depth study of lithics from a major urban center to date.

THE INDUS LITHIC INDUSTRY

The lithic industry of the Indus Bronze Age is "among the richest and most diverse industries known to archaeologists in the world" (Pelegrin 1994: 588). Here I provide a brief overview of the main studies of the Harappan period workshops in the Rohri Hills and other sites and introduce aspects of my work with the HARP collections to provide an initial model of the complete Indus lithic industry.

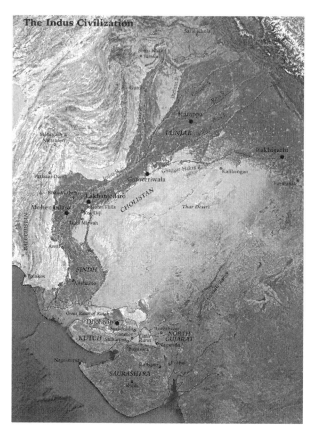

FIGURE 2.1. *Map of Indus region with location of sites and raw materials mentioned in the text*

Models of Production Techniques and Strategies

The Indus Tradition's technological complex and many of the related Chalcolithic neighbors were focused on blade and bladelet production. This production utilized a wide variety of techniques and skill sets including pressure flaking (punch technique), indirect and direct percussion, pressure retouch, heat treatment, and possibly indirect percussion by rebound or Khambhat (Cambay) technique (Kenoyer 1986, 1998; Pelegrin 1994). From as early as the seventh millennium BCE, pressure flaking has been a tradition in South Asia. Highly regular blades and bladelets were present by the time of incipient urbanism in the Indus region. Most scholars believe pressure techniques produced long blades (up to 20 cm long), although other techniques, such as indirect (punch) percussion, could have been used to produce shorter, less regular blades (Inizan and Lechevallier 1985, 1990, 1995; Marcon and Lechevallier 2001; Pelegrin 1994) and have been reproduced with good representation of known workshops (Briois et al. 2006).

The Rohri Hills Workshops

During the Harappan period in the Indus Tradition, Rohri Hills seems to have been the major center of production, although other geologically related smaller outcrops are increasingly identified (Biagi and Nisbet 2010; Biagi and Starini 2008; Law 2008). The Rohri Hills are a series of limestone terraces that stretch for 40 km in length (Biagi 2006). The range is approximately 45 km east of the modern-day course of the Indus (Biagi and Starini 2011). The Rohri Hills alone have 1,287 documented workshops (Shaikh et al. 2002); the knapping and extraction of chert materials date from the Middle Paleolithic to modern-day limestone mining (Biagi 2006; Biagi et al. 1997) (figures 2.2, 2.3).

Many of the sites at this important raw material source consist of quarrying activities and the mass production of blades and bladelets in multiple workshops (Biagi et al. 1997; Negrino et al. 1996). These workshops sometimes represent different phases of production where tools and debitage are found in situ, with the only disturbance seeming to be deflation of the landscape (figures 2.4, 2.5). There were at least two different strategies of chert blade production during the Indus period (Starini and Biagi 2011): "normal" subpyramidal or subconical prismatic blade core reduction and smaller "bullet" cores. The average length of the regular blades is 95 mm, while the bladelets struck off the "bullet" cores average 45 mm in length (Starini and Biagi 2011).

Blade Production

We have production "workshops" for each of these types of blades in the Rohri Hills region. Sites RH 480 (Negrino and Starini 1995) and RH 58 (Biagi and Pessina 1994) are two of the best-represented sites associated with the full-sized blades. The blades produced were long and very standardized, with uniform, regular, and straight parallel sides. In cross-section, the blades were often triangular or trapezoidal. The cores of regular blades were prepared by creating a crested ridge and striking off a large flake to create a flat platform. Estimates suggest that approximately twenty regular blades averaging roughly 95 mm resulted from one such core (Biagi and Starini 2011). Few complete blades remain at the workshops; most of the recovered products were blade fragments with a high proportion of proximal fragments (Biagi and Starini 2011).

FIGURE 2.2. *Rohri Hills landscape*

FIGURE 2.3. *Artifact scatters likely dating to the Paleolithic and Harappan periods*

The site of Kandharki-I, located in the Thar Desert outside of the Rohri Hills, is of particular importance because of the technological stages of manufacture there. The site dates to the pre-urban Kot Dijan period (Shaikh et al. 2002). Here, large cores and blades 11–13 cm long, such as those found at Mohenjo-daro (Biagi 1997), occur along with manufacturing waste (Shaikh et al. 2002). These samples are pink in color as a result of heat treatment (Shaikh et al. 2002). At the site of Kandharki, there are numerous extant pits in which pink stone and blue/black "over-fired" stone were heat-treated (Shaikh et al.

FIGURE 2.4. *Harappan period quarry sites*

2002). Spatially segregated manufacturing stages (Shaikh et al. 2002) suggest the division of labor. The Harappan period sites do not contain evidence of such large blades or cores (Shaikh et al. 2002).

Bladelet Production

Rather than rejuvenated cores having been repurposed to produce small blades, the small "bullet" cores are currently believed to have been a parallel industry, as seen at the Rohri Hills sites RH 59 (Biagi and Pessina 1994) and RH 862 (Negrino et al. 1996; Starini and Biagi 2006). Evidence suggests a

FIGURE 2.5.
Production areas in Rohri Hills region

similar *chaîne opératoire* for both industries. The bullet core–bladelet industry also employed flat platforms, and few complete bladelets were recovered from these sites (Biagi and Starini 2011). Some of these bladelets, if not all, were retouched into a type of bead micro-drill (Vidale et al. 1992).

The site of RH 862, located 3.5 km south of the Shadee Shaheed shrine (Biagi and Starini 2011), is a 120 m C-shaped distribution of features that include mines and multiple knapping areas (Biagi 1997). Site RH 862 was excavated by the Joint Rohri Hills Project. RH 862 was dated with Harappan period ceramic fragments and radiocarbon samples that date to 3870 ± 70 BCE (Biagi 1995; Starini and Biagi 2006). Much of the initial decortication of the chert nodules and the pre-forming of the core took place within the mine area or along its edge (evidenced by the large number of decortication flakes, crested ridge blades, and discarded pre-cores; Starini and Biagi 2011).

The workshops near the mining pits were associated with what seems to be the mass production of bladelets from bullet cores at Workshop 1 and resulted in a total of 446 kilos of lithic artifacts being recovered from this 120 m² site (Negrino et al. 1996; Starini and Biagi 2011). While the average sizes of these Harappan Rohri workshops range from only 15–150 m², they have artifact assemblages in the tens of thousands. For example, as many as 51,378 chert artifacts were recovered from Site 862 alone (Biagi 1997; Negrino et al. 1996; Starini and Biagi 2011).

Evidence for Production at Harappa

A vast majority of the site's assemblage are blades and blade fragment tools, with low frequencies of production evidence found in my study. However, production indicators such as various types of debitage and cores, both blade and bullet bladelet cores, are present but underrepresented in the sample. This underrepresentation is exasperated because many of the items are accessioned Harappa Museum objects, which were not included in my study. Further systematic reevaluation will be needed for a definitive understanding of the nature of production at the site. In my opinion, even considering sampling bias, there appears to be limited production of blades at the site of Harappa (table 2.3; figures 2.6, 2.7).

A further indirect measure of the low level of production at the site is the low frequency of cortex. While this is to be expected with blade-based assemblages, it illustrates that the few flakes and other debitage present were not likely the result of early production stages. When cortex is present, it is typically a small section near the proximal end (table 2.4).

Specialized Production and Standardization

While the variability and standardization of blade widths and thicknesses may be linked to many factors (Hirth and Andrews 2002), the creation of standardized blade widths and thicknesses by regulating the application of pressure requires a great deal of skill, particularly as the core is reduced (Titmus and Clark 2003). The regularity of blades in their thickness and width measurements has been used to argue for specialist producers at sites such as Tepe Hissar and Malyan in Iran (Kardulias 2003). Iranian chipped stone production may be the most closely analogous system of urban lithic production to the Indus system (Piperno 1973). The coefficient of variation (CV) at Harappa for width is 38.5, higher than those reported for any site in Iran and Greece examined by Kardulias, whose CV ranged from 14.3 to

FIGURE 2.6. *Sample of lithics including artifacts associated with primary and secondary production at Harappa. Photo credit, HARP.*

FIGURE 2.7. *Example of precore from Harappan Museum Collection. Photo credit, HARP.*

33.3 (see also Runnels 1985; table 2.5). However, the measurements of width used to support specialization in Iran are problematic, as the sample size was only 18 at Tepe Hissar (CV 14.3), particularly when compared to the over 10,000 tools in the sample from Harappa. The equation of standardization and technical knowledge with simplistic views of "specialization" is also problematic (Kenoyer et al. 1991).

TABLE 2.3. Count and percentage of Harappan (HARP) lithic sample by major artifact type

Artifact Type	Sample Count	Percentage (%)
Retouched blades and blade fragments	2,756	32.4
Edge-damaged blade and blade fragments	2,977	35.0
Unmodified blades and blade fragments	2,674	31.5
Edge-damaged flakes and flake fragments	17	0.2
Retouched flakes and flake fragments	23	0.3
Unmodified flakes and flake fragments	30	0.4
Cores and core fragments	3	0.04
Bullet cores	5	0.06
Core preparation flakes	6	0.07
Core trimming flakes	4	0.04
Crested ridge blades	4	0.04
Total	**8,499**	**100.00**

TABLE 2.4. Frequency of cortex in Harappan (HARP) sample

	Sample Count	Percentage (%)
No cortex	5,108	95
< 50% cortex	136	2.5
< 99% cortex	136	2.5
100% cortex	9	0.1
Not determinable	4	0.07
Total	**5,393**	

TABLE 2.5. Quantitative measures of blade tools from Harappan (HARP) sample

	Maximum Length	Maximum Thickness	Maximum Width
Mean (mm)	20.5	2.7	10.1
Standard deviation	11.6	1.3	3.9
Maximum (mm)	119.0	38.6	44.7
Minimum (mm)	0.67	0.54	0.95
Coefficient of variation	56.5	48.0	38.9
N	10,705	10,230	10,704

A better understanding of production strategies can also be achieved by plotting quantitative measures, such as the evidence of distinct production systems seen through bimodal distributions of widths in the Pre-Pottery Neolithic of the Levant and Anatolia (Binder 2007). The measurements and ratios are all continuous and share a similar distribution curve that is skewed left of normal. This continuous variation suggests that it is unlikely that different tools or blank types were preconceived by the manufacturers or consumers; and if there were clear-cut blade blank types, they were obscured through the process of use and re-sharpening before entering the archaeological record. Though the re-sharpening and use do not seem to have had a profound effect because the unmodified tools, which may have been used with materials that did not create macroscopically visible indications, have a distribution profile similar to the others. The visually continuous various ratios of length, thickness, and width were examined more carefully for signs of bimodal or multimodal divisions through the use of Gaussian functions and joint distribution. However, despite the use of these more powerful techniques, I did not determine the clusters to be salient or meaningful to the analysis or classification of the blade tools at Harappa.

Models of Distribution and Consumption

After the initial phases of production, these blades, or at least partially prepared cores, are believed to have been widely distributed to urban and rural consumers across the Indus Civilization and, to a lesser extent, to their Chalcolithic (or Mesolithic) neighbors (Cleland 1987; Gadekar et al. 2013, 2016; Inizan and Lechevallier 1990, 1997; Pelegrin 1994; Prabhakar et al. 2012), including Harappa (Law 2008).

Provisioning Strategies

The distribution of raw materials at Harappa, along with many other Indus reported sites, is consistent with models of direct access, specialized traders, or institutional procurement (Hirth et al. 2006), as a single source of raw material dominates. Of the chert objects, nearly 95 percent were made from Rohri-like cherts based on macroscopic evaluation. The utilization of Rohri-related cherts increases through time and completely dominates during the urban Harappan period 3, when virtually all chert can be assigned to Rohri-like sources (opaque gray 67%, n = 3,557; tan-brown 14%, n = 752; translucent gray 10%, n = 529; translucent tan-brown 3%, n = 170). I believe direct access models for Harappan provisioning are unfeasible because of the low levels of on-site production, the distance to raw material sources, and the relatively low value of the blades as indicated by their frequency and their low levels of sharpening and curation.

In light of the limited extant production evidence, distinguishing between institutionalized procurement and specialized traders and local producers (or itinerant provisioning producers) is difficult (Hirth 2008). However, one might view the corporate form of institutional procurement as a joint venture of a social group or network of specialists that aligns well with what we know of other crafts' interregional social-economic organization in the Indus region (Kenoyer 1989): the guilds (*s'reni*) of historic India (Majumdar 1977: 215–216; Majumdar and Mookerji 1920).

In contrast, indirect access to raw materials through trade is suggested during the pre-urban Ravi phase, when we have the most variability in the raw materials present (see figure 2.8; Kenoyer 2011; Law 2008). The non-Rohri gray-black chert (0.6%, n = 32) specifically, and potentially others, may be traced to the closer Salesar Formation of the Salt Range roughly 225 km north of the site (Law 2008; Law and Baqri 2003).

Transportation of Lithic Blades

Indus blades are rarely complete; instead, they are often segmented into fragments that have been called "typologically undiagnostic" (Méry et al. 2007: 1105). The nature of how these tools arrived at Harappa, as whole blades or pre-processed segments, can be evaluated in part by looking at the proportional representation of the different blade segments to each other following De León and colleagues (2009). Whole blade transport would be supported by a relatively even distribution ratio of distal, medial, and proximal segments, while processed blades would have uneven representation biased against generally less desirable proximal and distal segments. A true 1:1:1 ratio cannot be expected for whole blade transport, as their use and post-depositional patterns can alter the ratios (De León et al. 2009). De León and his colleagues suggest a distal to medial ratio of 2–3:1 and a proximal to distal ratio of 1:1 to be expected for whole blade trade. The ratio of medial to distal pieces at Harappa was 2:1 and the ratio of proximal to distal pieces was 1:1, consistent with both whole blade trade and local production of blades from cores and inconsistent with pre-processed blade segments arriving from elsewhere. Based on published data, other sites in the Indus may have used different systems for blade trade, but this cannot be conclusively argued at this time because of inconsistent collection and excavation strategies at some of the sites. The potential use of distal segments as drills increases their value in the Indus relative to other

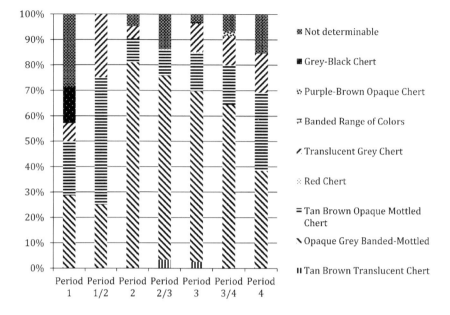

FIGURE 2.8. *Raw material by time period at Harappa. Macroscopically identified raw materials. Opaque gray banded-mottled, tan-brown opaque mottled, translucent gray, and tan-brown translucent samples of these materials were sourced by Law 2008 as originating in the Rohri Hills or geologically related sources.*

ethnographic and archaeological area traditions and may have encouraged whole blade or blade core transport or both (figures 2.9, 2.10).

Actors of Lithic Distribution

No formal model for the distribution of blades or the producers has been put forth; however, some scholars suggest that itinerant flintknappers were an important facet of a complex system (Inizan and Lechevallier 1995; Pelegrin 1994). There are relatively proportional examples of primary production, such as, cores and platform rejuvenation flakes, and secondary production, such as crested ridge blades (sensu De León et al. 2009) in my study sample and my survey of accessioned objects. The presence of both production types suggests that local craftspeople rather than itinerant producers were involved with local production, as cores could have traveled away from the site with itinerant producers. Although Hirth (2008) models multiple raw material sources as indicative of itinerant craftspeople, the geography and sourcing precision

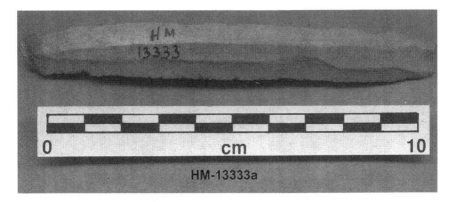

FIGURE 2.9. *Example of complete blade from Harappan Museum Collection. Photo credit, HARP.*

available in the Indus region compared to Mesoamerica do not make this a particularly useful distinction.

Distribution Methods

The primary mode of economic distribution of goods and commodities within the Indus region is yet to be demonstrated. The extent to which market, redistribution, and reciprocal systems of exchange were formalized is speculation linked to scholars' interpretations of how the political system was shaped (see Fairservis 1986; Jacobson 1986; Jarrige and Meadow 1992; Kenoyer 1994b; Possehl 1998; Shaffer 1982). It is not likely that either redistribution or reciprocal systems were used to distribute chipped stone materials or tools (see correlates proposed by Hirth 1998). No hoards of chipped stone tools have been found; further, they are one of the most commonly encountered classes of artifact and were not associated with specific site areas or contexts. This even distribution and the general homogeneity in the chipped stone are consistent with a marketplace exchange system (Hirth 1998), despite the lack of readily definitive marketplaces at Indus urban centers.

I suggest that the distribution of chipped stone and raw materials was noncentralized. The various macroscopic varieties of Rohri-like cherts were largely evenly distributed across the various Harappan mounds but unevenly distributed among proposed neighborhoods (Davis 2016). The northern neighborhoods of Mound ET and E, A, and C have a higher percentage of gray cherts, while the southern neighborhoods of E and ET, G, and D have higher percentages of tan cherts. In addition, some classes of unmodified tools, created through

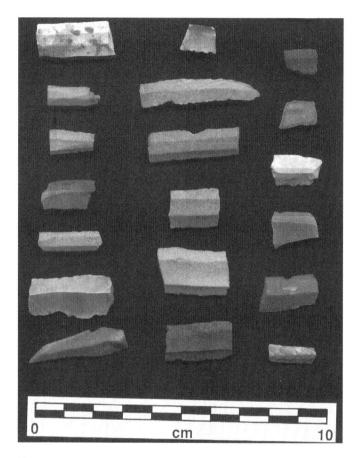

FIGURE 2.10. *Examples of blade segments and raw materials from HARP sample. Photo by M. Davis.*

a soft hierarchical classification system of attributes, demonstrate spatial correlation between otherwise distinct neighborhoods (Davis n.d.). However, not all patterns of unmodified tool classes, potentially distinct blade blanks, and raw material patterns were spatially contingent (see figure 2.11; tables 2.6, 2.7).

These relationships and distribution patterns transcended any form of district organization or administration. The fact that there is never any exclusivity for raw material types suggests that the ties linking those in charge of raw material acquisition to the consumer were informal and that there were no prohibitions on consumption or differential access to raw material networks. These long-standing market or merchant relationships with local consumers

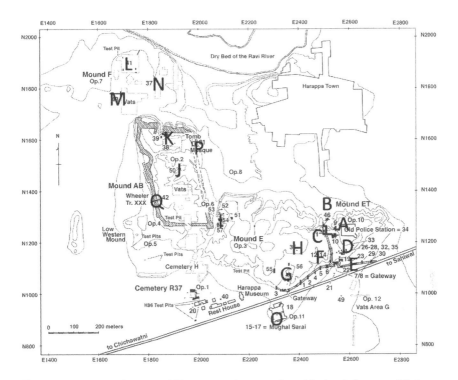

FIGURE 2.11. *Map of the site of Harappa with proposed neighborhoods (map modified from HARP excavation area map)*

may have some analogies to the intergenerational relationships between consumers and shopkeepers in modern-day markets in the region. At this time, however, there is no evidence to suggest a "market" with competing "pattherwallas." The spatial relationship of raw material consumption suggests that these intergenerational relationships may have existed at the interregional level, with consumers accessing stones that were the most convenient.

MODELS OF USE
Typological and Functional Studies

The function of Indus stone tools still requires further investigation. Stone tools were initially thought to be domestic all-purpose tools (Marshall 1931: 458) or ritual implements (Mackay 1938: 36). Because the vast majority of Indus blades do not conform to classic morphological types, there have been few typologies of the Indus stone tools, aside from the extensive and fruitful

TABLE 2.6. Ratios of blade segments at Indus sites.

Site	Proximal	Medial	Distal
Dholavira	2	7	1
Banawali	2	5	1
Kalibangan	2	5	1
Bagasara	1	2	1
Shikarpur	3	5	1
Mohenjo-daro	1	5	1
Cleland regional	2	5	1
Harappa HARP excavations	1	2	1

Data drawn from the following publications: Dholavira, Banawali, and Kalibangan (Inizan and Lechevallier 1990: 51; Inizan and Lechevallier 1995: 83, figure 4); Bagasara and Shikarpur (Gadeker et al. 2014: 145), the Dales excavations at Mohenjo-daro (Kenoyer 1984a: 131), Cleland's overall tabulation of blades without cortex at eight Harappan- and Early Harappan–related sites in the Indus (Cleland 1977: 232, table 4), and the present sample of the HARP excavations at Harappa.

While the HARP blades were originally recorded in the five state categories (proximal, proximal-medial, medial, distal-medial, and distal), these categories were collapsed (i.e., proximal-medial sections were counted with proximal) to make them comparable.

work with stone drills (Kenoyer and Vidale 1992). Cleland (1977; Hoffman and Cleland 1977) was the first to attempt to combine attribute analysis with classical typology by using the presence or absence of traits, including utilization and retouch, to define his types. Kenoyer (1984) conducted a more detailed examination of retouch and edge-damage patterns on Indus tool segments on 101 blades and blade fragments from the Dales excavations at Mohenjo-daro. My investigation (Davis n.d.) of tools created a functionally aimed attribute classification system, avoiding techno-typological aspects of earlier analysis, as such morphological types have limited or no bearing on the actual activities of tools (Bisson 2000; Chase 2008; Hardy et al. 2008; Holdaway and Douglass 2012; Rolland and Dibble 1990; Shea 1988, 1989; Tomaskova 2005). The tool classes and questions based on their spatial and temporal distribution will require future testing with targeted microwear analysis.

At this time, there has been limited use-wear analysis of any Indus Tradition stone tools. One high-powered microwear study of seven nearly complete blades from a pottery workshop at Nasharo during the Indus period (2500–2400 BCE) suggests that potters used the blades for trimming wheel-thrown pottery (Méry et al. 2007). A core with macroscopic polish, not from the workshop but also made of "Rohri-like" chert, was less strongly supported to have been used for burnishing or smoothing leather-hard pottery

TABLE 2.7. Spatial distribution of raw material by neighborhoods

Chert Type	NBHD A N	NBHD A %	NBHD B N	NBHD B %	NBHD C N	NBHD C %	NBHD D N	NBHD D %	NBHD E N	NBHD E %	NBHD G N	NBHD G %	NBHD H N	NBHD H %	NBHD I N	NBHD I %	NBHD J N	NBHD J %	NBHD K N	NBHD K %	NBHD L N	NBHD L %	NBHD M N	NBHD M %
Tan Trans	5	1.5	1	5.3	4	2.3	23	3.7	5	4.2	13	5.4	68	3.6	24	4	0	0.0	7	4.0	1	3	4	2.7
Opaque Gray	266	81.6	15	79.0	126	71.2	434	69.2	95	79.2	149	61.6	1,312	68.5	426	72.5	26	76.5	107	61.8	24	72.7	104	70.3
Opaque Tan	18	5.5	2	10.5	21	11.9	92	14.6	7	5.8	41	16.9	302	15.8	87	14.8	6	17.7	31	17.9	3	9.1	16	10.8
Red	0	0.0	1	5.3	0	0.0	3	0.5	1	0.8	2	0.8	3	0.2	2	0.3	1	2.9	4	2.3	0	0.0	2	1.3
Gray Trans	30	9.2	0	0.0	24	13.6	67	10.7	10	8.3	25	10.3	221	11.5	42	7.1	0	0.0	15	8.7	5	15.2	21	14.2
Band Colors	2	0.6	0	0.0	2	1.1	2	0.3	1	0.8	0	0.0	0	0.0	2	0.3	0	0.0	0	0.0	0	0.0	0	0.0
Purple-Brown	3	0.9	0	0.0	0	0.0	2	0.3	0	0.0	1	0.4	1	0.1	3	0.5	0	0.0	2	1.2	0	0.0	0	0.0
Gray-Black	2	0.6	0	0.0	0	0.0	4	0.6	1	0.8	3	1.2	7	0.4	1	0.2	1	2.9	7	4.0	0	0.0	1	0.7
Total	0.326		19		177		627		120		242		1,914		587		34		173		33		148	

(Méry et al. 2007). Three "endscrapers" collected in the Internazionale di Studi sul Mediterraneo e l'Oriente (IsMEO; 1982–1985) surface collection of the Moneer South East Area of Mohenjo-daro were reanalyzed, and it was found that two were used longitudinally and the third with a transverse scraping action. They show signs of reddish particulate matter on the ventral face and were likely hafted, possibly with a wooden handle (Vidale et al. 2013).

Current Evidence of Use of Tools at Harappa

The breakdown of the blade assemblage is roughly equally distributed among blades with retouch, blades with edge damage, and those with no macroscopic modification visible with a 10× lens. This differentiation among retouch, edge damage, and unmodified blades is a continuum rather than constituting discrete categories and is also the result of a complex history of manufacture, modification, use, discard, deposition, and storage. The intentionality of retouch can be difficult to determine, as it may result from purposeful modification of a tool or through use. Different motions, materials worked, and length of use can alternatively result in various degrees of edge micro-flaking. Classification of these blades as utilized tools or unused blades would require microscopic analysis. The sample of flakes has a higher proportion of unmodified representatives (n = 30) compared to retouched (n = 23) or edge-damaged flakes (n = 17). However, this is not a significant enough sample size to draw definitive conclusions about the use or lack of use of flakes as tools, expedient or otherwise (table 2.8).

Most of the edge flaking observed on blades was only marginally invasive. Of those tools with invasive retouch, 201 were found on distal portions of the blade, associated with drill-class tools. Normal retouch and edge damage was the most common form of edge modification. Normal backing retouch is associated with drilling and piercing tools. Unsurprisingly, proximal sections are more likely to be unmodified (table 2.9).

The edges of the blades exhibited low macroscopically visible polishes, and 92.8 percent of tools (n = 3,160) had no polish readily identifiable. Of the remaining tools, 176 (5.1%) had a slight polish, and only 2 percent (n = 69) had a well-formed polish usually associated with working materials with a high silica content (e.g., grasses, cereals, wood, antler, and bone). No significant variation was found when examining polish occurrence while looking at tools by state of the blade. The lack of sickle polish is important because unlike other early areas in which lithic use persists alongside metals, the tools at Harappa are not primarily linked to agricultural activities (Kardulias 2003).

TABLE 2.8. Invasiveness of edge modifications

	Edge-Damage Invasiveness	Retouch Invasiveness
Marginal	2,004	678
Invasive	13	287
Semi-invasive	220	295
Total	2,237	1,260

TABLE 2.9. Edge-damage class

	All	Proximal-Medial	Proximal	Medial	Distal-Medial	Distal
Normal	1,078	158	43	517	166	127
Inverse	349	55	13	192	49	29
Alternate	288	57	15	155	28	25
Alternating	325	51	26	173	31	7
Bifacial	106	21	1	44	20	12
Trampling	95	15	8	37	8	19
Total	2,241					

Stone tools were found widely in both residential and workshop contexts. The spatial analysis of attributes suggests that despite the overall lack of morphological variation, specialized tasks were enacted with these blades (Davis 2016, n.d.). Furthermore, the evident discrete spatial patterning of these tools suggests that by and large they were not used primarily as multipurpose tools, and they do not show high rates of retooling. The lack of tool conservation is further supported by the relatively functional average edge angle of 61.8° (s.d. 7.03), low extensiveness of retouch, and a width to thickness ratio of 4 to 1.

There seems to have been little discrimination in using the ventral or dorsal side of the blade for transverse activities that produced normal edge damage when the classes of edge modification are examined spatially. An even representation of all blade segments for each tool was present in spatially concentrated activity areas. This suggests that neither workshops nor domestic areas were targeting certain blade segments for different activities, outside of drilling workshops, but were using each section in the same manner. This pattern may encourage future study to see if some blade segmentation occurred through use, in contrast with a general perspective that blades were intentionally segmented (Gadekar et al. 2014; Inizan and Lechvallier 1995). Vidale and colleagues (2013) suggests that the presence of languette-form fractures in his study of the three blades from Mohenjo-daro supports tool breakage during use.

SUMMARY

The Indus lithic technological complex during the Urban period involved a variety of stages, processes, and specialists in a multifaceted and multiple actor system during the course of a tool's life history, from raw materials to use. Similar to other sedentary societies using stone tools, producers focused on blade and bladelet industries. The density of debris and segmentation of production at quarry and workshop sites suggests mass or industrial production of blades and bladelets by specialists in the Rohri Hills during the Bronze Age. It appears that most of the production was taking place at the site of raw material acquisition, away from archaeologically visible settlements, or at settlements near these raw material sources, such as Kandharki-I (Shaikh et al. 2002) and Kot Diji (Cleland 1977).

Finished blades and nearly finished cores were distributed across almost one million square kilometers. This distribution system was one of many that integrated people across regions and functions in both large urban centers and small villages, possibly facilitated by corporate social-economic group networks.

A wide variety of crafting and domestic tasks utilized these blades, despite the accessibility of copper, because the stone blades were not only efficient but also relatively cheap, flexible, and multifunctional. The high prevalence of blades suggests that mass manufacture and transport and adaptability to consumers were among the highest priorities for producers and distributors of the blades.

This model of the chipped stone industry for the Indus is preliminary, and significant testing is required through more detailed and directed studies of production at "consumer" sites, particularly to evaluate the production of blade tools at sites such as Harappa. Of equal importance, more microscopic use-wear studies are needed to address specific questions of the functions of stone tools, and regional evaluation is needed to discover potential political, economic, and social organizational variations that may be reflected in stone tool procurement and distribution systems.

ACKNOWLEDGMENTS

I would like to thank the organizers of the SAA session and editors of this volume, particularly Rachel Horowitz, for my inclusion and for useful feedback.

In Pakistan I thank the Shah Abdul Latif University Khairpur Archaeology Department, particularly Qasid Mallah and Ghulam Muhiuddin Vessar for their intellectual and literal guidance to archaeological sites in Sindh and their chipped stone tools, including those in the Rohri Hills. Special thanks for the research and excavations of the HARP team, which completely transformed our knowledge of the Indus Civilization. I am indebted to the team members for their excellent work and accumulation of a vast amount of precisely excavated and recorded data. Particular thanks to Dr. Jonathan Mark Kenoyer for his assistance with this project and reviewing drafts of this chapter. I would also like to thank the anonymous reviewers of this chapter and the government and peoples of Pakistan.

REFERENCES

Andrieu, C. 2014. "Maya Lithic Production." In *Encyclopaedia of the History of Science, Technology, and Medicine in Non-Western Cultures*, ed. Helaine Selin, 1–14. New York: Springer.

Aoyama, K. 2001. "Classic Maya State, Urbanism, and Exchange: Chipped Stone Evidence of the Copan Valley and Its Hinterland." *American Anthropologist* 103 (2): 346–360.

Aoyama, K. 2007. "Elite Artists and Craft Producers in Classic Maya Society: Lithic Evidence from Aguateca, Guatemala." *Latin American Antiquity* 18 (1): 3–26.

Barthélémy de Saizieu, B. 2003. *Les Parures de Mehrgarh: Perles et Pendentifs du Néolithique Préceramique a la Période pré-Indus: Fouilles 1974–1985*. Paris: Editions Recherche sur les Civilisations.

Belcher, W.R. 1991. "Fish Resources in an Early Urban Context at Harappa." In *Harappa Excavations 1986–1990: A Multidisciplinary Approach to Third Millennium Urbanism*, ed. R.H. Meadow, 107–120. Madison, WI: Prehistory Press.

Belcher, W.R. 1997. "Urban Provisioning and Social Relations: Fish Remains from the Urban Center of Harappa, Pakistan." Paper presented at the 67th annual meeting of the Society for American Archaeology, Nashville, TN, April 2–6.

Bhan, K., M. Vidale, and J.M. Kenoyer. 1994. "Harappan Technology: Theoretical and Methodological Issues." *Man and the Environment* 19 (1–2): 141–156.

Bhan, K.K., M. Vidale, and J.M. Kenoyer. 2002. "Some Important Aspects of the Harappan Technological Tradition." In *Archaeology of the Harappan Civilization*, ed. S. Settar and R. Korisettar, 223–272. Indian Archaeology in Retrospect, vol. 2. New Delhi: Indian Council of Historical Research.

Biagi, P. 1995. "An AMS Radiocarbon Date from the Harappan Flint Quarry-Pit 862 in the Rohro Hills (Sindh-Pakistan)." *Ancient Sindh* 2: 81–84.

Biagi, P. 1997. "Flint Assemblages from the Rohri Hills in British Collections." *Ancient Sindh* 2: 81–84.

Biagi, P. 2006. "The Archaeological Sites of the Rohri Hills (Sindh, Pakistan): The Way They Are Being Destroyed." *Web Journal on Cultural Patrimony* 2: 101–119.

Biagi, P., F. Negrino, and E. Starini. 1997. "New Data on the Harappan Flint Quarries of the Rohri Hills (Sindh-Pakistan)." In *Man and Flint: Proceedings of the VIIth International Flint Symposium*, ed. R. Schild and Z. Sulgostowska, 29–39. Warszawa, Poland: Warszawa Institute of Archaeology and Ethnology.

Biagi, P., and R. Nisbet. 2010. "The Prehistoric Flint Mines at Jhimpir in Lower Sindh (Pakistan)." *Antiquity Project Gallery* 84 (235): 67–81.

Biagi, P., and A. Pessina. 1994. "Surveys and Excavations in the Rohri Hills (Sindh-Pakistan): A Preliminary Report on the 1993 Campaign." *Ancient Sindh* 1: 13–76.

Biagi, P., and E. Starini. 2008. "The Bronze Age Indus Quarries of the Rohri Hills and Ongar in Sindh (Pakistan)." In *Geoarchaeology and Archaeomineralogy: Proceedings of the International Conference 29–30 October 2008, Sofia*, ed. R.I. Kostov, B. Gaydarska, and M. Gurova, 77–82. Sofia: St. Ivan Rilski.

Biagi, P., and E. Starini. 2011. "Technological Choices and Lithic Production in the Indus Period: Case Studies from Sindh (Pakistan)." *Iranian Archaeology* 2: 21–33.

Binder, D. 2007. "PPN Pressure Technology: Views from Anatolia." In *Technical Systems and Near Eastern PPN Communities*, ed. L. Astruc, D. Binder, and F. Briois, 235–243. Antibes, France: Éditions APDCA.

Bisson, M.S. 2000. "Nineteenth Century Tools for Twenty-First Century Archaeology? Why the Middle Paleolithic Typology of Francois Bordes Must Be Replaced." *Journal of Archaeological Method and Theory* 7 (1): 1–48.

Briois, F., F. Negrino, J. Pelegrin, and E. Starini. 2006. "Flint Exploitation and Blade Production during the Harappan Period (Bronze Age): Testing the Evidence from the Rohri Hills Mines (Sindh-Pakistan) through an Experimental Approach." In *Stone Age, Mining Age*, ed. G. Korlin and G. Weisgerber, 307–314. Bochum, Germany: Deutsches Bergbau-Museum.

Chabot, J., and J. Pelegrin. 2012. "Two Examples of Pressure Blade Production with a Lever: Recent Research from the Southern Caucasus (Armenia) and Northern Mesopotamia (Syria, Iraq)." In *The Emergence of Pressure Blade Making: From Origin to Modern Experimentation*, ed. P.M. Desrosiers, 181–198. New York: Springer.

Chase, P.G. 2008. "Form, Function, and Mental Templates in Paleolithic Lithic Analysis." Paper presented at the symposium From the Pecos to the Paleolithic: Papers in Honor of Arthur J. Jelinek, Society for American Anthropology Meetings, Vancouver, BC, March 26–30.

Clark, S.R. 2003. "Representing the Indus Body: Sex, Gender, Sexuality, and the Anthropomorphic Terracotta Figurines from Harappa." *Asian Perspectives* 42 (2): 304–328.

Cleland, J.H. 1977. "Chacolithic and Bronze Age Chipped Stone Industries of the Indus Region: An Analysis of Variability and Change." PhD dissertation, University of Virginia, Charlottesville.

Cleland, J.H. 1987. "Lithic Analysis and Culture Process in the Indus Region." In *Studies in the Archaeology of India and Pakistan*, ed. J. Jacobson, 91–116. Warmister, UK: Aris and Phillips.

Dales, G.F., and J.M. Kenoyer. 1991. "Summaries of Five Seasons of Research at Harappa (District Sahiwal, Punjab, Pakistan) 1986–1990." In *Harappa Excavations 1986–1990: A Multidisciplinary Approach to Third Millennium Urbanism*, ed. R.H. Meadow, 185–262. Madison: Prehistory Press.

Davis, M.A. 2016. "Stone Tools as Indicators of Socio-Economic Variability at Harappa, Pakistan." In *Contextualizing Material Culture in South and Central Asia in Pre-Modern Times: Papers from the 20th Conference of the European Association for South Asian Archaeology and Art Held in Vienna from 4th to 9th July 2010*, ed. V. Widorn, U. Franke, and P. Latschenber, 51–65. Turnhout, Belgium: Brepols.

Davis, M.A. n.d. "The Social Urban Landscape of Harappa: Stone Tools and Neighborhoods." PhD dissertation, University of Wisconsin–Madison.

De León, J.P., K.G. Hirth, and D.M. Carballo. 2009. "Exploring Formative Period Obsidian Blade Trade: Three Distribution Models." *Ancient Mesoamerica* 20 (1): 113–128.

Edens, C. 1999. "The Chipped Stone Industry at Hacinebi: Technological Styles and Social Identity." *Paleorient* 25 (1): 23–33.

Fairservis, W. 1986. "Cattle and the Harappan Chiefdoms of the Indus Valley." *Expedition* 28 (2): 43–50.

Frahm, E. 2014. "Buying Local or Ancient Outsourcing? Locating Production of Prismatic Obsidian Blades in Bronze-Age Northern Mesopotamia." *Journal of Archaeological Science* 41: 605–621.

Gadekar, C., P. Ajitprasad, and M. Madella. 2013. "Crested Ridge Technique and Lithic Assemblage from Datrana, Gujarat." *Heritage: Journal of Multidisciplinary Studies in Archaeology* 1: 16–28.

Gadekar, C., S.V. Rajesh, and P. Ajithprasad. 2014. "Shikarpur Lithic Assemblage: New Questions Regarding Rohri Chert Blade Production." *Journal of Lithic Studies* 1 (1): 137–149.

Gadekar, C., S.V. Rajesh, and P. Ajithprasad. 2016. "A Comparison of Lithic Assemblages Belonging to Economically Diverse Settlements Flourishing during Mid-Third Millennium BCE Gujarat." *Herita* 3: 44–53.

Hardy, B.L., M. Bolus, and N.J. Conard. 2008. "Hammer or Crescent Wrench? Stone-Tool Form and Function in the Aurignacian of Southwest Germany." *Journal of Human Evolution* 54 (5): 648–662.

Hartenberger, B., S. Rosen, and T. Matney. 2000. "The Early Bronze Age Blade Workshop at Titriş Höyük: Lithic Specialization in an Urban Context." *Near Eastern Archaeology* 63 (1): 51–58.

Hartenberger, B., and C. Runnels. 2001. "The Organization of Flaked Stone Production at Bronze Age Lerna." *Hesperia* 70 (3): 255–283.

Hirth, K.G. 1998. "The Distributional Approach: A New Way to Identify Marketplace Exchange in the Archaeological Record." *Current Anthropology* 39 (4): 451–476.

Hirth, K.G. 2008. "The Economy of Supply: Modeling Obsidian Procurement and Craft Provisioning at a Central Mexican Urban Center." *Latin American Antiquity* 19 (4): 435–457.

Hirth, K.G. 2012. "The Organizational Structures of Mesoamerican Obsidian Prismatic Blade Technology." In *The Emergence of Pressure Blade Making: From Origin to Modern Experimentation*, ed. P.M. Desrosiers, 401–415. New York: Springer.

Hirth, K.G., and B. Andrews, eds. 2002. *Pathways to Prismatic Blades: A Study in Mesoamerican Obsidian Core-Blade Technology*. Los Angeles: Cotsen Institute of Archaeology Press.

Hirth, K.G., B. Andrews, and J.J. Flenniken. 2006. "A Technological Analysis of Xochicalco Obsidian Prismatic Blade Production." In *Obsidian Craft Production in Ancient Mexico*, ed. K.G. Hirth, 63–95. Salt Lake City: University of Utah Press.

Hirth, K.G., G. Bondar, M.D. Glascock, A.J. Vonarx, and T. Daubenspck. 2006. "Supply Side Economics: An Analysis of Obsidian Procurement and the Organization of Workshop Provisioning." In *Obsidian Craft Production in Ancient Central Mexico*, ed. K.G. Hirth, 115–136. Salt Lake City: University of Utah Press.

Hoffman, B.C., and H.M.-L.-L. Miller. 2014. "Production and Consumption of Copper-Base Metals in the Indus Civilization." *Journal of World Prehistory* 22 (3): 237–264.

Hoffman, M.A., and J.H. Cleland. 1977. *Excavations at the Harappan Site of Allahdino: The Lithic Industry at Allahdino*. Papers of the Allahdino Expedition 2. New York: American Museum of Natural History.

Holdaway, S., and M. Douglass. 2012. "A Twenty-First Century Archaeology of Stone Artifacts." *Journal of Archaeological Method and Theory* 19 (1): 101–131.

Inizan, M.-L., and M. Lechevallier. 1985. "La Taille du Silex par Pression a Mehrgarh, Pakistan: La Tombe d'un Tailleur?" *Paleorient* 11 (1): 111–118.

Inizan, M.-L., and M. Lechevallier. 1990. "A Techno-Economic Approach to Lithics: Some Examples of Blade Pressure Debitage in the Indo-Pakistani Subcontinent."

In *South Asian Archaeology, 1987*, ed. M. Taddei and P. Callieri, 43–59. Rome: Internazionale di Studi sul Mediterraneo e l'Oriente.

Inizan, M.-L., and M. Lechevallier. 1995. "A Transcultural Phenomenon in the Chalcolithic and Bronze Age Lithics of the Old World: Raw Material Circulation and Production of Standardized Long Blades, the Example of the Indus Civilization." *South Asian Archaeology* 1: 77–86.

Inizan, M.-L., and M. Lechevallier. 1997. "A Transcultural Phenomenon in the Chalcolithic and Bronze Age Lithics of the Old World: Raw Material Circulation and Production of Standardized Long Blades: The Example of the Indus Civilization." In *South Asian Archaeology 1995*, ed. B. Allchin, and R. Allchin, 77–85. New Delhi: Oxford and IBH.

Jacobson, J. 1986. "The Harappan Civilization: An Early State." In *Studies in the Archaeology of India and Pakistan*, ed. J. Jacobson, 137–173. New Dehli: Oxford and IBH.

Jarrige, C., J.-F. Jarrige, R.H. Meadow, and G. Quivron. 1995. *Mehrgarh Field Reports 1975 to 1985—From the Neolithic to the Indus Civilization*. Karachi: Department of Culture and Tourism, Government of Sindh and the French Foreign Ministry.

Jarrige, J.-F., and R.H. Meadow. 1980. "The Antecedents of Civilization in the Indus Valley." *Scientific American* 243 (2): 122–137.

Jarrige, J.-F., and R.H. Meadow. 1992. "Mélanges Fairservis: A Discourse on Relations between Kachi and Sindh in Prehistory." In *South Asian Archaeology Studies*, ed. G.L. Possehl, 163–178. New Delhi: Oxford and IBH.

Kardulias, P.N., 2003. "Stone in an Age of Bronze: Lithics from Bronze Age Contexts in Greece and Iran." In *Written in Stone: The Multiple Dimensions of Lithic Analysis*, ed. P.N. Kardulias and R.W. Yerkes, 113–124. Lanham, MD: Lexington Books.

Kenoyer, J.M. 1984a. "Chipped Stone Tools from Mohenjodaro." In *Frontiers of the Indus Civilization*, ed. B.B. Lal and S.P. Gupta, 118–131. New Delhi: Books and Books.

Kenoyer, J.M. 1984b. "Shell Working Industries of the Indus Civilization: A Summary." *Paléorient* 10 (1): 49–63.

Kenoyer, J.M. 1986. "The Indus Bead Industry: Contributions to Bead Technology." *Ornament* 10 (1): 18–23.

Kenoyer, J.M. 1989. "Socio-Economic Structures of the Indus Civilization as Reflected in Specialized Crafts and the Question of Ritual Segregation." In *Old Problems and New Perspectives in the Archaeology of South Asia*, ed. J.M. Kenoyer, 183–192. Madison: Wisconsin Archaeological Reports.

Kenoyer, J.M. 1991a. "Urban Process in the Indus Tradition: A Preliminary Model from Harappa." In *Harrapa Excavations 1986–1990: A Multidisciplinary Approach* to *Third Millennium Urbanism*, ed. R.H. Meadow, 29–60. Madison, WI: Prehistory Press.

Kenoyer, J.M. 1991b. "The Indus Valley Tradition of Pakistan and Western India." *Journal of World Prehistory* 5 (4): 331–385.

Kenoyer, J.M. 1994a. "Faience from the Indus Valley Civilization." *Ornament* 17 (3): 36–39, 95.

Kenoyer, J.M. 1994b. "The Harappan State: Was It or Wasn't It?" In *From Sumer to Meluhha: Contributions to the Archaeology of South and East Asia in Memory of George F. Dales Jr.*, ed. J.M. Kenoyer, 71–80. Madison: Department of Anthropology, University of Wisconsin.

Kenoyer, J.M. 1995. "Shell Trade and Shell Working during the Neolithic and Early Chalcolithic at Mehrgarh." In *Mehrgarh Field Reports 1974–1985: From Neolithic Times to the Indus Civilization*, ed. C. Jarrige, J.-F. Jarrige, R.H. Meadow, and G. Quivron, 566–581. Karachi: Department of Culture and Tourism, Government of Sindh and the French Foreign Ministry.

Kenoyer, J.M. 1997. "Early City-States in South Asia: Comparing the Harappan Phase and Early Historic Period." In *The Archaeology of City States: Cross Cultural Approaches*, ed. D.L. Nichols and T.H. Charlton, 51–80. Washington, DC: Smithsonian Institution Press.

Kenoyer, J.M. 1998. *Ancient Cities of the Indus Valley Civilization*. Karachi: Oxford University Press.

Kenoyer, J.M. 2005. "Bead Technologies at Harappa, 3300–1900 BC: A Comparative Summary." In *South Asian Archaeology 1*, ed. C. Jarrige and V. Lefevre, 157–170. Paris: Editions Recherche sur les Civilisations-ADPF.

Kenoyer, J.M. 2007. "Stone Beads in Ancient South Asia—7000–600 BC: A Comparative Approach to Technology, Style, and Ideology." In *The Global Perspective of Beads and Beadwork: History, Manufacture, Trade, and Adornment*, ed. J. Allen and V. Hector, 1–12. Istanbul: Kadir Has University.

Kenoyer, J.M. 2008. "Indus Urbanism: New Perspectives on Its Origin and Character." In *The Ancient City: New Perspectives on Urbanism in the New and Old World*, ed. J. Marcus and J.A. Sabloff, 183–208. Santa Fe, NM: School for Advanced Research Press.

Kenoyer, J.M. 2011. "Regional Cultures of the Greater Indus Valley: The Ravi and Kot Diji Phase Assemblages at Harappa, Pakistan." In *Cultural Relations between the Indus and the Iranian Plateau during the Third Millennium BCE Indus Project, Research Institute for Humanities and Nature*, ed. T. Osada and M. Witzel, 165–217. Cambridge: Cambridge University Press.

Kenoyer, J.M. 2014. "New Perspectives on the Indus Tradition: Contributions from Recent Research at Harappa and Other Sites in Pakistan and India." In

Sindhu-Sarasvati Valley Civilization: New Perspectives: A Volume in Memory of Dr. Shikaripur Ranganatha Rao, ed. N. Rao, 500–535. Los Angeles: Nalanda International.

Kenoyer, J.M., and R.H. Meadow. 1997. "Excavations at Harappa 1986–97: A Brief Overview." *Punjab Journal of Archaeology and History* 1: 61–73.

Kenoyer, J.M., and H.M.-L. Miller. 1997. "Metal Technologies of the Indus Valley Tradition in Pakistan and Western India." In *The Archaeometallurgy of the Asian Old World,* ed. V.C. Pigott, 107–151. Philadelphia: University of Pennsylvania Museum.

Kenoyer, J.M., and M. Vidale. 1992. "A New Look at Stone Drills of the Indus Valley Tradition." In *Materials Issues in Art and Archaeology III: Symposium Held April 27– May 1, 1992, San Francisco, California, USA,* ed. P.B. Vandiver, 495–518. Cambridge: Cambridge University Press.

Kenoyer, J.M., M. Vidale, and K.K. Bhan. 1991. "Contemporary Stone Beadmaking in Khambhat, India: Patterns of Craft Specialization and Organization of Production as Reflected in the Archaeological Record." *World Archaeology* 23 (1): 44–63.

Law, R.W. 2008. "Inter-Regional Interaction and Urbanism in the Ancient Indus Valley: A Geologic Provenience Study of Harappa's Rock and Mineral Assemblage." PhD dissertation, University of Wisconsin, Madison.

Law, R.W. 2011. *Inter-Regional Interaction and Urbanism in the Ancient Indus Valley: A Geological Provenience Study of Harappa's Rock and Mineral Assemblage.* Occasional Paper 11, Linguistics, Archaeology, and the Human Past. Kyoto, Japan: Research Institute for Humanities and Nature.

Law, R.W., and S. Baqri. 2003. "Black Chert Source Identified at Nammal Gorge, Salt Range." *Ancient Pakistan* 14: 34–40.

Mackay, E.J.H. 1938. *Further Excavations at Mohenjo-daro I–II.* New Delhi: Munshiram Manoharlal.

Majumdar, R.C. 1977. *Ancient India.* Delhi: Motilal Banarsidass.

Majumdar, R.C., and R. Mookerji. 1920. *Corporate Life in Ancient India.* Poona, India: Oriental Book Agency.

Marcon, V., and M. Lechevallier. 2001. "Lithic Industries of the Indo-Iranian Borderlands: Technological Approach of Blade Debitage in the Assemblages of Mehrgarh, Nausharo, and Miri Qalat in Balochistan, Pakistan." In *South Asian Archaeology 1997,* ed. M. Taddei and G. De Marco, 215–235. Rome: Istituto italiano per l'Africa e l'Oriente.

Marshall, J. 1931. *Mohenjo-daro and the Indus Civilization I–III.* London: Arthur Probsthain.

Meadow, R.H., and J.M. Kenoyer. 1993. "Excavation at Harappa 1992 and 1993." *Pakistan Archaeology* 28: 55–102.

Meadow, R.H., and J.M. Kenoyer. 2001. "Harappa Excavations 1998–1999: New Evidence for the Development and Manifestation of the Harappan Phenomenon." In *South Asian Archaeology 1999*, ed. K.R. van Kooij and E.M. Raven. Leiden. Groningen, Netherlands: Egbert Forsten.

Meadow, R.H., J.M. Kenoyer, and R.P. Wright. 1997. "Harappa Archaeological Research Project: Harappa Excavations 1997." Report submitted to the Department of Archaeology and Museums, Government of Pakistan.

Meadow, R.H., J.M. Kenoyer, and R.P. Wright. 2001. "Harappa Archaeological Research Project: Harappa Excavations 2000–2001." Report submitted to the Department of Archaeology and Museums, Government of Pakistan.

Méry, S., P. Anderson, M.L. Inizan, M. Lechevallier, and J. Pelegrin. 2007. "A Pottery Workshop with Flint Tools on Blades Knapped with Copper at Nausharo (Indus Civilisation, ca. 2500 BC)." *Journal of Archaeological Science* 34 (7): 1098–1116.

Miller, H.M.-L. 1996. "The Distribution of High-Temperature Manufacturing at Harappa, Pakistan (3rd Mill. BCE)." Paper presented at the Society for American Archaeology Meeting, New Orleans, LA, April 18–22.

Miller, H.M.-L. 1999. "Pyrotechnology and Society in the Cities of the Indus Valley." PhD dissertation, University of Wisconsin, Madison.

Miller, H.M.-L. 2000. "Reassessing the Urban Structure of Harappa: Evidence from Craft Production Distribution." In *South Asian Archaeology 1997*, ed. M. Taddei and G. De Marco, 77–100. Rome: l'Istituto Italiano per l'Africa e l'Oriente.

Miller, H.M.-L. 2004. "The Indus Talc-faience Complex: Types of Material, Clues to Production." In *South Asian Archaeology 1999*, ed. K.R. van Kooij and E.M. Raven, 111–122. Leiden: Netherlands International Institute of Asian Studies.

Moholy-Nagy, H., and B.A. Álvarez-Sandoval. 2011. "Observations on the Use-Life Trajectory of Lithic Artifacts at Tikal, Guatemala." In *The Technology of Maya Civilization: Political Economy and Beyond in Lithic Studies*, ed. Z.X. Hruby, G.E. Braswell, and O. Chinchilla Marzariegos, 30–36. Sheffield, UK: Equinox.

Negrino, F., C. Ottomano, E. Starnni, and G.M. Veesar. 1996. "Excavations at Site 862 (Rohri Hills, Sindh, Pakistan): A Preliminary Report of the 1995 and 1997 Campaigns." *Ancient Sindh* 3: 67–104.

Negrino, F., and E. Starini. 1995. "A Preliminary Report of the 1994 Excavations on the Rohri Hills (Sindh-Pakistan)." *Ancient Sindh* 2: 55–80.

Pelegrin, J. 1994. "Lithic Technology in Harappan Times." In *South Asian Archaeology 1993*, ed. A. Parpola and P. Koskikallio, 587–598. Helsinki: Suomalainen Tiedeakatemia.

Piperno, M. 1973. "The Lithic Industry of Tepe Yahya: A Preliminary Typological Analysis." *East and West* 23 (1–2): 59–74.

Possehl, G.L. 1998. "Sociocultural Complexity without the State: The Indus Civilization." In *Archaic States*, ed. G. Feinman and J. Marcus, 261–291. Santa Fe, NM: School of American Research Press.

Possehl, G.L. 2002. *The Indus Civilization: A Contemporary Perspective*. Walnut Creek, CA: Altamira.

Prabhakar, V.N., R.S. Bisht, R.W. Law, and J.M. Kenoyer. 2012. "Stone Drill Bits from Dholavira—A Multi-faceted Analysis." *Man and Environment* 37 (1): 8–25.

Rolland, N., and H.L. Dibble. 1990. "A New Synthesis of Middle Paleolithic Variability." *American Antiquity* 55 (3): 480–499.

Rosen, S.A. 1997. *Lithics after the Stone Age: A Handbook of Stone Tools from the Levant*. Walnut Creek, CA: Altamira.

Runnels, C. 1985. "The Bronze-Age Flaked-Stone Industries from Lerna: A Preliminary Report." *Hesperia: The Journal of the American School of Classical Studies at Athens* 54 (4): 357–391.

Shafer, H.J., and T.R. Hester. 1991. "Lithic Craft Specialization and Product Distribution at the Maya Site of Colha, Belize." *World Archaeology* 23 (1): 79–97.

Shaffer, J.G. 1982. "Harappan Commerce: An Alternative Perspective." In *Anthropology in Pakistan*, ed. S. Pastner and L. Flam, 166–210. Ithaca, NY: Cornell University Press.

Shaffer, J.G. 1984. "The Indo-Aryan Invasions: Cultural Myth and Archaeological Reality." In *The People of South Asia: The Biological Anthropology of India, Pakistan, and Nepal*, ed. J.R. Lukacs, 77–90. New York: Plenum.

Shaffer, J.G. 1992. "The Indus Valley, Baluchistan, and Helmand Traditions: Neolithic through Bronze Age." In *Chronologies in Old World Archaeology*, ed., R. Ehrich, 441–464. Chicago: University of Chicago Press.

Shaikh, N., Q.H. Mallah, and G.M. Veesar. 2002. "Recent Discoveries of Sites/Industrial Complexes in Thar, Rohri Hills, and Adjacent Plains: Regional Perspective." *Ancient Sindh* 7: 27–66.

Shea, J.J. 1988. "Spear Points from the Middle Paleolithic of the Levant." *Journal of Field Archaeology* 15 (4): 441–450.

Shea J.J. 1989. "A Functional Study of the Lithic Industries Associated with Hominid Fossils in the Kebara and Qafzeh Caves, Israel." In *The Human Revolution: Behavioural and Biological Perspectives on the Origins of Modern Humans*, ed. P. Mellars and C. Stringer, 611–625. Edinburgh: Edinburgh University Press.

Starini, E., and P. Biagi. 2006. "Excavations at the Harappan Flint Quarry 862 on the Rohri Hills (Sindh, Pakistan)." *Der Anschnitt* 19: 1–8.

Starini, E., and P. Biagi. 2011. "The Archaeological Record of the Indus (Harappan) Lithic Production: The Excavation of RH862 Flint Mine and Flint Knapping

Workshops on the Rohri Hills (Upper Sindh, Pakistan)." *Journal of Asian Civilizations* 34 (2): 1–61.

Titmus, G.L., and J.E. Clark. 2003. "Mexica Blade Making with Wooden Tools: Recent Experimental Insights." In *Mesoamerican Lithic Technology: Experimentation and Interpretation*, ed. K.G. Hirth, 72–97. Salt Lake City: University of Utah Press.

Tomaskova, S. 2005. "What Is a Burin? Typology, Technology, and Interregional Comparison." *Journal of Archaeological Method and Theory* 12 (2): 79–115.

Vidale, M. 1995. "Early Beadmakers of the Indus Tradition: The Manufacturing Sequence of Talc Beads at Mehrgarh in the 5th Millennium BC." *East and West* 45 (1–4): 45–80.

Vidale, M. 2000. *The Archaeology of Indus Crafts: Indus Craftspeople and Why We Study Them*. Rome: Istituto Italiano per l'Africa e l'Oriente.

Vidale, M. 2005. "La formazione degli stati arcaici nella valle dell'Indo: le ipotesi ei dati archeologici." *Annali dell'Università Degli Studi Di Napoli L'Orientale. Rivista Del Dipartimento Di Studi Asiatici E Del Dipartimento Di Studi E Ricerche Su Africa E Paesi Arabi* 65: 197–255.

Vidale, M. 2010. "Aspects of Palace Life at Mohenjo-Daro." *South Asian Studies* 26 (1): 59–76.

Vidale, M., J.M. Kenoyer, and K.K. Bhan. 1992. "A Discussion of the Concept of 'chaîne opératoire' in the Study of Stratified Societies: Evidence from Ethnoarchaeology and Archaeology." In *Ethnoarchaeology: Justifications, Problems, and Limits*, ed. A. Gallay, 181–194. Juan-Le-Pins, France: Centre De Recherches Archéologiques.

Vidale, M., and H. Miller. 2001. "On the Development of Indus Technical Virtuosity and Its Relation to Social Structure." In *South Asian Archaeology, 1997*, ed. M. Taddei and G. De Marco, 115–132. Rome: l'Istituto Italiano per l'Africa e l'Oriente.

Vidale, M., A. Siviero, G. Sidoti, G. Guida, and G. Priori. 2013. "Three End-Scrapers from Mohenjo-Daro (Pakistan)." In *Unconformist Archaeology: Papers in Honor of Paolo Biagi*, ed. Elisabetta Starini, 119–129. Oxford, UK: Archaeopress.

Wright, R.P. 2010. *The Ancient Indus: Urbanism, Economy, and Society*. Cambridge: Cambridge University Press.

3

The Importance of Being Ad Hoc

Patterns and Implications of Expedient Lithic Production in the Bronze Age in Israel

Francesca Manclossi and Steven A Rosen

In the southern Levant, the introduction, development, and increasing availability of copper and copper alloys (tin bronzes, arsenical bronzes, and other combinations) during the Chalcolithic and Bronze Ages (ca. 4500–1200 BCE) did not immediately cause the cessation of the production and use of flint tools for either specialized or domestic activities. Chipped stone tools continued to be systematically produced at least through the middle of the Iron Age (ca. tenth century BCE). Only with the spread of iron technology and its ready accessibility for a large range of functions, including most notably as sickles, did systematic production of chipped stone tools cease. The reasons for the continued use of chipped stone tools over such a long span when metals were available are varied and include the material attributes of flint versus metal tools, the technological structures of production of the different materials, and the economic and social structures of production and distribution (e.g., Rosen 1996, 1997: 151–166).

In particular, Bronze Age lithic assemblages are characterized by three main components: a formal and standardized production of sickle blades used for harvesting; a large cortical flake industry, restricted to the Chalcolithic and Early Bronze Ages (fifth through third millennia BCE), whose primary function in the settled zone seems to have been related to cult; and the manufacture of non-diagnostic ad hoc tools produced and used in domestic contexts. The first component

DOI: 10.5876/9781607328926.c003

consists of the specialized production of Canaanean blades during the Early Bronze Age (fourth–third millennia BCE) (Manclossi et al. 2016; Rosen 1997: 44–60, 107–109) and of large geometric sickle elements during the Middle and Late Bronze Ages and indeed into the Iron Age (second–first millennia BCE) (Rosen 1997: 44–60, 111–112). These specialized production systems reflect technological transformations and different production/distribution systems, which changed through time but were functionally equivalent. The cortical flake industry, which produced tabular scrapers, was based on desert production by pastoral groups and import into the settled zone, a kind of regional production specialization (e.g., Abe 2008; Müller-Neuhof 2013; Quintero et al. 2002; Rosen 1983, 1997: 71–80, 109), although not necessarily based on intensive production (but compare Rosen 1997 with Abe 2008). This system also shows chronological changes in various attributes and changes in the structures of production and distribution over time. In contrast to the technological and social variability evident over time and space in the sickle and tabular scraper systems, the ad hoc component remained stable over large expanses and long time periods. If it represents on one hand the expedient and opportunistic production of tools (cf. Binford 1973, 1977) used for a wide range of domestic tasks with little production standardization, on the other hand, it shows long-term technological patterns that reflect little change over time.

In this study we focus on this third component that, although simple, is quantitatively dominant in the (well-collected) lithic assemblages from the proto- and early Historic periods in the region. Although domestically and expediently produced, with little obvious standardization (e.g., Cauvin 1968; Rosen 1997: 115, 158), the ad hoc tools can be characterized using technological criteria and parameters that discern recurrent patterns in lithic manufacture (e.g., Boëda 1991; Boëda et al. 1990; Inizan et al. 1995; Pelegrin 1995; Soressi and Geneste 2011). Our observations derive from the analysis of the lithic assemblages of three sites: Tel Yarmuth, Tel Safi, and Ashkelon (Manclossi 2016).

The formal tool types from the Bronze and Iron Ages, the sickle segments and tabular scrapers, are generally found in assemblages only as finished or semi-finished knapped products without other waste elements connected with their manufacture (the result of varying kinds of specialized off-site manufacture). In contrast, the ad hoc industry exhibits all the stages of the *chaîne opératoire* with tools, debitage, waste, and cores (figure 3.1), clearly reflecting the domestic contexts of their manufacture and use.

In analysis of all the products of the reduction sequence of this ad hoc industry, our aim is to recognize technological patterns and define behaviors that can contribute to a better understanding of a non-standardized, apparently

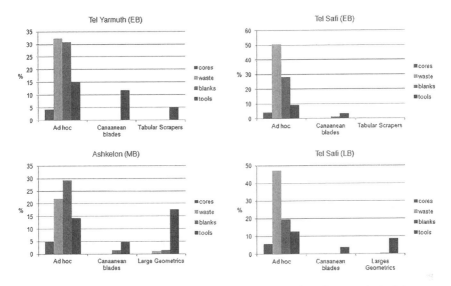

FIGURE 3.1. *Frequencies of the ad hoc industry according to the techno-typological classes produced in the various steps of the reduction sequence.*

random production. The key point is that production is, in fact, non-random. Despite the morphometric and typological heterogeneity, the ad hoc assemblage represents a coherent industry, resulting from basic knapping strategies based on a few rules and simple flaking schemes.

RAW MATERIAL

Recognition of the geological origin of the flint is important not only for identifying the source of the raw materials (e.g., Andrefsky 1994), but it also has implications for knapping strategies because the size, shape, and quality of the flint influence the knapper's options and choices (e.g., Allard 2003; Geneste 1991; Perlès 1990). Raw material is characterized macroscopically according to cortex, texture, color, and internal homogeneity. Cortex is the external surface, generally calcareous, covering the flint. In particular, its presence and characteristics reflect the geological processes in the formation of sedimentary rocks as well as post-formation processes. Flint from primary deposits has fresh cortex, and the analysis of its shape can indicate whether the original blocks were nodules or blocks derived from beds of flint. In secondary deposits, flint is altered by natural post-depositional processes, such as battering on river cobbles. In the ad hoc industry, flint most commonly appears as cobbles with damaged cortex, often rolled and sometimes rounded. Furthermore, flint from secondary deposits comes in smaller-size cobbles than natural nodules or beds (a primary morphometric constraint for the knapped products) and presents less internal homogeneity and more irregularities (e.g., fissures and cracks), which condition the quality of the knapping. The examination of all the cortical elements of the ad hoc industry (on both cores and flakes) shows a selection almost exclusively of flint coming from secondary deposits, generally rounded cobbles available in the immediate vicinity of the site. The cortex is rarely fresh, but damaged and irregular with abrasions or naturally smoothed surfaces, and there are other alterations such as patina and naturally polished surfaces, all indicating post-depositional processes. When there is no cortex, the presence of numerous cracks and fissures as a result of the mechanical movement of the blocks confirms the use of secondary deposits of raw material. Given the use of such secondary deposits, it is not surprising that raw materials are heterogeneous and vary from a fine-grained translucent flint to a less fine-grained brown-gray and to coarser and multi-colored materials: gray, white, beige and brown, light or dark.

The analysis of the texture of the ad hoc products and cores shows a clear dominance of fine/medium-grained flint (figure 3.2). Coarse-grained flint is rare, and other types of raw material, such as limestone, were little exploited. This suggests that not all the cobbles available in the vicinity were collected, and the almost exclusive presence of flint with texture appropriate to knapping indicates clear selection of raw materials. Nevertheless, a fine/medium-grained texture does not automatically mean good quality, and other elements such as fissures, cracks, and inclusions may compromise production. The high frequency of internal irregularities may indicate that the selection of raw material was not strictly limited to specific materials and that the inner homogeneity of the flint was not considered necessary to obtain the desired products and tools.

CORES

The second aspect of this study focuses on the ad hoc cores, which are almost always oriented toward flake production. When blade removals are visible, they are simply long flakes detached during the same reduction sequence as the flakes. Core size and shape vary depending on the nature of the raw material and the intensity of reduction, although they are generally small or medium-sized (figure 3.3). Although the small dimensions represent the final core sizes, indirect elements, such as the presence of cortex and the similar size of removal scars on the cores and the knapped products, suggest that these

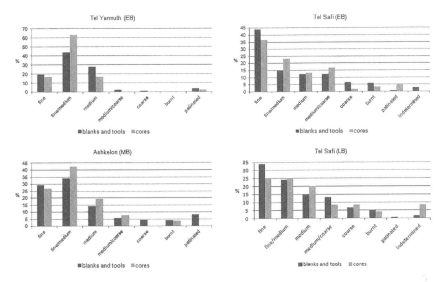

FIGURE 3.2. *Frequencies of different types of texture of raw material used for the ad hoc industry.*

dimensions are only slightly smaller than the original blocks. Even if intensively exploited, the cores were probably not big.

In addition to the final core dimensions, the analysis of length, width, and thickness shows strong linear correlations between each measurement (figure 3.3), indicating that core shape, regardless of the specific dimension, is constant. This suggests that very specific shapes, more or less oval, were initially selected for reduction and the reduction sequence did not focus on a particular dimension but, instead, all dimensions were reduced in tandem.

The cores show only minimal technological investment, as indicated in the absence of any preparation and maintenance flakes (in the assemblages only a few flakes are clearly detached with the intent to remove very hinged surfaces and correct the knapping faces). The detachment of the flakes was conducted after the creation of a plain or simple striking platform, or directly from a cortical surface, without other adjustments. The same lack of investment is reflected in some of the apparent reasons for core discard, such as (1) the presence of irregularities and flaws revealed within the core during the course of reduction (e.g., cracks, fissures, and inclusions), (2) knapping errors that rendered continued reduction impossible (e.g., large hinged scars), and (3) reduction beyond the parameters, allowing continued knapping (e.g., the development of too large an angle between the striking platform and the knapping

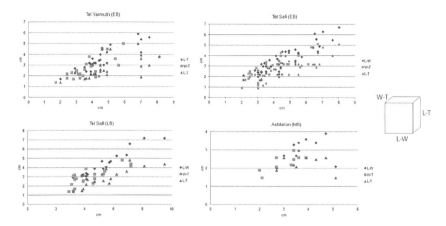

FIGURE 3.3. *Ad hoc core dimensions.*

surface). In most of these cases the cores could have been used for producing more flakes through core rejuvenation, but the knappers did not invest in them, preferring simply to change the block of flint.

Despite this simple technology, the analysis of the cores—including striking directions, core rotation and orientation, the relative chronology of the removals, and how these are integrated with one another—permits recognition of some recurrent themes and the definition of general patterns of reduction.

Flake scars can be divided into two categories: single isolated removals and linked removals forming a series. The majority of the cores have at least one series of contiguous removals sharing the same striking platform. The cores are classified according to the number of knapping sequences and isolated removals and by observing the exploited surfaces. The cores indeed have different polyhedral shapes, but if we consider their geometric volume without considering their shape, we can count the number of surfaces involved in the flaking considering both the series and the isolated removals. Isolated removals may be present either on the same knapping surface as the series or on different surfaces, and a single knapping surface may show one or more series (figure 3.4).

Using these parameters, we can see that the cores mostly have one or two series, usually using one or two knapping surfaces, and that the isolated removals are detached on different knapping surfaces. The order of the detachments shows that the series are independent. Once one sequence is completed, the block seems to be regarded as a new core, and the knapping continues with a new series, or isolated removals, on the surface where the technical criteria permit detachment of new flakes, generally without previous modifications.

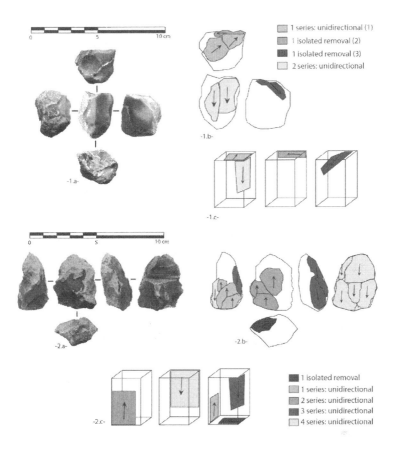

FIGURE 3.4. *Technological analysis of ad hoc cores showing isolated removals and series of contiguous removals: 1a. core from Tel Safi (LB), 1b. technological reconstruction, 1c. box diagram of volumetric reconstruction, 2a. core from Tel Safi (EB), 2b. technological reconstruction, 2c. box diagram of volumetric reconstruction.*

There were four different potential knapping sequence permutations (figure 3.5): (1) A new series was knapped on a new surface in no relation to the previous one; (2) the striking platform of the first sequence was used a second time for a new series on a different knapping surface; (3) the negatives of the first series were used as a striking platform for a new sequence; and (4) a new series was knapped on the same knapping surface as the first one but using a different striking platform.

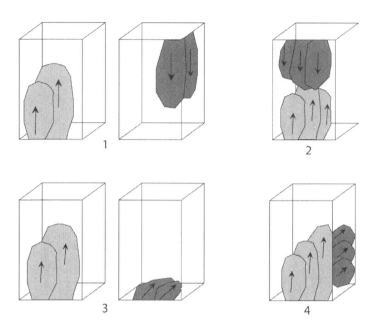

FIGURE 3.5. *Ad hoc core permutations: 1. two series on different surfaces, 2. two series sharing the same knapping surface but a different striking platform, 3. two series sharing the same striking platform but on a different knapping surface, 4. the negatives of one series are used as a striking platform for a new series.*

Other than the different combinations, which vary according to the number of series and the volumetric exploitation of the cores, there are no direct linkages between the removals that do not belong to the same sequence. Series sharing the same knapping surface or used as a striking platform for subsequent sequences were not planned but are the result of an additional flaking scheme (see Boëda 2012) characterized by the succession of varying knapping sequences (figure 3.6).

Because each series corresponds to an independent reduction sequence, we can analyze them separately considering the number of the removals and the direction of the detachments, observing some recurrent patterns.

The sequences are generally short, with only two or three removals, although exceptions with more than three removals are not unusual. In general, if there are more than three negatives, the scars are often hinged (e.g., figure 3.6.1a, center, showing final hinged removal). This suggests that the longer sequences

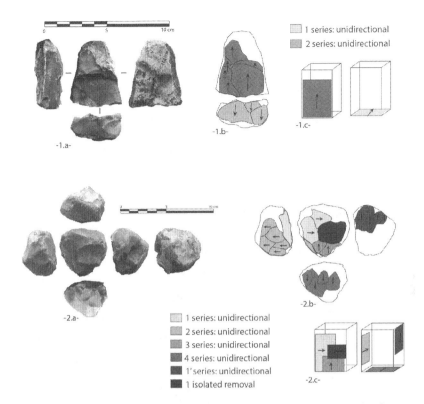

FIGURE 3.6. *Technological analysis of ad hoc cores: 1a. core from Tel Safi (EB), 1b. technological reconstruction, 1c. box diagram of volumetric reconstruction, 2a. core from Ashkelon (MB), 2b. technological reconstruction, 2c. box diagram of volumetric reconstruction.*

are not the result of intentionally long reduction sequences but are more likely the effect of repetitive production errors and attempts to rectify them. The fact that the final removals are generally hinged supports this hypothesis and explains why so many cores were discarded after relatively little reduction.

Considering the direction of the scars, there is a marked dominance of unidirectional series. Other possibilities, although less frequent, are (1) radial sequences with removals coming from the perimeter of the knapping surface (or part of it); (2) a bidirectional pattern, where the sequence is composed of removals detached on the same knapping surface but from opposite striking platforms; and (3) an alternating pattern, where the series is composed of removals each of which is detached using the previous one as a striking platform (figure 3.7).

This analysis shows that the different cores share a common general pattern reflecting a very simple knapping strategy—direct percussion with a hard hammer stone—which does not require deep knowledge and skills, as well-reflected in the frequent mistakes (mostly hinge fractures) and unsuccessful removals. The pebble/core was generally not completely exploited and was not prepared, and flaking was initiated directly on the cortical surfaces or from a plain striking platform previously initiated. Using direct percussion, the knappers detached a few flakes, usually linked in a short series sharing the same knapping surface and striking platform. When the surfaces were no longer suitable (generally because of hinged negatives, irregularities in the flint, or the exhaustion of the good angle between the striking platform and the knapping surface), the flaking was continued by turning the core and starting a new series.

FLAKED PRODUCTS

Beyond the description of the cores, the reconstruction of the knapping strategies requires a complementary analysis of all knapped products. On one hand, some aspects of the knapping technology can be better defined by observing the unretouched and retouched flakes together, and on the other, it is important to recognize the criteria affecting the selection of blanks that were then modified into tools. These elements permit recognition of the technical behaviors of flintknappers in terms of procedures, strategies, and choices (e.g., Bailly 2006; Desrosiers 1991; Pelegrin et al. 1988; Perlès 1991).

Regarding technique, identifiable by the features present on the knapped products, especially the proximal ends (Tixier 1967), the utilization of direct percussion has already been suggested from the core analyses. The absence of any preparation, necessary for other techniques, is confirmed by the presence of cortical and plain platforms. The big platforms and pronounced bulbs, as well as the well-marked impact points inside the striking platforms, suggest the utilization of hard hammer stones. The elevated incidence of flaking mistakes indicates poor control of the force exerted for detaching the flakes, and is another clue indicating the use of generally unskilled hard hammer direct percussion.

The analysis of the dorsal patterns and their relationship with the knapping axis corresponds well to the picture obtained from the study of the cores. The majority of the flakes have unidirectional dorsal scars, and in general, the last dorsal negative is aligned with the knapping axis. Other patterns (perpendicular, bidirectional, multi-directional) are usually associated with hinge fractures or irregularities in the flint that do not allow continuation of the sequence and require changing the striking platform.

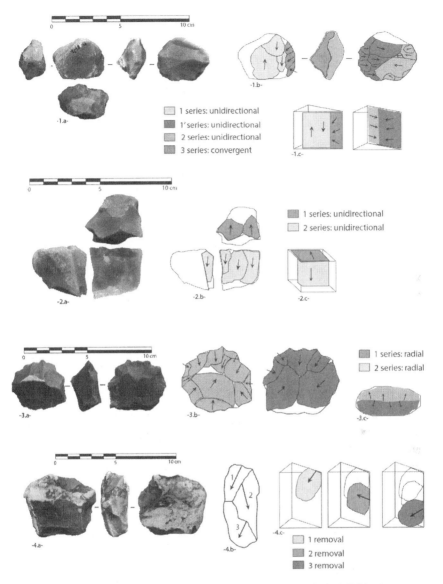

FIGURE 3.7. *Technological analysis of ad hoc cores: 1a. core from Tel Safi (LB), 1b. technological reconstruction, 1c. box diagram of volumetric reconstruction, 2a. core from Ashkelon (MB), 2b. technological reconstruction, 1c. box diagram of volumetric reconstruction, 3a. core from Tel Safi (LB), 3b. technological reconstruction, 3c. box diagram of volumetric reconstruction, 4a. core from Tel Safi (LB), 4b. technological reconstruction, 4c. box diagram of volumetric reconstruction: three alternate removals.*

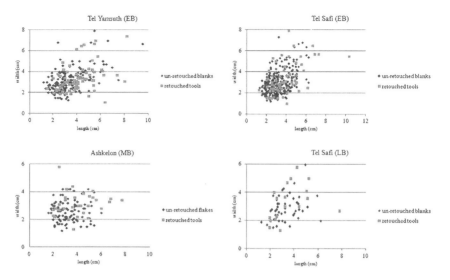

FIGURE 3.8. *Retouched and unretouched flake dimensions.*

Beyond the technological characterization of the knapped products, the second goal of our study is to compare the unretouched and retouched flakes in order to evaluate the criteria for the selection of blanks then transformed into tools. The variables taken into account are dimensions, position in the reduction sequence, and incidence of eventual knapping mistakes.

The examination of the size of blanks and tools shows that although there is overlap in retouched and unretouched flake length and width dimensions, the longest flakes were more often retouched (figure 3.8).

This offers insight into the actual selection process, indicating that the largest pieces were clearly preferred but also that there seems to have been a lower threshold for the small pieces. Given typical correlation between flake dimensions, it is likely that the determining criterion was length or cutting edge and that the differences in other dimensions resulted from correlation with length. In this context it is also worth noting that the strong correlations between different dimensions of the cores are far less evident among the flake products, indicating that the core shape only partially influenced flake shape. In fact, the great variability in flake shape (reflected in the lesser correlation between the flake dimensions) probably reflects the low level of technical control of the flaking process.

The position of the retouched tools in the reduction sequence is our second criterion of analysis, which can be established by considering both the cortex

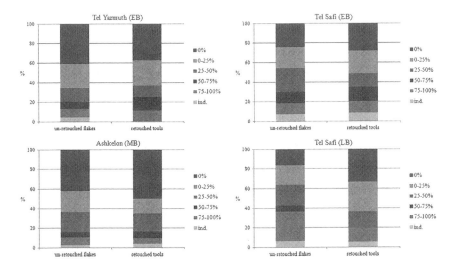

FIGURE 3.9. *Proportion of cortex on flakes.*

distribution and the number of dorsal negatives. According to the distribution of cortex, primary flakes (flakes with greater than 50% cortex on the dorsal surface) as well as flakes with lower proportions of cortex were transformed into tools, even if the group of flakes without cortex, corresponding to final removals of the sequence, seems to have been preferred (figure 3.9). This suggests that the cortical flakes were not primary flakes in the classical sense; they were not detached during an initial step of the reduction sequence in order to remove cortex and prepare the cores but were already flakes used as potential blanks. Thus decortication was not a specific stage in the flaking sequence during which desired blanks were specifically produced for the manufacture of tools; rather, all the knapped products had the potential for use and retouch, a sequence that represents the opportunistic production of flakes later selected for specific tasks and uses.

Considering the number of dorsal scars, we can observe two different normal distributions, one of the unretouched flakes and the other of the retouched tools (figure 3.10). These data seem to indicate that blanks detached in the more advanced stages of the core exploitation were more often chosen for modification into tools.

Finally, in accord with the previous observations of the incidence of flaking mistakes, it is important to stress that the high number of dorsal scars often depends on the presence of hinged fractures or other anomalies. The use of

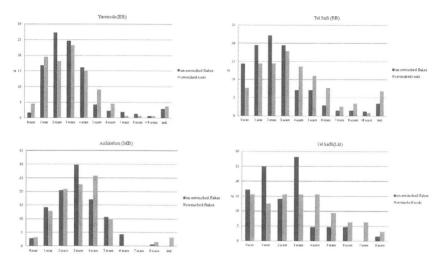

FIGURE 3.10. *Scar patterns plotted against flakes and flake tools.*

irregular flakes, then, suggests that the presence of flaking mistakes did not affect knappers' decisions, and these blanks were not automatically discarded. On the contrary, these flakes were apparently more retouched than the others, perhaps a result of the need for greater modification to be useful.

Among the retouched flakes, in general, using typological lists, less than 50 percent can be defined as notches, scrapers, drills, borers, or denticulates (e.g., Cauvin 1968). Even these classified types are variable, and they often overlap and are certainly not standardized. Usually, the tools show simple retouch varying in delineation, extent, distribution, and position and can be classified only as retouched flakes (figure 3.11). In general, the retouch did not significantly modify the original blanks and is present on the more suitable edges that required little transformation. For example, the cortical lateral edges and plunging terminations were rarely retouched. In contrast, natural sharp edges or portions of them were commonly retouched.

DISCUSSION AND CONCLUSIONS

It is important to stress that we define as tools (*les outils*) all artifacts showing intentional retouch that created specific shapes and edge delineations. Unmodified flakes that, although used, do not show retouch that can be construed as intentional modification and all the other flakes presenting damaged edges that derived from some type of utilization are not included in the tool

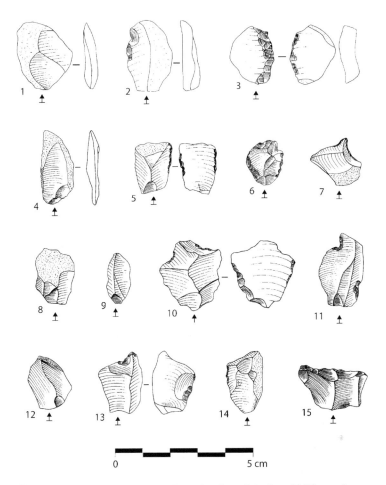

FIGURE 3.11. *Typical ad hoc blanks and tools: 1. flake from Tel Yarmuth (EB), 2. flake from Tel Safi (LB), 3. flake from Tel Safi (LB), 4. retouched flake from Ashkelon (MB), 5. awl from Ashkelon (MB), 6. retouched flake from Ashkelon (MB), 7. denticulate from Tel Yarmuth (EB), 8. denticulate from Tel Safi (LB), 9. scraper from Tel Safi (EB).*

category (e.g., Binder 1987). However, this last group, defined by some scholars as *a posteriori tools* (Bailly 1995) because their edge morphology is the result not of intentional modification but instead of their utilization, is often ignored by archaeologists because the tools are difficult to recognize and define. The high percentage of flakes without intentional retouch *might* indicate that this group composed the majority of the flakes effectively used, and this should be considered in some types of analysis. Indeed, our study suggests that retouch was not the first intent of the knappers producing ad hoc tools and that pieces were retouched only when necessary to create suitable edges where they were not automatically created in the production of blanks.

In different contexts, especially in examining the evolution of sedentary societies in North America, expedient technologies have been tied to decreasing levels of mobility (e.g., Johnson 1996; Parry and Kelly 1987). Ad hoc production as defined here is not tied to increased sedentism but can be traced to the increasing complexity of production systems evident at least by the Chalcolithic period, if not somewhat earlier, immediately preceding the periods reviewed here and thousands of years after the evolution of sedentary farming villages (Rosen 1996, 1997: 103–115). Essentially, ad hoc production arises as the second side of the coin of production specialization (e.g., Astruc 2005; Astruc et al. 2006; Binder and Perlès 1990; Burnez-Lanotte and Allard 2012; Perlès 1990). As the more formal tools that required special skills for their manufacture became invested in specialized systems, knapping expertise in the general population was no longer requisite. Although edged tools of flint were still needed, the skills needed to produce them were not great. With the ready accessibility of flint throughout the region, ad hoc production flourished.

To summarize, the simple ad hoc technology described here suggests that people with knowledge of only the most basic knapping principles and rules produced flakes for a wide range of domestic activities that required sharp cutting tools (e.g., McConaughy 1979, 1980 for microwear study of such tools at the Early Bronze Age site of Bab edh Dhra in Jordan). It is probable that knappers, also likely the users, detached short series of flakes and then selected the most appropriate for the particular task at hand. The limited number of retouched flakes and their morphometric variability may indicate that the knappers were focused more on the particulars of the working edge than on the shape of the entire implement. They produced blanks with natural sharp edges and used them without important modification of their volume and shape. Once produced and used, the ad hoc tools were quickly discarded without any investment in maintenance for later use.

The uniformity and stability in the ad hoc production system through the Early, Middle, and Late Bronze Ages—almost three millennia—indicates the maintenance of common technical behaviors that did not change in parallel to other technological transformations, either within the flint system or outside it (e.g., the introduction of metallurgy), or in response to significant sociopolitical changes, such as the rise of cities and states. This diachronic continuity reflects a stable technological substrate. The low technical investment and the elementary production/consumption system represent domestic contexts (Hendon 1996), widespread within the society that for millennia played a leading role in the daily life of ancient people.

ACKNOWLEDGMENTS

We are grateful to Rachel Horowitz and Grant McCall for organizing the session on lithics in complex societies at the annual meeting of the Society for American Archaeology, for inviting us to participate, and for comments on the manuscript. We thank our colleagues who directed the excavations at the various sites from which the assemblages analyzed here were derived—Haskel Greenfield, Aren Maeir, Daniel Master, and Pierre de Miroschedji—for graciously allowing us access to their collections. This work has been part of Francesca Manclossi's doctoral research at Université Paris X, Nanterre, and Ben-Gurion University of the Negev.

REFERENCES

Abe, Masashi. 2008. "The Development of Urbanism and Pastoral Nomads in the Southern Levant—Chalcolithic and Early Bronze Age Stone Tool Production Industries and Flint Mines in the Jafr Basin, Southern Jordan." PhD dissertation, University of Liverpool, UK.

Allard, Pierre. 2003. "Economie des matières premières des populations rubanées de la Vallée de l'Aisne." *Les matières premières lithiques en Préhistoire, actes de la table ronde internationale d'Aurillac (Cantal), 20–22 juin 2002*. Préhistoire du Sud-Ouest, supplément 5: 15–26.

Andrefsky, William, Jr. 1994. "Raw Material Availability and the Organization of Technology." *American Antiquity* 59 (1): 21–34.

Astruc, Laurence. 2005. "Avant-propos." In *Au-delà de la notion de technologie expédiente: outillages lithiques et osseux au Néolithique, actes de la table ronde du 15 mars 2004, Nanterre, Maison de l'archéologie et de l'ethnologie*, 175–227. Cahiers des thèmes transversaux. Paris: Archéologies et Sciences de l'Antiquité V.

Astruc, Laurence, François Bon, Vanessa Léa, Pierre-Yves Milcent, and Sylvie Philibert, eds. 2006. *Normes techniques et pratiques sociales: de la simplicité des outillages pré- et protohistorique*. Antibes, France: Editions APDCA.

Bailly, Maxence. 2006. "Faire simple: oui, mais comment? Production lithique et dynamique des relations sociales dans le Néolithique moyen et le Néolithique final de l'arc jurassien." In *Normes techniques et pratiques sociales: de la simplicité des outillages pré- et protohistoriques*, ed. Laurence Astuc, François Bon, Vanessa Léa, Pierre-Yves Milcent, and Sylvie Philibert, 35–47. Antibes, France: Editions APDCA.

Binder, Didier. 1987. *Le Néolithique ancien provençal: typologie et technologie des outillages lithiques*. Paris: Centre National de la Rechere Scientifique.

Binder, Didier, and Catherine Perlès. 1990. "Stratégies de gestion des outillages lithiques au Néolithique." *Paléo* 2: 257–283.

Binford, Lewis R. 1973. "Interassemblage Variability: The Mousterian and the 'Functional' Argument." In *The Explanation of Culture Change: Models in Prehistory*, ed. Colin Renfrew, 227–253. Pittsburgh: University of Pittsburgh Press.

Binford, Lewis R. 1977. "Forty-Seven Trips: A Case Study in the Character of Archaeological Formation Process." In *Stone Tools as Cultural Markers: Change, Evolution, and Complexity*, ed. Richard V.S. Wright, 24–36. Canberra: Australian Institute of Aboriginal Studies.

Boëda, Eric. 1991. "Approche de la variabilité des systèmes de production lithique des industries lithiques du Paléolithique inférieur et moyen: chronique d'une variabilité attendue." *Technique et Culture* 17–18: 37–79.

Boëda, Eric. 2012. *Techno-logique & technologie: une paléo-histoire des objets lithiques tranchants*. Paris: Archéo-éditions.

Boëda, Eric, Jean-Michel Geneste, and Liliane Meignen. 1990. "Identification des chaînes opératoires lithiques de Paléolithique Ancien et Moyen." *Paléo* 2: 43–80.

Burnez-Lanotte, Laurence, and Pierre Allard. 2012. "Avant Propos: Productions domestiques versus spécialisées au Néolithique et Chalcolithique, finalité technique et fonction sociales: question d'échelle?" *Bulletin de la société préhistorique française* 109 (2): 211–219.

Cauvin, Jacques. 1968. *Les outillages lithiques néolithiques de Byblos et du littoral libanais*. Paris: Université de Paris.

Desrosiers, Sophie. 1991. "Sur le concept de chaîne opératoire." In *Observer l'action technique: des Chaînes opératoires, pour quoi faire*, ed. Hélène Balfet, 21–25. Paris: Centre National de la Rechere Scientifique.

Geneste, Jean-Michel. 1991. "L'approvisionnement en matières premières dans les systèmes de production lithique: la dimension spatiale de la technologie." *Tecnologia y Cadenas operativas liticas: Treballs d'arqueologie* 1: 1–36.

Hendon, Julia A. 1996. "Archaeological Approaches to the Organization of Domestic Labor: Household Practice and Domestic Relation." *Annual Reviews of Anthropology* 25: 45–61.

Inizan, Marie-Louise, Michèle Reduron-Ballinger, Hélène Roche, and Jacques Tixier. 1995. *Technologie de la pierre taillée: Préhistoire de la pierre taillé, tome 4*. Meudon, France: Le Cercle de Recherches et d'Etudes Préhistoriques.

Johnson, Jay K. 1996. "Lithic Analysis and Questions of Cultural Complexity." In *Stone Tools, Theoretical Insights into Human Prehistory*, ed. George H. Odell, 159–180. New York: Plenum.

Manclossi, Francesca. 2016. "De la pierre aux métaux: dynamiques des changements techniques dans les industries lithiques du Levant Sud (4e–1er millénaire av. J. Ch.)." PhD dissertation, Université Paris Ouest Nanterre la Défense and Ben-Gurion University of the Negev, Paris, France, and Beersheba, Israel.

Manclossi, Francesca, Steven A. Rosen, and Pierre de Miroschedji. 2016. "The Canaanean Blades from Tel Yarmuth: A Technological Analysis." *Paléorient* 42: 53–79.

McConaughy, Mark. 1979. *Formal and Functional Analysis of Chipped Stone Tools from Bab edh Dhra*. PhD dissertation, University of Pittsburgh, Pittsburgh, PA..

McConaughy, Mark. 1980. "Chipped Stone Tools [from Bab edh Dhra]." *Bulletin of the American Schools of Oriental Research* 240: 53–58.

Müller-Neuhof, Bernd. 2013. "Southwest Asian Late Chalcolithic/Early Bronze Age Demand for 'Big-Tools': Specialized Flint Exploitation beyond the Fringes of Settled Regions." *Lithic Technology* 38: 220–236.

Parry, William J., and Robert L. Kelly. 1987. "Expedient Core Technology and Sedentism." In *The Organization of Core Technology*, ed. Jay K. Johnson and Carol A. Morrow, 285–304. Boulder: Westview.

Pelegrin, Jacques. 1995. *Technologie lithique: le châtelperronien de Roc-de-Combe (Lot) et de La Côte (Dordogne)*. Paris: Centre National de la Rechere Scientifique.

Pelegrin, Jacques, Claudine Karlin, and Pierre Bodu. 1988. "Chaînes opératoires: un outil pour le préhistorien." In *Technologie préhistorique*, ed. Jaques Tixier, 55–62. Paris: Centre National de la Rechere Scientifique.

Perlès, Catherine. 1990. "L'outillage de pierre taillée néolithique en Grèce: approvisionnement et exploitation des matières premières." *Bulletin de correspondance hellénique* 114: 1–42.

Perlès, Catherine. 1991. "Économie des matières premières et économie du débitage: deux conceptions opposées?" *Rencontres internationales d'archéologie et d'histoire d'Antibes* 11: 35–45.

Quintero, Leslie, Philip Wilke, and Gary Rollefson. 2002. "From Flint Mine to Fan Scraper: The Late Prehistoric Jafr Industrial Complex." *Bulletin of the American Schools of Oriental Research* 327: 17–48.

Rosen, Steven A. 1983. "The Tabular Scraper Trade: A Model for Material Culture Dispersion." *Bulletin of the American Schools for Oriental Research* 249: 79–86.

Rosen, Steven A. 1996. "The Decline and Fall of Flint." In *Stone Tools, Theoretical Insights into Human Prehistory*, ed. George H. Odell, 129–158. New York: Plenum.

Rosen, Steven A. 1997. *Lithics after the Stone Age*. Walnut Creek, CA: Altamira.

Soressi, Marie, and Jean-Michel Geneste. 2011. "The History and Efficacy of the Chaine Opératoire Approach to Lithic Analysis: Studying Techniques to Reveal Past Societies in an Evolutionary Perspective." *Paleoanthropology* 2011: 334–350.

Tixier, Jacques. 1967. "Procédés d'analyse et questions de terminologie dans l'étude des ensembles industriels du Paléolithique récent et de l'Epipaléolithique en Afrique du Nord-Ouest." In *Background to Evolution in Africa*, ed. Walter W. Bishop and Desmond F. Clark, 771–820. Chicago: University of Chicago Press.

4

Leaving No Stone Unturned

Expedient Lithic Production among Preclassic Households of San Estevan, Belize, and K'o and Hamontún, Guatemala

Jason S.R. Paling

Through the Middle, Late, and Terminal Preclassic periods (1000 BCE–250 CE), settlements in the Maya lowlands experienced increased social complexity and size. Sociopolitical and economic complexity were marked by indications of state-like institutions, such as the centralization of political authority, the development of stratified social organizations, appearance of ritual and cosmological systems, and the creation of writing systems. Amplified populations and urban growth among lowland centers may be attributed to agricultural advances, exploitation of local resources, and development of trade and communication networks. Early settlement along river systems and wetland areas during the Early Preclassic period (2500–1000 BCE) created opportunities for sustained subsistence, but later these areas were natural corridors for the movement of trade items and new ideas. The production of local resources and finished goods, as well as the control of trade networks, formed a basis for the requisite accumulation of wealth, prestige, and power, which was mobilized to facilitate these increases in complexity. Early commodities, such as lithic tools, thereby served as key industries related to and useful for the analysis of sociopolitical development. In this chapter, stone tool exchange networks, production industries, and tool usage from the sites of San Estevan in northern Belize and K'o and Hamontún in northeastern Guatemala will be evaluated and analyzed to create a clearly delineated system that may

DOI: 10.5876/9781607328926.c004

help to describe the economic conditions that surrounded this fluorescence of complexity.

From the Middle Preclassic period (1000–300 BCE) on, household or cottage industries became eclipsed by specialized production communities that infiltrated regional economic networks, measured by visible changes in architectural and ceramic production (Brady et al. 1998; Callaghan 2008; Doyle 2013; Sheets 1979a, 1979b; Willey et al. 1967). By the Late Preclassic period (300 BCE–150 CE), flake stone tools (e.g., chert and chalcedony) played a key role in many dimensions of daily life, from the gathering of agricultural surplus to the construction of small homes or large-scale monuments. Waste debris of tool production has been noted from a variety of archaeological contexts, from emerging Maya lowland monumental centers such as Tikal (Moholy-Nagy 1985, 1991), Altar de Sacrificios (Smith 1950), Cerros (Mitchum 1986), and El Mirador (Fowler 1987) but also among small agrarian villages like K'axob (McAnany and Peterson 2004) and Pulltrouser Swamp (Hammond 1991; Shafer 1983). Studies of regional and long-distance economic systems were initiated after the discovery of Colha (see Eaton et al. 1994; Hammond 1973, 1982; Hester 1985; Hester and Shafer 1984, 1994; Masson 2000; Roemer 1991; Shafer 1991), where later archaeological investigations conducted by the Colha Project revealed dense workshop deposits associated with Late Preclassic platforms and *aguada* groups (King 2000; Roemer 1984; Shafer and Hester 1983, 1986, 1991). These lithic debitage studies demonstrated uniformity in the production volume, standardization of production, and standardization of tool form, thereby signifying mass production (Drollinger 1989; Shafer 1991: 31; Shafer and Hester 1983, 1986, 1991), a key indicator of economic complexity.

Colha (figure 4.1) is located within a band of fine-grained chert. This outcrop of chert is commonly known as the Colha, or Northern Belize Chert-bearing Zone (NBCBZ) (Cackler et al. 1999; Tobey 1986; Tobey et al. 1994). The zone contains cherts, which were particularly favored by craft specialists at Colha from the Preclassic through the Postclassic periods. In the Late Preclassic period, lithic production at Colha shifted from household production to standardized production of agrarian tools, such as oval bifaces and tranchet-bit adzes, as well as the production of ritual/ceremonial objects such as stemmed macroblades and eccentrics (Drollinger 1989; Hester and Shafer 1984, 1994; Potter 1991; Potter and King 1995; Shafer 1991; Shafer and Hester 1983, 1986). The presence of these tools among neighboring agricultural villages and civic-ceremonial centers such as Cerros (Mitchum 1991, 1994), Cuello (McSwain 1991a, 1991b), Santa Rita Corozal (Dockall and Shafer 1993), Pulltrouser Swamp (Shafer 1983), and K'axob (McAnany 1986, 1989) suggests

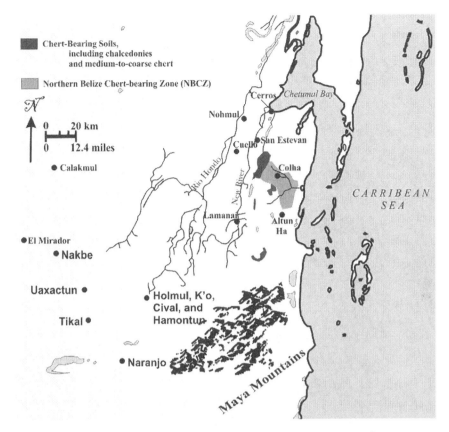

FIGURE 4.1. *Northern Belize Chert-bearing Zone (NBCBZ) and chert- and chalcedony-bearing soils in northern Belize*

that northern Belize witnessed centralized craft production as well as an integrated regional distributional economy at every level of society by the Late Preclassic period. The appearance of ritual/ceremonial objects produced from visually similar NBCBZ materials among elite contexts as far away as Altar de Sacrificios in the Rio Pasion area of northwestern Guatemala (Willey 1972; Willey et al. 1965) also supports the theory that NBCBZ materials were incorporated into long-distance trade networks controlled by the political elite.

New lithic tool and debitage data from Late Preclassic period household deposits from San Estevan, located in northern Belize, and from K'o and Hamontún in northeastern Guatemala (figure 4.2) provide an opportunity to understand complex regional and interregional interactions across

FIGURE 4.2. Map of Maya area, showing the location of San Estevan and Holmul region

two politically independent regions in the central Maya lowlands. Preclassic lithic refuse collected from variable social household group middens at K'o, Hamontún, and San Estevan serve as the means to interpret inter- and intra-regional economic strategies implemented across the Maya lowlands through time.

ERSTWHILE THOUGHTS OF HIERARCHY AND HETERARCHY ECONOMIES

A dichotomy between elite and non-elite interests in chipped stone economies led to contrasting arguments: one group disputed that elites were not interested in utilitarian production and consumption (Masson 2000; McAnany 1992, 1993, 1995; Potter and King 1995; Rice 1987; Sheets 2000; West

2002), while others consider a strong role for elite involvement in utilitarian economies (Aldenderfer 1991; Aoyama 1999, 2001; Kovacevich 2006; Moholy-Nagy 1997). Because chert tools are ubiquitously found throughout the Maya lowlands, McAnany (1992: 93) proposes that stone tools were incorporated and exchanged in separate economies devoid of elite interest. Kovacevich (2006) argues that chert may have been accessible by all levels of Maya populations among Maya Classic period sites; however, at Piedras Negras, eccentric chert objects may have been so rare as to become symbolic fetishized objects deserving of elite ritual caching (Hruby 2006). For his part, Hirth (2009: 16) acknowledges that the political elite would have promoted the production of both utilitarian and prestige goods when the distribution of these goods reinforced their social position.

A single chert artifact may, over its lifetime, have been consigned to numerous different organizations; from a gift to a commodity, it may have been a prestige, inalienable, or utilitarian object. A stone artifact might have been circulated or non-circulated through elite and non-elite economies or may have been plundered, recycled, or stolen (Appadurai 1986). Chert stone tools were essential to daily Preclassic life, but how can one account for the ways these items circulated through early social systems? Smith (2004: 77) argues that political economies are open systems concerned with inequality and social classes and that they invoked ways to explain the role of elites in expropriating resources from the broader population through manipulation of social and demographic environments. These economies also focus on processes of local historical change rather than on broad processes of cultural evolution.

Maya economic systems were not simple and were composed of intricate vertical and horizontal interactions that changed over regions and through time. Pluralistic economic models that intermingled simultaneously have been proposed for the development of social complexity. Potter and King (1995) proposed that hierarchical and heterarchical economic systems operated independently among Classic period Maya centers, as elites did not regulate and control utilitarian production. El Ceren (Sheets 2000) exemplifies multiple independent vertical and horizontal modes of production and exchange systems where many non-elite households produced utilitarian goods to augment their trading capacity in low-level intra-site and inter-site exchanges.

Most early Mesoamerican households were probably provisioned through a variety of acquisitive acts (vertical and horizontal), including trading and bartering, reciprocal gifting, redistributive exchanging, and various other kinds of resource gathering. Within political economies, the means to mobilize craft production and the subsequent distribution and consumption of chert commodities may travel along hierarchical lines. While political economies clearly benefited the local consolidation of power and wealth through centralizing economic surplus, other forms of political and economic interactions may have coexisted.

PRODUCTION: FORMAL AND INFORMAL

Modes of production and craft specialization are central to the interaction between political and domestic economies. The political economy thrives where craft specialization is well developed because crafts feed directly into such an economy (Feinman and Nicholas 2004). There is also a well-documented relationship between craft specialization and social stratification (Brumfiel and Earle 1987; Clark 1986; Peregrine 1991; Robb 1999; Service 1962: 148). The presence of specialized occupations and craft specialization has been considered a hallmark of state-level society (Clark and Parry 1990), although Smith (2004: 82) has made a recent case that specialization has come to be an interchangeable term with craft production. Production can be a complicated process, as craft production involved multiple consumption spheres—such as households, communities, and elite palaces—and may have included personal gifting, been a part of tribute obligations, or been used for commercial exchange or barter at the local, regional, or interregional scale (Brumfiel 1991; Clark and Houston 1998; Clark and Parry 1990; Costin 1998; Feinman and Nicholas 2004).

Specialized production has often been divided into two categories: independent or attached craft specialization (Brumfiel and Earle 1987; Clark and Parry 1990). Categories of attached and independent specialization have been devised as a means of understanding the social affiliations of producers (Brumfiel and Earle 1987; Costin 1986; Inomata 2001a; Smith 2004: 83). Attached specialization is synonymous with production sponsored by elite patronage (Clark and Parry 1990; Costin 1991), and attached specialists generally produce prestige goods, wealth items, or weapons (Kovacevich 2006: 67). Attached production was an important component among the Classic period Maya elite; most notably, ceramists have argued that the making of fine polychrome serving ware found throughout the Maya realm was carried out by attached specialists (Ball 1993; Reents-Budet 1998).

Independent specialization refers to subsistent and utilitarian production for unspecified groups by persons outside elite control (Masson 2002; McAnany et al. 2002; Smith 2004). Independent specialists can possess a relatively high degree of autonomy over the terms under which they create and exchange products with consumers or intermediaries. Hirth (2009: 13) has adopted the view that small-scale, part-time specialized household craft production was an important component of most pre-modern domestic economies. Hirth (2009) considers intermittent crafting a part-time effort measured by the amount of labor committed to craft production and quantified by the amount of production materials recorded and their diversity among households.

Mesoamerican households may have served as the center of utilitarian production (Ball 1993: 265; Berdan et al. 2003: 106; Freidel 1981: 377; King and Potter 1994; McAnany 1993, 1995) and in most accounts were more autonomous. Regarding lithic craft production in the Maya realm, there is considerably more emphasis on the social relationship between producers and consumers (Clark and Parry 1990; Costin 1991; McAnany 1995; Potter and King 1995; Shafer and Hester 1983, 1986, 1991). Investigations of Late Preclassic lithic production and distribution in northern Belize indicate that agricultural chert tools were primarily produced at Colha and distributed through regional economic networks. McAnany (1989: 343) modeled this localized relationship as a "ring," where political centers were consumers of subsistent and utilitarian goods from secondary centers and communities that encircled them. While these producer-consumer interactions were more prominent in later periods throughout the Maya lowlands (see Ball 1993; Fry 1980; Rands and Bishop 1980; Rice 1987), "producer-consumer" models developed with the discovery of Colha's extensive lithic workshops (Hester and Shafter 1994; Shafer and Hester 1983, 1986, 1991).

Shafer and Hester (1983, 1986, 1991) contend that large-scale specialized production had occurred at Colha and that craft production was carried out by independent specialists. Lithic goods were divided between two consumer types—primary consumers and peripheral consumers—and exchange was carried out by "professional traders" (Hester and Shafer 1994: 53; see also Gibson 1989: 133; McAnany 1986: 269). It is hard to distinguish between a "petty" and a "professional" trader when the scales and value of goods vary. Whether through "petty" or "professional" traders, Preclassic period centers and agricultural areas have been identified as recipients of exported Colha lithics, while Tikal, Uaxactún, and El Mirador have been identified as outlying centers that have recovered Colha-like eccentrics and stemmed macroblades (Hester and Shafer 1994; Kidder 1947; McAnany 1989; Moholy-Nagy 1991; Willey 1972).

Outlying peripheral centers, such as Santa Rita Corozal, Cerros, Pulltrouser Swamp, and K'axob, may have served as recipients of Colha's finished lithic goods, which were maintained by similar formal tool assemblages and an apparent lack of lithic debitage that would indicate early reduction sequences of formal tool manufacturing. At Santa Rita Corozal, located 70 km north of Colha, formal tools composed a considerable portion of the Late Preclassic lithic assemblage (Dockall and Shafer 1993). Production of these types of formal tools at Santa Rita Corozal was negated. Only a portion (25.2 %) of the lithic debitage was composed of local chalcedony, while the greatest portion (74.8 %) of the total debris was composed of chert. Of the entire chert and chalcedony Late Preclassic debitage sample, 71.7 percent of all chert flakes and 90.0 percent of all chalcedony flakes, respectively, were non-cortical flakes. Furthermore, lithic debris failed to provide evidence of manufacturing failures (Dockall and Shafer 1993: 168). This would imply that formal tools may have been imported into Santa Rita rather than manufactured locally. Local production did occur, but it involved production of expedient tools fashioned from small exhausted flake cores made of chalcedony, along with tools made from recycled formal bifaces (Dockall and Shafer 1993: 170–172).

Although Lewenstein (1987: 202) surmised that Late Preclassic households at Cerros produced and maintained a wide range of lithic implements for their own use, Mitchum's (1991, 1994) later analysis of tools at Cerros suggests that residents of Cerros also imported formal tools from Colha. Cerros, like Santa Rita Corozal, was part of the Late Preclassic coastal trade network that linked the center with Colha. Residents of Cerros may have also imported chert nodules and large cortical flakes for the production of informal or expedient tools (Mitchum 1994: 49). Mitchum (1994) recognized that recycling and resharpening of formal tools also occurred among Cerros households. Formal tool resharpening and manufacturing of expedient tools from local chalcedony sources were also identified by McAnany (1986, 1989; McAnany and Peterson 2004) among Preclassic period households at Pulltrouser Swamp (Shafer 1983) and K'axob. The identification of manufacturing debris has led Speal (2006: 93) to reconsider producer-consumer models that fail to embrace the importance of expedient ad hoc formal tool technologies among Preclassic period households. Speal (2006: 13) proposes that standards of quantification for the ratio of early-stage reduction (ESR) debris to total diagnostic flakes may be a more robust measurement for understanding interregional and diachronic economic change. Within the same framework, this type of study was conducted earlier on the lithic debitage of Middle to Late Preclassic period deposits at Cuello.

Studies of Preclassic period debitage at Cuello revealed changing regional economic systems. McSwain's (1991a, 1991b) study of Preclassic lithic assemblages indicated that most formal and expedient tools were made of locally available chalcedonies in the Middle Preclassic period. By the Late Preclassic period, oval bifaces, stemmed macroblades, and tranchet-bit adzes appeared and were composed primarily of northern Belize chert (McSwain 1991b). A study of 2,194 flakes (McSwain 1991b: 343) corroborates this transition. Of this sample, 603 (27.5%) flakes were of northern Belize chert. These flakes had little to no cortex on dorsal surfaces and were thinner compared to the majority of the debitage assemblage, which was composed of locally available chalcedony; they were also greater in size and included flakes that contained greater amounts of cortex. McSwain (1991b: 346) recognizes that northern Belize chert tools could have traveled through regional economic mechanisms by way of producer sites but proposes that since most tools and debris were composed of local raw materials, residents of Cuello could have also imitated regional tool styles to meet local needs. McSwain (1991b) notes that cortical flakes decreased from the Middle to Late Preclassic periods as the level of standardization among formal tools increased, implying that Cuello was likely integrated into the regional economic lithic sphere fronted by Colha. Hester and Shafer (1994: 56) later assert that Cuello was a typical consumer site and that any NBCBZ flake debris was a product resulting from the recycling and resharpening of Colha products.

At Saktunha, Speal (2005, 2006) proposed that residents produced the majority of lithic tools from imported NBCBZ chert. The site dates to the Terminal Classic period; nevertheless, Speal determined that large quantities of early-stage reduction flakes recovered from Saktunha household middens could indicate a low dependency on Colha products. Other northern Maya lowland sites may not have been dependent solely on Colha products and may have served as producers, as first suggested by McSwain and proposed at Saktunha.

In the Petén, lithic debitage found in construction fill at Tikal has been disputed as a production site because the number of lithic tools per meter of fill is substantially lower than that found at Colha (Potter and King 1995). Earlier, McAnany (1989: figure 3) proposed that Tikal was a peripheral consumer, as elite residents imported ritual/symbolic items. Lithics, manufactured at Colha, found their way into elaborate Preclassic elite burials and other contexts (Hester and Shafer 1994; Moholy-Nagy 1991). Chipped stone production was still an important economic means among centers in the Petén, as evident by the refuse found in construction fill and the discovery of substantial outcrops neighboring major monumental centers (Aldenderfer 1991; Hruby 2006; Kovacevich 2006; Lewis 2003; Moholy-Nagy 1991; Paling et al. 2009). High-quality crypto-crystalline debitage found in the construction fill of elite structures (Fowler 1987; Moholy-Nagy 1991, 1994, 1997), in elite middens

(Aldenderfer 1991), or associated with elite burial rituals (Hruby 2006; Willey et al. 1965) implies hierarchical economic systems with production that is either attached or independent but still monitored by elite households.

McAnany (1989: 342) also recognized the existence of "core" models, which implies that production took place within urbanized centers. Based on the quantity and types of lithic debitage and tools recovered from Middle Preclassic period sheet middens, Paris (2012: 133) has submitted that Middle Preclassic period lithic production at San Estevan was "independent, small-scale, and relatively unskilled, and could have been carried out by a mixture of part-time specialists working seasonally in conjunction with agriculture (Hagstrum 2001), or [by] non-specialists." At El Pedernal and El Pilar, Classic period lithic workshops have been identified (Ford and Olson 1989; Lewis 1995, 1996, 2003). Formal tools were produced from local materials, and finished goods were exchanged regionally. Similar patterns have been recognized at Tikal (King and Potter 1994; Moholy-Nagy 1997) and Piedras Negras (Hruby 2006), but the degree of domestic or production autonomy is not well understood. The existence of both forms of contrasting independent lithic specialization indicates that multiple forms of craft specialization existed; moreover, attached and independent specializations are not mutually exclusive.

Not only could elites directly influence production, but indirect forms of influence were also common, particularly where political structures were heterarchically organized or elite political influence was relatively weak (Berdan 2003: 95; Berdan et al. 2003: 106; Crumley 2003; Graham 2002: 414; McAnany et al. 2002). In many early states, craft production was done in or around the house (household industry) or in workshops connected with the house (Feinman and Nicholas 2000). As most household productivity may have coincided with and been limited by other seasonal or annual subsistence activities (e.g., agriculture) or service duties (labor, military, other), Hirth distinguishes between levels (single or multiple) of domestic production.

Multicrafting is measured by the diversity of activities occurring within a household (Costin 2001; Hirth 2006, 2009) and is a form of intensive craft production that can combine with other subsistence activities to create a more diversified form of intermittent crafting (Hirth 2009: 22). Although multicrafting activities have been most perceptible among Classic and Postclassic period economies (McAnany 1995; Murata 2010; Widmer 2009), Preclassic households may also have engaged in diverse crafting operations. Hirth (2009: 22) specifies that intermittent crafting and multicrafting are not mutually exclusive; rather, crafting fell along a continuum dependent on household circumstances and fluctuated over time, place, and space.

Since production is measured on an individual household-by-household basis, vis-à-vis other activities and based on how important craft production was, this study of craft production accounts for household agency. By trying to best fit production into a multitude of overlapping typologies, one may get the impression that emerging craft specialization evolved along a single unilineal course. An examination of the production choices carried out by each household provides a more nuanced understanding of external political and economic pressures.

THE SITES

Northern Belize Region: San Estevan

San Estevan, the archaeological site and modern town, is located on the New River, Belize, in the eastern Maya lowlands. The site and town are sandwiched between two of the largest marshlands in the region, and the area immediately surrounding San Estevan contains rich clays, which are well suited for agricultural cultivation (Romney 1959). The richly organic soils surrounding San Estevan was likely one of many factors in early and also modern settlement in this area.

The earliest archaeological investigations at San Estevan were carried out by William Bullard (1965) in the 1960s. Bullard mapped the civic-ceremonial center, excavated and restored two Early Classic structures (I and II) on Plaza A, and established the first architectural categorization for the region. The site map of San Estevan was further expanded by Normand Hammond (1973, 1975) during the 1973–1974 British Museum and Cambridge University Corozal Survey Project. Mapping and excavation continued at San Estevan in 1989 and 1990, conducted by Laura Levi (1996, 2002). Levi's political configurations have led to considerable debate regarding political organization in the region. Focusing on the architectural layout of outlying residential structures at San Estevan and Pulltrouser Swamp, Levi (2002) has argued that by the Classic period the region encompassing San Estevan, Kokeal, and K'axob formed a single political unit, while the area surrounding Tibaat and Nohmul formed another polity. Despite the expansion of elite households during the Late Preclassic period, there is no consensus about the political organization of northern Belize during this period. Scarborough (1991) has argued that there were four large states in the region (Cerros, Lamanai, Colha, and Nohmul) that assumed control over secondary centers, like San Estevan, and tertiary villages or communities (like K'axob and Pulltrouser Swamp), while McAnany (1995, 2004a) has argued that scores of politically independent entities of different sizes and varying levels of political complexity coexisted.

Recent excavations were led by Robert Rosenswig in 2002 and by the University of Albany–SUNY Archaeological Field School in 2005 and 2008. Excavations recovered lithic materials from Middle and Late Preclassic midden deposits. Substantial Late Preclassic and Classic period ceremonial and residential architecture has led Rosenswig and Kennett (2007) to propose that second-order polities were perhaps independent polities interacting and competing with large centers. San Estevan's increasing political complexity during the Late Preclassic period (Rosenswig and Kennett 2007) is demonstrated by its architectural intensification, evidenced by the San Estevan ballcourt and the Mound XV pyramid (Rosenswig 2007). This pattern represents the emergence of complex political systems during the Late Preclassic period in the region (Freidel 1979; Rosenswig and Kennett 2007).

The Holmul Region: K'o and Hamontún

The Holmul region is located in the Petén region of northeastern Guatemala, approximately 15 km west of the Belizean border and 80 km south of the Mexico border. Since 2000, extensive archaeological investigations in the Holmul region have been carried out under the direction of Francisco Estrada-Belli and the Holmul Archaeological Project (Estrada-Belli 2000, 2014). Intensive excavation projects have revealed evidence of continuous occupation for nearly 1,900 years, from the early Middle Preclassic to the Terminal Classic (1000 BCE–900 CE), with major construction episodes occurring in the Late and Terminal Preclassic and the Early and Late Classic periods. Intensive mapping operations of Holmul's site center and the surrounding settlements have led to the discovery of additional archaeological sites, two of which were K'o and Hamontún.

John Tomasic surveyed and mapped K'o's site core and all surrounding patio groups within 800 m^2 of the epicenter. Tomasic (2006; Estrada-Belli 2005) carried out excavations of selected patio groups within the site core, test excavations of a stratified random sample of patio groups outside the core, and intensive excavation of some of these groups to refine the settlement and construction chronology. Tomasic's work at K'o (Paling 2009; Rangel 2009; Tomasic 2006, 2008, 2009a; Tomasic and Estrada-Belli 2008; Tomasic et al. 2008, 2009a, 2009b) has established that the earliest occupation of the site occurred in the late Middle Preclassic (600–350 BCE). The majority of K'o's public architecture was constructed during the Terminal Preclassic through the early facet of the Early Classic period (200–600 CE).

Survey and mapping operations at Hamontún (Paling et al. 2009) revealed Middle to Late Preclassic period occupation. Similar to Tomasic's work, which identified refuse middens adjacent to residential structures at K'o (Tomasic 2008, 2009b), middens among Hamontún's residential structures were targeted to collect lithic materials. An outcrop of medium to coarse-grained chert located along "La Riverita" (Paling et al. 2009) was also investigated; this outcrop is known locally as "El Pedernal" and is found 6 km northeast of Hamontún. The coloration of the chert varies from mottled opaque buffs and creams to tans, light browns, and light grays, while surface nodules range in size from cobbles (10–15 cm long) to small stones (x ≤ 10 cm).

TECHNICAL DESCRIPTION OF THE LITHIC TYPOLOGY

In this study, lithic debitage was sorted through mass analysis using 2 inch, 1 inch, 0.5 inch, and 0.25 inch nested screens (see Ahler 1989; Masson 1989, 2001; Michaels 1986; Roemer 1984). The separation of debitage samples by gradient size and cross-sample comparisons of counts and weights provides a direct relationship to the manufacturing stage. Within those gradients, debitage was individually analyzed by type (flake or shatter), raw material type, raw material color, percentage of cortex on the dorsal surface (0 percent, 1–24 percent, 25–49 percent, and over 50 percent), patination, edge damage, and fire damage. Greater amounts of cortex on the dorsal side of large flakes often indicate initial reduction flakes derived from nodule or core reduction, while smaller flakes with little to no cortex indicate the final stages of reduction. Fire damage is present with obvious physical property changes that were believed to improve flaking quality among knappers (Crabtree 1964), while each flake was examined for edge damage using a 10× hand lens to determine if flakes were also utilized as unmodified, expedient tools. Utilized flakes have been identified among other lithic debitage assemblages (McSwain 1991a, 1991b; Speal 2005, 2006), and the degree to which households recycle broken materials or production debris may reinforce the varying aspects of household organization, production locales, craft production, access to raw materials, and household status and wealth.

The lithic tool assemblages were broadly grouped into five technological classes: bifaces, unifaces, blades, secondary tools, and production tools, which include cores, hammerstones, and pre-form tools. The following variables were recorded for each tool: provenance, artifact, number, tool type, section, material type, material color, breakage type, percentage of cortex, heat treatment, evidence of recycling, type and location of edge damage, patina, shape plan and profile, length, width, thickness, weight, and working-edge angles (if applicable). Bifaces, characteristic of tools worked on both the dorsal and ventral sides, can be either formal (Clark 1988; Shafer 1991) or informal, meaning they are made from flakes or recycled from larger bifaces or cores (Potter 1991). Formal bifaces are also identified as having relatively even, symmetrical flakes removed from both faces on the lateral and distal edges, while informal or expedient bifaces are roughly elliptical in cross-section; they are often smaller and less symmetrical and they have less even flake removal patterns than formal bifaces (Paris 2007: 79). Among the San Estevan, K'o, and Hamontún lithic assemblages, expedient bifaces were further sorted by morphological categories, which included discoidal, elliptical, elongated, thick-truncated or elongated, thin-truncated, exhausted-miniature, irregular-single bifacial edge, and fragmentary.

Chert unifacial tools are knapped on one side, more often than not on the dorsal rather than the ventral side of the flake. Unifaces vary widely in form, and in this work, unifaces are categorized by shape, form, or angle of distal edge. Blades are twice as long as they are wide and are not bifacially worked. Blades also vary in size, from large macroblades to small microblades or flake blades. Preclassic period lithic assemblages also include secondary, or ad hoc, tools. These tools appear to have been recycled from other tools such as bifaces, unifaces, and cores. Expedient unifaces, like formal unifaces, have reduction flake scars on only one surface; generally, although not always, this is the dorsal surface. Use-wear and damage (i.e., utilized flakes) are not sufficient to classify a tool as a uniface. Unifaces are created by the same processes as flakes; however, unifaces are flakes with retouch, the exception being blades. Unifaces have been found at K'axob, Colha, Cuello, and Pulltrouser Swamp (McAnany 2004b: 287; McSwain 1991a; Potter 1991; Shafer 1983). Expedient unifaces in the San Estevan lithic assemblage are highly variable in size, shape, quality, percentages of cortex, thickness, and edge angle. It is nearly impossible to avoid associating these types of tools with a particular function, as technological and morphological traits often correlate with a particular function. This large and varying assemblage was categorized around morphological traits and by hypothetical functional traits and included the categories of gravers, notches, perforators, scrapers, and denticulates. See table 4.1 for technical descriptions of the formal or informal subcategories noted among the K'o, Hamontún, and San Estevan lithic assemblages.

TABLE 4.1. Technological descriptions of Preclassic lithic tools

Technological Class		Description	Notable References	Figure
Bifaces	**Oval bifaces** Also referred to as General utility tools, biface celts, choppers, ovate bifaces–thick, or Puleston axe	Characterized by distinctive teardrop shape, have a length that is two and a half times the width, are bi-convex in shape at the cross-section, and have an even, symmetrical bifacial removal pattern of flakes from both faces on the lateral and distal edges.	Anderson 1976; Hester 1985; Kidder 1947: 5; Kovacevich 2006: 359; Mitchum 1986: 106; Shafer 1983, 1990, 1994: 141; Shafer and Hester 1983; Thompson 1991; Willey 1965; Wilk 1977	Figure 4.3
	General Utility Bifaces (GUBs)	Characterized by a symmetrical, thick bifacial profile with dulled, slightly convex lateral edges. GUBs also exhibit a wide D-shape configuration with a truncated midsection and are generally more oval than oval bifaces, as they are less tapered toward the proximal end.	Shafer 1983	Figure 4.4
	Tranchet-bit tools Also referred to as Tranchet Axe and "Orange-Peel Adze"	Triangular in shape, plano-convex in profile, have a sloping (from dorsal to ventral) shear working edge, and can be the same length and thickness as oval bifaces. Distal cutting edge would be 65 to 70 degrees and was presumably used as an adze, not an ax.	Hester 1976; Rovner and Lewenstein 1997; Shafer 1983, 1991: 33, 1994; Shafer and Hester 1983	
	Polished bifacial celt	Characterized by a symmetrical, bifacial, elliptical cross-section; bifacially knapped into shape and finished by abrasion. Polishing removes evidence of facets and creates finer lateral and distal edges.	Shafer 1994	Figure 4.5
	Bipointed bifaces Also referred to as elongated bifaces, narrow bifaces, or chisels	Bipointed bifaces are narrow and convex toward the proximal and distal ends and have a lenticular to slightly plano-convex cross-section profile. At the midpoint the pieces have nearly parallel lateral sides.	Rovner and Lewenstein 1997: 20, figure 6h; Shafer 1991: 38	

continued on next page

TABLE 4.1—continued

Technological Class	Description	Notable References	Figure
Small bifaces Also referred to as miniature bifaces	Small bifaces are symmetrical and bi-convex but incredibly small in size. It is likely that small bifaces are a product of heavy use and recycling operations and are probably not a true formal tool category.	Paris 2007	
Eccentrics	Eccentrics demonstrate the highest level of skill and craftsmanship. eccentric flints can take on the form of gods, weapons, animals, or other symbolic matter and are found among elite ceremonial contexts. At San Estevan, eccentrics have irregular shapes, are partially worked, and consist of a uniform bifacially knapped edge. Small eccentrics have been noted in Cuello assemblage (McSwain 1991a).	Estrada-Belli 2005; Fash 1991; Hester and Shafer 1994; Hruby 2006; Moholy-Nagy 2003; Shafer 1983, 1991; Shafer and Hester 1983, 1986, 1991; Willey 1972	Figure 4.6
Phase 1 and phase 2 biface pre-forms	These are bifaces that were never completely finished. Phase 1 bifaces are bifacially reduced by hard-hammer percussion, have a rough flake removal pattern, are irregular in outline and shape, and show greater amounts of cortex than Phase 2 pre-forms. Phase 2 pre-forms are less irregular in outline and shape and contain some cortex but may also have some evidence of lateral or distal edge use-wear damage.		
Expedient bifaces	Expedient bifaces show asymmetrical flake removal along lateral, distal, and/or proximal ends; have a greater percentage of cortex ($x > 25\%$), are roughly elliptical in cross-section; and are irregular in shape. Use-wear shows no distinctive single purpose. They can be either recycled from broken formal bifaces or unifacial tools or composed from a large primary or secondary flake and had flakes removed to create a bifacial working edge.	McAnany and Peterson 2004; McSwain 1991a; Shafer 1994	Figure 4.7

continued on next page

TABLE 4.1—continued

Technological Class		Description	Notable References	Figure
Unifaces	**T-shaped unifaces**	Characterized as having a tapered bifacially or unifacially flaked stem and a wide, straight, sharp-angled distal edge.	McAnany and Peterson 2004; McSwain 1991a; Paris 2007: 84; Shafer 1983, 1994	
Blades	**Prismatic Blades**	Specialized flakes with parallel or near parallel lateral edges. Generally more than twice as long as they are wide.		Figure 4.8
	Macroblades	Macroblades are generally twice as long as they are wide characteristically have pronounced medial dorsal ridges that run the length of the specimen and are created by hard-hammer percussion.	Shafer 1991	Figure 4.9
	Stemmed Macroblades	Large macroblades with stems that are bifacially worked that run approximately one-third the total length and have a long, tapered point.	Peterson 2001; Shafer 1991, 1994	Figure 4.10
Secondary Tools	**Graver**	Functional term that describes elongated flakes with one or multiple ridges for incising or engraving activities. They are as thick as they are wide, often created by hard-hammer percussion of edges from unidirectional cores, and triangular in cross-section, which allows for one sharp lateral edge with a broad, strong spine.		
	Notches	Made from retouched flakes or recycled tool fragments, characterized by the removal of a single or multiple concave notch in or toward the distal end of a flake. Notches are created by direct pressure flaking, and use-wear must be present in the groove.	Lewenstein 1987; Paris 2007: 87	Figure 4.11

continued on next page

TABLE 4.1—continued

Technological Class		Description	Notable References	Figure
	Perforators Also referred to as Graver-on blade and include types noted as elongated, burin spall, or spur perforators	Characterized as having an elongated body that tapers to a pointed distal end. Perforators are thick and triangular, square, or trapezoidal in cross-section, and they have use-wear on the distal tip.	Kovacevich 2006: 364; McAnany and Peterson 2004; McSwain 1991a; Mitchum 1994; Rovner and Lewenstein 1997: 22	Figures 4.12 and 4.13
	Scrapers Include end, side, opposed lateral, pyramidal, and discoidal types	Manufactured from flakes, blades, or recycled tools and have steep, pronounced edge angles. Scrapers come in various non-standardized shapes and sizes and were categorized in this study by edge angle.	Kovacevich 2006: 362; Paris 2007; Rovner and Lewenstein 1997; Stoltman 1978: 11	
	Denticulates	Similar to notches but have multiple U-shaped cavities notched along a working edge. The spacing between notches creates small rectangular protrusions that resemble a row of teeth.		Figure 4.14
Production Tools	**Tested Cobble**	Nodules of chert, chalcedony, or quartz with one to three flakes removed. Large thin flakes may have served as the primary lithic reduction stages for the production of expedient flakes or more formally recognized tools.		
	Cores Include polyhedral, bifacial, bipolar, blade, burin, and unidirectional core types	Cores begin as nodules of varying quality, from coarse to fine-grained siliceous cryptocrystalline materials, and are reduced to create flakes. Characterized by the lithic reduction techniques of producing flakes.		Figure 4.15
	Hammerstones	Hammerstones are generally spherical in cross-section and show heavy macroscopic battering or crushing damage. In this study hammerstones were subcategorized by material types, size, shape, and morphology.		Figure 4.16

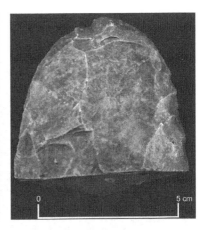

FIGURE 4.3. *Thin oval biface from San Estevan*

FIGURE 4.4. *General Utility Biface from Hamontún*

FIGURE 4.5. *Polished bifacial celt distal fragment from San Estevan*

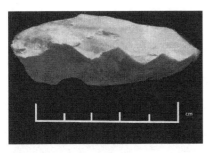

FIGURE 4.6. *Eccentric from San Estevan*

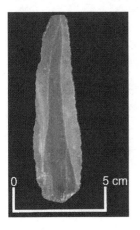

FIGURE 4.7. *Informal biface from San Estevan*

FIGURE 4.8. *Chert blade from San Estevan*

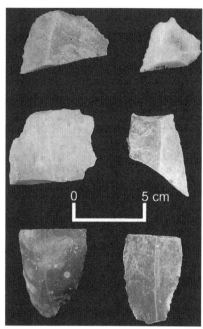

FIGURE 4.11. *Notch from K'o*

FIGURE 4.10. *Stemmed macroblade*

FIGURE 4.9. *Proximal, medial, and distal fragments of macroblades from San Estevan*

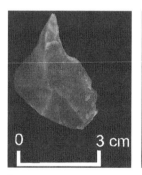

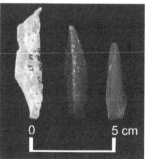

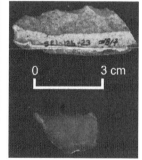

FIGURE 4.12. *Spur notched perforator*

FIGURE 4.13. *Burin spall perforators from San Estevan*

FIGURE 4.14. *Denticulates from San Estevan*

FIGURE 4.15. *Polyhedral cores*

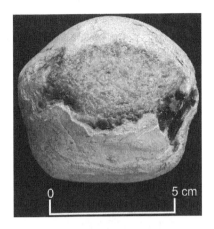

FIGURE 4.16. *Spherical hammerstone from Hamontún*

LITHIC DISCUSSION

A total of 16,084 Preclassic chert artifacts were examined and 9,611 (59.76%) of those artifacts comprised the San Estevan lithic assemblage. The greatest concentration of lithic materials came from early Middle Preclassic midden contexts and includes 210 tools (see table 4.2), of which the greatest material type for all Middle Preclassic tools includes medium-grained cherts (40.48%, n = 85) and chalcedony (38.57%, n = 81). The late Middle Preclassic tool assemblage includes 85 pieces and a more uniform distribution of raw material sources: medium-grained chert (40%, n = 34), fine-grained northern Belize chert (24.70%, n = 21), chalcedony (28.23%, n = 24), and quartz blends (7.05 %, n = 6). The Late Preclassic lithic assemblage also constitutes a significant share of the assemblage (39.59%, n = 192), but unlike the previous epochs, medium-grained chert tools dominate this period, at 56.25% (n = 108).

The Preclassic period K'o lithic assemblage included 4,733 (29.43%) artifacts. Nearly a fifth (18.85%, n = 59) of the K'o tool assemblage dates to the Middle Preclassic period. The foremost material type from this period includes 28 tools (47.56%) constructed from coarse-grained or quartz-blend cherts, 22 pieces (37.29%) made from medium-grained chert, and 9 tools (15.25%) made of chalcedony. The greatest concentration of Preclassic lithic tools was recovered from Late Preclassic contexts and includes 176 tools (56.23%) predominantly manufactured from medium-grained chert (n = 97, 55.11%), coarse-grained chert and quartz blends (n = 55, 31.25%), chalcedony (n = 22, 12.5%), and hardened limestone (n = 2, 1.14%). The most evident material change occurred from the Middle to the Late Preclassic, as tools were fashioned from better-quality material—from coarse-grained to medium-grained chert. A quarter of the entire Preclassic period K'o lithic assemblage (n = 78, 24.92%) dates to the Terminal Preclassic period, during which tools are equally constructed from medium-grained (n = 32, 41.03%) and coarse-grained/quartz-blended cherts (n = 35, 44.87%). As in previous epochs, chalcedony was consistently utilized, at around 14.1 percent (n = 11) of the Terminal Preclassic tool assemblage.

The Preclassic period Hamontún lithic assemblage consists of 1,740 (10.81%) artifacts. The greatest portion of the assemblage did, however, come from Middle Preclassic period midden contexts and includes 46 tools. Among Middle Preclassic period tools, the most prominent construction material type recorded was medium-grained chert (60.87%), followed by coarse-grained/quartz blends (34.78%). Among Late Preclassic tools, the foremost raw material source was also medium-grained chert (76.67%), followed by coarse-grained/quartz blends (16.67%) and chalcedony (3.33%).

The most commonly recognizable formal tool technologies throughout northern Belize during the Middle and Late Preclassic periods include oval bifaces, tranchet-bit adzes, and polished celts. San Estevan joins other sites such as Cerros, Cuello, El Pozito, K'axob, Kichpanha, Nohmul, Pulltrouser Swamp, and Santa Rita Corozal (Dockall 1994; Hester and Shafer 1984; McAnany and Peterson 2004; McSwain 1991a, 1991b; Mitchum 1994; Potter 1991; Shafer 1979, 1982, 1983; Shafer and Hester 1983, 1986, 1991) in having a well-documented oval biface assemblage. At San Estevan, thick oval bifaces dominate the entire formal biface tool assemblage (53.49%, n = 23) from the early Middle to Late Preclassic periods. In the early Middle Preclassic period, oval bifaces at San Estevan are composed primarily of chalcedony and medium-grained chert. By the Late Preclassic period (see table 4.2), a veritable explosion of formal tools fashioned from fine-quality NBCBZ cherts appears in household middens.

Compared to lithic assemblages recovered from K'o, in Hamontún a scarcity of formal bifaces is observed (table 4.2). Thick oval bifaces are the only recognized formal bifacial tools recovered from Middle through Terminal Preclassic period middens at K'o, while only a single thick oval biface was recovered from a Middle Preclassic household at Hamontún. This variation between northern and central Maya lowland centers can be a product of many interconnected factors. General Utility Bifaces, bipointed bifaces, and polished bifacial celts may be reflective of regional tool technologies that did not extend into the Petén. Perhaps the fact that formal tools associated with agricultural activities were not recovered from neighboring household middens in the Petén reflects the distance of agricultural plots from tool production or refurbishing sites, which may not be the case when one examines the quantity of expedient bifaces recovered from middens at these sites.

INFORMAL BIFACES

Expedient bifaces top thick oval bifaces as the largest number of tools recovered from Preclassic period deposits at San Estevan. Of the entire Preclassic period San Estevan lithic assemblage, 19.59 percent (n = 95) of all tools were expedient bifaces, the greatest portion of which was found among early Middle Preclassic and Late Preclassic contexts. Elongated, thick-truncated bifaces were the most common type found and were largely produced from medium-grained cherts—early Middle Preclassic (eMP, 75%; n = 3), late Middle Preclassic (lMP, 50%; n = 3), and Late Preclassic (LP, 80%; n = 12)—but were also manufactured from fined-grained NBCBZ chert.

Among the entire Preclassic K'o lithic assemblage, 15.66 percent (n = 49) of all tools were expedient bifaces, the greatest portion of which was found among Late Preclassic period contexts. Elongated, thick-truncated bifaces were the most common type found and were largely produced from medium-grained cherts but were also manufactured from chalcedony and coarse-grained cherts. Elongated, thick-truncated, expedient bifaces appear as early as Middle Preclassic period contexts (n = 5) but explode in number during the Late Preclassic period (n = 14) and continue to be recovered from Terminal Preclassic period contexts (n = 7). Elongated, thin-truncated bifaces appear as early as the Late Preclassic period (n = 2) and were generally manufactured from medium-grained cherts and chalcedony but were found entirely composed of coarse to quartz-blended cherts among Terminal Preclassic period deposits (n = 3). The biface tool typology is dominated by fragmentary bifaces recovered from Middle Preclassic through Terminal Preclassic period middens. It is impossible to determine the original design of these bifaces, but they were primarily composed of medium-grained cherts (n = 9) and also of coarse chert and chalcedony.

Elongated, thick-truncated expedient bifaces constitute 21.05 percent of the total Hamontún Preclassic lithic assemblage. At K'o, again, this category comprised 15.66 percent of all Preclassic tools, with the majority of elongated, thick-truncated expedient bifaces composed mainly of medium-grained cherts and found in greater quantity among Late Preclassic households. At Hamontún, elongated, thick-truncated expedient bifaces are also composed of medium-grained chert (68.75 %) but are predominantly recovered from Middle Preclassic household midden contexts (n = 13). The decline

TABLE 4.2. Frequency of each tool type across each site and period

Tool Types	San Estevan Early Middle Preclassic	San Estevan Late Middle Preclassic	San Estevan Late Preclassic	K'o Middle Preclassic	K'o Late Preclassic	K'o Terminal Preclassic	Hamontún Middle Preclassic	Hamontún Late Preclassic	Grand Total
Formal bifaces									
Oval biface–thick	6	7	10	2	2	2	1		30
Oval biface–thin			1						1
General Utility Biface	1		6	2	2				11
Tranchet-bit adze			1						1
Polished bifacial celt	3	1	1						5
Bipointed biface	1	2							3
Small biface				1	1				2
Eccentric	1	1	1						3
Pre–form–Phase I					1		1		2
Constricted adze						1			1
Expedient bifaces									
Discoidal biface	2	3				1			6
Elongated–thick–truncated	4	6	15	5	14	7	13	3	67
Elongated–thin–truncated	1	1	4		2	3			11
Exhausted–miniature biface	4		3						7
Irregular	6	1	4						11

continued on next page

TABLE 4.2—continued

Tool Types	San Estevan Early Middle Preclassic	San Estevan Late Middle Preclassic	San Estevan Late Preclassic	K'o Middle Preclassic	K'o Late Preclassic	K'o Terminal Preclassic	Hamontún Middle Preclassic	Hamontún Late Preclassic	Grand Total
Fragmentary	15	3	22	4	10	3		3	60
Unifaces									
Uniface	6	1	6	1	2	1		1	18
Blades	20	15	7	6	12	6	1		67
Macroblade	4	1	3	3	2	3		1	17
Stemmed blade	2	1	3	3	3	1		3	16
Expedient unifaces									
Graver	6		1	1	1				9
Notch	3	2	7						12
Perforator–spur	1	3	4	1		1			11
Perforator–burin spall	8	4	1		1		1	1	16
Scraper–end					3				3
Scraper–side	3				3	1			7
Scraper–opposed lateral		1							1
Scraper–discoidal								1	1
Denticulate	1	1	1	4	5	1	1	1	15
Production									
Tested cobble			5						5

continued on next page

TABLE 4.2—continued

Tool Types	San Estevan Early Middle Preclassic	San Estevan Late Middle Preclassic	San Estevan Late Preclassic	K'o Middle Preclassic	K'o Late Preclassic	K'o Terminal Preclassic	Hamontún Middle Preclassic	Hamontún Late Preclassic	Grand Total
Polyhedral core	46	14	31	17	43	30	11	8	200
Polyhedral core-exhausted	5	3	5	2	16	5	6	3	45
Bifacial core	5	2	2	5	7	2	2		25
Bipolar core	5		4		9	3	1	1	23
Blade core	1		3		3				7
Pyramidal core					5	1			6
Burin	5	1	1		1	1	1		10
Hammerstone–poly. core	38	9	30		17	5	3	2	104
Hammerstone–spherical	6	2	8		4		2	1	23
Hammerstone–irregular	1		1	2	7			1	12
Hammerstone–groundstone			1						1
Mano							1		1
Total	210	85	192	59	176	78	46	30	876

in expedient bifaces among Hamontún's households from the Middle to the Late Preclassic may be a reflection of household activities and production strategies, but among household at K'o, expedient bifaces continued to be important throughout the Preclassic period.

Blades and Unifaces

Prismatic blades found among the San Estevan lithic assemblage ranged in size from 2 to 15 centimeters in length, from 0.5 to 5 centimeters in width, and from 0.1 to 3 centimeters in thickness. Of the San Estevan lithic assemblage, only a very small percentage (× < 2%) of all blades showed any resharpening along lateral edges. Early Middle Preclassic blades were composed of an assortment of material types, including chalcedony (30%, n = 6), medium-grained chert (25%, n = 5), fine-grained NBCBZ chert (20%, n = 4), and quartz blends (25%, n = 5). Late Middle Preclassic and Late Preclassic period blades are not as diverse and are composed primarily of medium- to fine-grained cherts. Likewise, throughout the Preclassic period, macroblades (n = 7) are made predominantly of medium-grained chert and chalcedony. Blades were produced at San Estevan, just not on a large scale. Blade cores were recovered from early Middle Preclassic (n = 1) and Late Preclassic (n = 3) contexts. The blade core of the early Middle Preclassic was recycled from a large broken tool made of fine-grained northern Belize chert. Blade cores were recovered from Late Preclassic contexts, and all three were composed of chalcedony.

Prismatic blades comprise 7.67 percent of the entire Preclassic K'o lithic assemblage (n = 24) and are manufactured primarily of coarse to quartz-blended cherts. The greatest concentration of chert prismatic blades was recovered from Late Preclassic period contexts (n = 12), but equal amounts were recovered from Middle and Terminal Preclassic period deposits (n = 6). Large macroblades were present among all Preclassic period deposits and were primarily composed of coarse-grained cherts in the Middle Preclassic period but were found fashioned only from medium-grained cherts among Late Preclassic period contexts. Finally, amid Terminal Preclassic period household contexts, macroblades were fashioned from a wide variety of raw materials. Stemmed blades (n = 7) were omnipresent and were manufactured from medium- to coarse-grained cherts. Blade cores were discovered among the K'o lithic assemblage but noted only in Late Preclassic period contexts (n = 3). Like the majority of blades recovered, Late Preclassic period blade cores were composed entirely of coarse to quartz-blended cherts.

At Hamontún, formal unifaces make up a small percentage of the Middle Preclassic lithic assemblage (2.17%), but by the Late Preclassic, unifaces appear more frequently. It is apparent that formal and expedient bifaces and formal unifaces were less of a concern for Hamontún households, but when we consider that over 50 percent (56.52%) of the entire lithic assemblage was production tools and that the expedient unifaces constituted the same relative proportion of lithic assemblages as was the case at San Estevan and K'o (table 4.3), perhaps the same crafting activities were occurring among households at Hamontún.

Expedient Second-Order Tools

Second-order tools, such as perforators, gravers, and scrapers, comprised nearly a tenth (9.69%, n = 47) of the entire siliceous Preclassic period tool assemblage of San Estevan. Second-order tools, again, are informal, ad hoc, or expedient tools recycled from broken formal tools or purposely prepared flakes from polyhedral cores or burins that show some form of modification. Second-order tools show little evidence for standardization or specialization in manufacturing and may indicate a variety of recycling operations, including edge resharpening, percussion flaking, or retouch. These types of tools not only illustrate a greater variety of recycling techniques but are also more disposed to be multipurpose tools and to demonstrate a variety of use-wear patterns. Second-order tools, such as spurs, gravers, and perforators, were identified among Preclassic lithic assemblages at Cerros (Mitchum 1991, 1994), Colha (Potter 1991), Cuello (McSwain 1991a), K'axob (McAnany 2004b), and Pulltrouser Swamp (Shafer 1983); they were manufactured or recycled from flakes, burins, blades, and bifaces. These types of tools, along with notches (Lewenstein 1987), were believed to have been used in woodworking and shellworking activities at these sites.

Formal and expedient bifaces, unifaces, cores, and blades tended to be the most commonly recycled tool forms among the San Estevan lithic assemblage. The most prevalent tools reprocessed were polyhedral cores that were turned into hammerstones (eMP, n = 38; lMP, n = 9; LP, n = 30). Large bifaces were also transformed into hammerstones but also into smaller expedient bifaces or unifaces, and these unifaces were recycled into small expedient bifaces or burins and scrapers, while broken blades were retouched and turned into perforators.

At San Estevan, second-order tools were predominately composed from local medium-grained cherts (42.55%, n = 20) and chalcedonies (42.55%, n = 20). The most recognized second-order tools from early Middle Preclassic

TABLE 4.3. Percentage of tool classes across each site and period

	San Estevan		
Technological Classes	Early Middle Preclassic	Late Middle Preclassic	Late Preclassic*
Formal bifaces	5.71	12.79	10.42
Expedient bifaces	15.25	16.28	25.00
Unifaces	15.24	20.93	9.90
Expedient unifaces	10.48	12.79	7.29
Production	53.33	36.05	7.29
Total Tools	**n = 210**	**n = 86**	**n = 192**

	K'o		
	Middle Preclassic	Late Preclassic	Terminal Preclassic
Formal bifaces	8.47	3.41	3.85
Expedient bifaces	15.25	14.77	17.95
Unifaces	22.03	10.80	14.10
Expedient unifaces	10.17	7.39	3.85
Production	44.07	63.64	60.26
Total Tools	**n = 59**	**n = 176**	**n = 78**

	Hamontún	
	Middle Preclassic	Late Preclassic
Formal bifaces	4.35	0
Expedient bifaces	28.26	20.00
Unifaces	2.17	16.67
Expedient unifaces	6.52	10.00
Production	56.52	53.33
Total Tools	**n = 46**	**n = 30**

* Other has not been included; therefore, totals may not equal 100 percent.

contexts included gravers, spurs, and burin spall perforators. These tool types are found continuously among San Estevan contexts through the late Middle Preclassic into the Late Preclassic periods. It has been proposed that burin spall drills recovered from Middle Preclassic period assemblages from Colha and Kichpanha served as drills for shell-working activities (Gibson 1986; Potter 1991). *Strombus* shell beads and pendants (France 2008: 103–104) were recovered from San Estevan (Suboperations 3a, 3c, 3d, 6a, 6i, 8, 9c, 13l, 13h, and 14b), as were gravers, spurs, and burin spall perforators. Of the seven burins recovered from Preclassic period deposits, the majority (n = 5) were found in early Middle Preclassic contexts. This possibly suggests that early Middle Preclassic period households in the site center of San Estevan were engaged in shell production and that this activity continued into the Late Preclassic period.

Second-order tools (7.03% of entire assemblage, n = 22) recovered from Preclassic period deposits at K'o are above all composed from local medium-grained cherts, followed by coarse to quartz-blended cherts and chalcedonies. The most recognized second-order tools are denticulates (n = 10). It is unclear whether the use-wear patterns of these pieces reflect serration or smoothing activities, but this expedient unifacial tool type was continuously found among K'o contexts from the Middle and Late Preclassic periods and into the Terminal Preclassic period. Of any second-order tool, denticulates are found in greater numbers among K'o's Middle and Late Preclassic households than among similar temporal households at San Estevan or Hamontún.

As early as the Late Preclassic period, end and side scrapers appeared among household contexts. Burin spall perforators and burins also appeared at this time, although a spur perforator was recovered from a Middle Preclassic deposit. The burin spall was composed of coarse-grained chert, while both burins were composed of local medium-grained chert.

Second-order tools were retrieved from Preclassic contexts at Hamontún. Denticulates and perforators, spur and burin spall make up 6.58 percent of the total lithic assemblage. All three Middle Preclassic secondary tools were recovered from late Middle Preclassic construction fill within the northernmost structure of Group 18 at Hamontún. Excavation of middens associated with this structure, HAM.T.15, revealed fragments of worked freshwater shell and a single worked fragment of pink *Spondulus* shell (Paling et al. 2009). As at San Estevan, these tools are possibly linked to shell-working activities but also illuminate a similar behavior of shell production activities among households within the site centers of both San Estevan and Hamontún as early as the Middle Preclassic period. Denticulates, discoidal scrapers, and burin spall perforators were also recovered from Late Preclassic contexts but at different loci.

Production Tools

The bulk of the San Estevan Preclassic period lithic assemblage is composed of artifacts associated with production and includes cores, hammerstones, tested cobbles, and pre-forms (48.25%, n = 234). Polyhedral cores (eMP, n = 46; lMP, n = 14; LP, n = 31) constituted nearly 40 percent of the production assemblage. Medium-grained chert (40.17%, n = 94) was the preferred material type of Preclassic San Estevan cores, followed by chalcedony cores (26.92%, n = 63) and, to a lesser extent, fine-grained northern Belize chert (5.55%, n = 13) and quartz blends (5.98%, n = 14). Along with cores, the entire Preclassic assemblage included 96 hammerstones, the majority of which were recycled polyhedral cores (n = 77). Hammerstones, like cores, were found ubiquitously from early Middle Preclassic through Late Preclassic contexts. Chalcedony (57.29%, n = 55) was the prevailing material type for hammerstones at San Estevan during the Preclassic period. Hammerstones were fashioned from medium-grained chert (n = 32), quartz (n = 8), and hardened limestone (n = 1), but no hammerstones of fine-grained northern Belize chert were recorded.

Polyhedral cores varied greatly in weight from the Middle to Late Preclassic periods at San Estevan. The mean weight of early Middle Preclassic polyhedral cores was 88.34 grams with a standard deviation of 45.54 grams, while the mean weight of late Middle Preclassic cores was 79.23 grams (dev. of 36.10 grams), and a mean weight of 61.86 grams of polyhedral cores resulted from or was associated with the Late Preclassic period (dev. of 24.98 grams). By the Late Preclassic period, polyhedral cores were approximately 20 grams (average 17.37 grams) lighter than late Middle Preclassic and 26.48 grams lighter than early Middle Preclassic polyhedral cores. This variance can be attributed to Late Preclassic households obtaining chalcedonies and medium-grained chert nodules from an overexploited band within the Cryptocrystalline Pebble Zone neighboring San Estevan. Otherwise, this change could be reflective of a technological change in the Late Preclassic period in which households were more greatly reliant on flake technologies than during the Middle Preclassic.

Similar to San Estevan, the K'o lithic assemblage was composed mainly of artifacts associated with production and included cores, hammerstones, and pre-forms (59.42%, n = 186). Polyhedral cores and exhausted polyhedral cores constituted the greatest proportion, at 36.01 percent of the production assemblage. Medium-grained chert (48.39% of production tools) was the preferred material type of K'o cores, followed by coarse-grained cores (34.41 %) and chalcedonies (16.13 %). The assemblage also included 38 hammerstones, the majority of which were recycled polyhedral cores. Unlike San Estevan, production tools were not found equally in number or ubiquitously through time. Only 13.98 percent of all production tools were recovered from the Middle Preclassic; however, among Late Preclassic period contexts, an elevated increase in production material (60.75 %) was recorded. There was also a noticeable elevation in the types of production tools recovered, including pyramidal, bifacial, and bipolar cores, as well as spherical hammerstones and pre-forms. This variability continued into the Terminal Preclassic (see table 4.2).

The mean length of Middle Preclassic polyhedral cores at K'o was 6.89 centimeters with a standard deviation of 1.50 centimeters, a mean thickness of 4.64 centimeters (dev. 3.13 centimeters), and an average weight of 168.18 grams (dev. 199.49 grams). Late Preclassic polyhedral cores at K'o were 6.37 centimeters in length (dev. 2.66 centimeters), with a mean thickness of 3.56 centimeters (dev. 2.06 centimeters) and a mean weight of 226.07 grams (dev. 573.52 grams); among Terminal Preclassic polyhedral cores, they averaged 6.83 centimeters in length (dev. 2.09 centimeters), 3.7 centimeters in thickness (dev. 1.52 centimeters), and 188.14 grams in weight (dev. 203.92 grams). By quantity and weight, polyhedral cores among Preclassic K'o households were the greatest in the Late Preclassic period, but they were slightly smaller in size.

The volume of production tools in relation to all other tools was again apparent among the Hamontún lithic assemblage. Production tools (n = 43) made up 56.58 percent of the entire collection, 19 of which were polyhedral cores and 9 of which were exhausted polyhedral cores. Production tools were composed primarily of medium-grained chert (60.47% of all production tools) but also of coarse-grained chert (37.21 %) and chalcedonies (2.33 %). The assemblage includes 9 hammerstones, the majority of which were recycled polyhedral cores. Among the Middle Preclassic perod Hamontún lithic assemblage, there is greater variability of production tools, including bifacial and bipolar cores, as well as various hammerstone types. This marked variability of production tools was only recognized by the Late Preclassic period at K'o but appeared earlier at Hamontún.

The mean length of Middle Preclassic polyhedral cores was 6.73 centimeters (dev. of 1.65 centimeters), and they had a mean thickness of 4.14 centimeters (dev. of 1.43 centimeters) and weighed 196.89 grams on average (dev. 185.85 grams). Late Preclassic polyhedral cores averaged 6.19 centimeters in length (dev. 1.11 centimeters), 3.96 centimeters in thickness (dev. 1.31 centimeters), and 132.58 grams in weight (dev. 89.58 grams). Although slightly greater in number (n = 12), Late Preclassic polyhedral cores were smaller in size and weight than those in the Middle Preclassic period. Residences at Hamontún were exploiting local resources as early as the Middle Preclassic, and variance among Late Preclassic households may reflect this earlier exploitation of larger nodules of local sources; however, when compared to K'o, polyhedral cores found among Late Preclassic household middens were significantly larger in size and weight. This variance in size and weight from the Middle to Late Preclassic periods, during which K'o polyhedral cores were increasing and Hamontún polyhedral cores were decreasing, may be reflective of shifting sociopolitical and economic networks between secondary and primary centers in the Holmul region, as Cival experienced a hegemonic collapse in the Late Preclassic period. This notion could be reified with complementary lithic debitage data.

Production Debris

Lithic debitage from San Estevan included 9,124 pieces, 60 percent of all flakes in this study (table 4.4). In the early Middle Preclassic period, most lithic debitage (76.9%) lacked or had little cortex and fell into the 0.2–0.25 inch size grades. Late Middle Preclassic non-cortical lithic debitage rose to 82.9 percent but fell into the 0.5–1.0 size categories, followed by 0.25 inch debitage. Most flakes were determined to be primarily secondary bifacial reduction flakes. In the Late Preclassic period, the percentage of debitage that lacked cortex again rose, to 90.59 percent of the total assemblage. Most flakes fell into the 0.25–0.5 inch size grades. While most flakes were too shattered to allow us to determine their type (28.78%, n = 78), the majority of Late Preclassic flakes were pressure flakes (21.9 %, n = 61), followed by tertiary bifacial reduction flakes (19.19%, n = 52). Three tranchet flakes (1.1%) were recovered from Late Preclassic middens. The greatest concentrations of utilized flakes were noted in the early Middle Preclassic period (table 4.5) but were also recovered from household middens in the late Middle and Late Preclassic.

Lithic debitage recovered from Preclassic period household contexts at K'o totaled 4,420 (29.06%) pieces. Among the Middle Preclassic lithic debitage, most lacked cortex (67.39%) and fell into the 0.5 inch size grade, followed by the 0.25 inch category. In the Late Preclassic period, the amount of lithic debitage with cortex dropped slightly, to 65.36 percent of the entire Late Preclassic period lithic debitage assemblage, but the majority of debitage continued to fall into the 0.5 inch size category; however, 1.0 inch size flakes did appear in greater quantity at this time. Among Terminal Preclassic period lithic debitage, nearly an equal amount of non-cortical (51.77 %) and cortical debitage (48.23 %) was noted. Most debitage fell into the 0.5–1.0 inch size grades, where most 1.0 inch debitage contained cortex. Unlike San Estevan, the greatest quantity of utilized flakes at K'o was recovered from Late Preclassic period middens.

Among Hamontún's Middle Preclassic lithic debitage, most (66.97 %) lacked cortex and fell between the 0.5–1.0 inch size grades. By the Late Preclassic, the amount of cortex on debitage increased to 76.69 percent of the total Late Preclassic lithic debitage assemblage. Unlike K'o during the Late Preclassic, most lithic debitage at Hamontún fell primarily between the 0.5–0.25 inch categories. When we consider that polyhedral cores recovered from Middle and Late Preclassic middens at Hamontún were also decreasing in size but

TABLE 4.4. Frequency of non-cortical versus cortical lithic debitage across each site and period

Inches	San Estevan Early Middle Preclassic Non-Cortical (0%–24% cortex)	Cortical (25%–100% cortex)	San Estevan Late Middle Preclassic Non-Cortical (0%–24% cortex)	Cortical (25%–100% cortex)	San Estevan Late Preclassic Non-Cortical (0%–24% cortex)	Cortical (25%–100% cortex)	Grand Total
2	47	41	16	9	25	14	152
1	735	358	279	76	339	97	1,884
0.5	2,071	596	332	56	613	83	3,751
0.25	1,347	266	223	37	910	39	2,822
< 0.25	94	26	25	2	367	1	515
Total	4,294	1,287	875	180	2,254	234	9,124

Inches	K'o Middle Preclassic Non-Cortical (0%–24% cortex)	Cortical (25%–100% cortex)	K'o Late Preclassic Non-Cortical (0%–24% cortex)	Cortical (25%–100% cortex)	K'o Terminal Preclassic Non-Cortical (0%–24% cortex)	Cortical (25%–100% cortex)	
2	12	23	43	100	31	47	256
1	96	91	410	345	97	113	1,152
0.5	411	210	985	437	103	64	2,210
0.25	247	48	362	79	17	8	761
< 0.25	7	2	25	6	1	0	41
Total	773	374	1,825	967	249	232	4,420

Inches	Hamontún Middle Preclassic Non-Cortical (0%–24% cortex)	Cortical (25%–100% cortex)	Hamontún Late Preclassic Non-Cortical (0%–24% cortex)	Cortical (25%–100% cortex)			
2	13	22	9	10			54
1	125	76	155	75			431
0.5	193	72	357	105			727
0.25	36	11	336	65			448
< 0.25	0	0	2	2			4
Total	367	181	859	257			1,664

TABLE 4.5. Utilized flakes

	San Estevan		
	Early Middle Preclassic	Late Middle Preclassic	Late Preclassic
Total	169	49	53

	K'o		
	Middle Preclassic	Late Preclassic	Terminal Preclassic
Total	18	102	32

	Hamontún	
	Middle Preclassic	Late Preclassic
Total	37	36

at K'o, debitage and polyhedral cores in the Late and Terminal Preclassic periods were larger, with much of the debitage associated with early production, it is evident that there was a shift in production. Utilized flakes were recovered equally from middens from both Middle and Late Preclassic period Hamontún households, as were modified, informal unifaces and production tools. There was an obvious decrease in the appearance of expedient and formal bifaces from Middle to Late Preclassic period Hamontún lithic assemblages.

DISCUSSION OF FINDINGS AND CONCLUDING THOUGHTS

Artifacts associated with lithic production can denote levels of production among households and demonstrate inter- and intra-regional production activities. The type and volume of early- to late-stage production debris and refurbishing debris can also demonstrate varying producer versus consumer households both within a site and between sites (Paling 2016). Preclassic San Estevan households had access to local sources of medium- to coarse-grained cherts and chalcedony, and most production activities revolved around the creation of expedient bifaces and a diverse flake tool technology.

Although some formally recognized tools were recovered from Middle Preclassic contexts at San Estevan, the majority of tools recovered included broken expedient bifaces, formal unifaces (blades and macroblades), and expedient, ad hoc unifaces made of medium- to coarse-grained cherts and chalcedonies. The early Middle Preclassic lithic assemblages also included a combination of debitage and production tools made of medium-grained chert and chalcedonies. Residents at San Estevan were likely obtaining production materials from neighboring outcrops of poorer-quality cherts and chalcedonies. It is likely that at these outcrops cobbles were tested and selected, early reduction sequences occurred on-site, and pre-forms and cores were brought back for late-stage bifacial reduction for the creation of informal bifacial farming tools. The large proportion of polyhedral and exhausted cores further indicates that lithic production was small-scale to accommodate a variety of multicrafting activities that required a modified flake technology.

By the Late Preclassic period, a significant portion of the tool assemblage continued to be composed of medium-grained chert (56.25%, n = 108) and again included production tools such as cores and hammerstones, expedient bifaces, blades and macroblades, and expedient, ad hoc secondary tools. Late Preclassic debitage shifted away from early stages of bifacial reduction. Most flakes recovered from midden deposits were pressure flakes (21.9%, n = 61) and tertiary bifacial reduction flakes (19.19%, n = 52) that were less than 0.5 inch in size. These types and the three tranchet flakes recovered from Late Preclassic middens indicate resharpening and repurposing activities. The variety of formal tools found among residential middens escalated. Most of these formal tools were made of fine-grained northern Belize chert (see figure 4.3), linking San Estevan to Colha workshops and regional economic systems.

Paris (2012) recognizes that many of the formal bifacial tool types and expedient, ad hoc unifacial flaking tools closely resembled tools found in Middle Preclassic period deposits at neighboring sites in northern Belize. Paris (2012) attributes this shared pattern to general production practices and technologies, as well as knapping strategies shared by sites throughout the region. The exchange of tool-making knowledge may have superseded or been later passed from the northern central lowlands, as many of the tools recovered from Middle and Late Preclassic midden deposits at K'o and Hamontún in the Petén are similar in design and likely in purpose to those found in the north.

In the Holmul region, the production of formal and expedient tools in the Preclassic was small-scale. The lithics were also composed of locally available medium- to coarse-grained cherts and chalcedonies. Thick oval bifaces and General Utility Bifaces were the only formal bifacial tools identified from early household midden materials. The physical properties of the materials point to local production and not to long-distance exchange from northern Belize. That is not to say that bifaces were unimportant to Preclassic residents of Holmul. As at San Estevan, early bifacial tool production in the Petén lacked mass production and standardization.

Middle and Late Preclassic lithic debitage indicated that the primary stages for cortical reduction did not occur at households in this region either. Secondary and tertiary bifacial reduction flakes were the most commonly recognized flakes recovered from Middle and Late Preclassic household midden deposits at K'o and Hamontún; however, in the Terminal Preclassic period, Group 38, a Plaza Plan 2 civic-residential patio group located in the northwest corner of K'o, indicates that early-stage production did occur among households (Paling 2016). Perhaps primary production staging activities occurred among households at the periphery of communities and emerging civic-ceremonial centers. At San Estevan and Hamontún, most investigations focused on residential groups close to the site center. More likely, Estrada-Belli (2011) proposes that Cival was a major center during the Late Preclassic, then during the Terminal Preclassic period (350 BCE–250 CE) the regional seat of power shifted from Cival to Holmul (Callaghan 2008; Estrada-Belli 2003, 2005). During the Terminal Preclassic period, Holmul continued to expand in size and regional power, and Cival's influence waned. Regional secondary civic-ceremonies, such as Hamontún, may have been subjected to declining and shifting socioeconomic and political order.

The recovery of production tools among Preclassic households in the Petén suggests that households engaged in a variety of forms of craft production, but in the grander picture, such flake tool technology appears to have been part of a greater interregional strategy. What was thought to be flake tool technology shared only among Preclassic sites in northern Belize appears among early communities in the Petén. Among early communities in the Petén and the northern Maya lowlands, most households were involved in the small-scale production of informal tools that may reflect preparation for agricultural activities or other household economic organization, such as craft production.

Investigations of lithic assemblages across the central and northern Maya lowlands demonstrate that these three sites had not only diverse but also heterogeneous modes of lithic production, but it is apparent that households across the region and throughout the Preclassic shared an expedient flaking technology. Multicrafting was clearly present among households as early as the Middle Preclassic period. In the Late Preclassic period, imported and standardized formal bifacial tools were introduced to San Estevan; as other activities incorporating this economic shift appeared, local production of ad hoc, expedient informal flake tools continued. At K'o and Hamontún, household production of flake tools occurred throughout the Preclassic period. While little evidence supports the idea that formal bifacial tools made from NBCBZ materials were exchanged into the region through long-distance trade routes, formal and informal bifacial tools were important and were manufactured from local sources. By the Late Preclassic period, shifting socioeconomic and political reorganization was influencing production activities at K'o and Hamontún. By the Terminal Preclassic period, raw materials were introduced and early-stage production of tools was carried out among some households at K'o, while at Hamontún, household production of modified and unmodified flakes continued. This increase in the plurality of production, as well as the diversity of production of formal household tools and the continuation of informal household tool production, parallels social complexity. It was the very appearance of multiple modes of economic complexity that while used simultaneously, constituted the markers for the development of hierarchy and led to the complexity seen in Mesoamerica in later periods.

ACKNOWLEDGMENTS

I wish to thank Marilyn Masson, Robert Rosenswig, John Tomasic, and Francisco Estrada-Belli for providing the opportunity for me to conduct this research. Special thanks to Amanda Silva and Justin Lowry for their thoughtful comments and suggestions, as well as to Elizabeth Paris for "cobbling" the way (pun intended) at San Estevan. Some of this research was supported by the National Science Foundation (NSF Dissertation Improvement Grant #0921021) and the Christopher DeCormier Scholarship for Mesoamerican fieldwork.

REFERENCES

Ahler, Stanley A. 1989. "Mass Analysis of Flaking Debris: Studying the Forest Rather Than the Tree." *Archaeological Papers of the American Anthropological Association* 1 (1): 85–118.

Aldenderfer, Mark. 1991. "The Structure of Late Classic Lithic Assemblages in the Central Petén Lakes Region, Guatemala." In *Maya Stone Tools*, ed. Thomas R. Hester and Harry J. Shafer, 119–142. Madison, WI: Prehistory Press.

Anderson, John. 1976. "Notes on the Pre-Columbian Chert Industry of Northern Belize." In *Maya Lithic Studies: Papers from the 1976 Belize Field Symposium*, ed. Thomas R. Hester and Norman Hammond, 151–176. San Antonio: Center for Archeological Research, University of Texas.

Aoyama, Kazuo. 2001. "Classic Maya State, Urbanism, and Exchange: Chipped Stone Evidence of the Copán Valley and Its Hinterland." *American Anthropologist* 103 (2): 346–360.

Aoyama, Kazuo. 1999. *Ancient Maya State, Urbanism, Exchange, and Craft Specialization: Chipped Store Evidence from the Copan Valley and the La Entrada Region, Honduras*. Pittsburgh: University of Pittsburgh Press.

Appadurai, Arjun. 1986. "Introduction: Commodities and the Politics of Value." In *The Social Life of Things: Commodities in Cultural Perspective*, ed. Arjun Appadurai, 3–63. Cambridge: Cambridge University Press.

Ball, Joseph W. 1993. "Pottery, Potters, Palaces, and Polities: Some Socioeconomic and Political Implications of Late Classic Maya Ceramic Industries." In *Lowland Maya Civilization in the Eighth Century AD*, ed. Jeremy Sabloff and John Henderson, 243–272. Washington, DC: Dumbarton Oaks.

Berdan, Frances F. 2003. "The Economy of Postclassic Mesoamerica." In *The Postclassic Mesoamerican World*, ed. Michael E. Smith and Francis F. Berdan, 93–95. Salt Lake City: University of Utah Press.

Berdan, Frances F., Marilyn A. Masson, Janine Gasco, and Michael E. Smith. 2003. "An International Economy." In *The Postclassic Mesoamerican World*, ed. Michael E. Smith and Frances F. Berdan, 96–108. Salt Lake City: University of Utah Press.

Brady, James, Joseph Ball, Ronald Bishop, Duncan Pring, Norman Hammond, and Rupert Housley. 1998. "The Lowland Maya Protoclassic: A Reconsideration of Its Nature and Significance." *Ancient Mesoamerica* 9: 17–38.

Brumfiel, Elizabeth M. 1991. "Weaving and Cooking: Women's Production in Aztec Mexico." In *Engendering Archaeology: Women and Prehistory*, ed. Joan M. Gero and Margaret W. Conkey, 224–251. Oxford: Blackwell.

Brumfiel, Elizabeth M., and Timothy K. Earle. 1987. "Specialization, Exchange, and Complex Societies: An Introduction." In *Specialization, Exchange, and Complex Societies*, ed. Elizabeth M. Brumfiel and Timothy K. Earle, 1–9. Cambridge: Cambridge University Press.

Bullard, William R., Jr. 1965. *Stratigraphic Excavations at San Estevan, Northern British Honduras*. Royal Ontario Museum, Occasional Paper 9. Toronto: University of Toronto Press.

Cackler, Paul R., Michael D. Glascock, Hector Neff, Harry Iceland, K. Anne Pyburn, Dale Hudler, Thomas R. Hestor, and Beverly M. Chiarulli. 1999. "Chipped Stone Artefacts, Source Areas, and Provenance Studies of the Northern Belize Chert-Bearing Zone." *Journal of Archaeological Science* 26: 389–397.

Callaghan, Michael. 2008. "Technologies of Power: Ritual Economy and Ceramic Production in the Terminal Preclassic Period Holmul Region, Guatemala." PhD dissertation, Vanderbilt University, Nashville, TN.

Clark, John E. 1986. "From Mountains to Molehills: A Critical Review of Teotihuacan's Obsidian Industry." In *Research in Economic Anthropology*, Supplement 2, ed. Barry L. Isaac, 23–74. Greenwich, CT: JAI.

Clark, John E. 1988. *The Lithic Artifacts of La Libertad, Chiapas, Mexico: An Economic Perspective*. New World Archaeological Foundation. Provo, UT: Brigham Young University.

Clark, John E., and Stephen D. Houston. 1998. "Craft Specialization, Gender, and Personhood among the Postconquest Maya of Yucatan, Mexico." *Archaeological Papers of the American Anthropological Association* 8 (1): 31–46.

Clark, John E., and William J. Parry. 1990. "Craft Specialization and Cultural Complexity." *Research in Economic Anthropology* 12, ed. Barry L. Isaac, 289–346. Greenwich, CT: JAI.

Costin, Cathy L. 1986. "From Chiefdom to Empire State: Ceramic Economy among the Prehistoric Wanka of Highland Peru." PhD dissertation, University of California, Los Angeles.

Costin, Cathy L. 1991. "Craft Specialization: Issues in Defining, Documenting, and Explaining the Organization of Production." *Archaeological Method and Theory* 3: 1–56.

Costin, Cathy L. 1998. "Introduction: Craft and Social Identity." *Archaeological Papers of the American Anthropological Association* 8 (1): 3–18.

Crabtree, Donald E. 1964. "Notes on Experiments in Flintknapping: 1-Heat Treatment of Silica Materials." *Tebiwa* 9 (1): 3–39.

Crumley, Carole L. 2003. "Alternative Forms of Social Order." In *Heterarchy, Political Economy, and the Ancient Maya: The Three Rivers Region of the East-Central Yucatán Peninsula*, ed. Vernon L. Scarborough, Fred Valdez Jr., and Nicholas Dunning, 136–145. Tucson: University of Arizona Press.

Dockall, John E. 1994. "Oval Biface Celt Variability during the Maya Late Preclassic." *Lithic Technology* 19 (1): 52–68.

Dockall, John E., and Harry J. Shafer. 1993. "Testing the Producer-Consumer Model for Santa Rita Corozal, Belize." *Latin American Antiquity* 4 (2): 158–179.

Doyle, James A. 2013. "The First Maya Collapse: The End of the Preclassic Period at El Palmar, Petén, Guatemala." PhD dissertation, Brown University, Providence, RI.

Drollinger, Harold D., Jr. 1989. "An Investigation of a Late Preclassic Maya Chert Workshop from Colha, Belize." Master's thesis, Texas A&M University, College Station.

Eaton, Jack D., Thomas R. Hester, and Fred Valdez Jr. 1994. "Notes on Eccentric Lithics from Colha and Northern Belize." In *Continuing Archeology at Colha, Belize*, ed. Thomas R. Hester, Harry J. Shafer, and Jack D. Eaton, 257–266. Studies in Archeology 16, Texas Archeological Research Laboratory. Austin: University of Texas.

Estrada-Belli, Francisco. 2000. "Archaeology Investigations at Holmul, Guatemala: Report of the First Field Season May–June 2000." Report submitted to the Instituto de Antropología e Historia, Guatemala City, Guatemala.

Estrada-Belli, Francisco. 2003. "Anatomia de Holmul: Su ciudad y territorio." In *XVI Simposio de Investigationes Arqueologicas en Guatemala, 2002*, ed. Juan Pedro Laporte, Barbara Arroyo, Hector Escobedo, and Hector Mejia, 263–273. Guatemala City: Museo Nacional de Arqueologia y Etnologia.

Estrada-Belli, Francisco, ed. 2005. "Investigationes Arqueologicas en la Region de Holmul, Petén Guatemala: Informe Preliminar de la Temporada 2005." Report submitted to the Instituto de Antropología e Historia, Guatemala City, Guatemala.

Estrada-Belli, Francisco. 2011. *The First Maya Civilization: Ritual and Power before the Classic Period.* New York: Routledge.

Estrada-Belli, Francisco, ed. 2014. "Investigationes Arqueologicas en la Region de Holmul, Petén: Holmul y Cival: Informe Preliminar de la Temporada 2014." Report submitted to the Instituto de Antropología e Historia, Guatemala City, Guatemala.

Fash, William L. 1991. *Scribes, Warriors, and Kings: The City of Copan and the Ancient Maya.* London: Thames and Hudson.

Feinman, Gary M., and Linda M. Nicholas. 2000. "High-Intensity Household-Scale Production in Ancient Mesoamerica: A Perspective from Ejutla, Oaxaca." In *Cultural Evolution: Contemporary Viewpoints,* ed. Gary M. Feinman and Linda Manzanilla, 119–144. New York: Kluwer.

Feinman, Gary M., and Linda M. Nicholas. 2004. "Unraveling the Prehispanic Highland Mesoamerican Economy: Production, Exchange, and Consumption in the Classic Period Valley of Oaxaca." In *Archaeological Perspectives on Political Economies,* ed. Gary M. Feinman and Linda M. Nicholas, 167–188. Salt Lake City: University of Utah Press.

Ford, Anabel, and Kristen Olson. 1989. "Aspects of Ancient Maya Household Economy: Variation in Chipped Stone Production and Consumption." In *Prehistoric Maya Economies of Belize,* ed. Patricia A. McAnany and Barry Isaac, 185–214. Research in Economic Anthropology Supplement 4. Greenwich, CT: JAI.

Fowler, William R., Jr. 1987. *Analysis of the Chipped Stone Artifacts of El Mirador, Guatemala.* Notes of the New World Archaeological Foundation 5. Provo, UT: New World Archaeological Foundation, Brigham Young University.

France, Elizabeth L. 2008. "Shell Tools and Debitage from San Estevan." In *The San Estevan Project, 2008,* ed. Robert M. Rosenswig, 99–106. Albany: Institute of Mesoamerican Studies Publication 15, University at Albany, State University of New York.

Freidel, David A. 1979. "Cultural Areas and Interaction Spheres: Contrasting Approaches to the Emergence of Civilization in the Maya Lowlands." *American Antiquity* 44: 6–54.

Freidel, David A. 1981. "The Political Economics of Residential Dispersion among the Lowland Maya." In *Lowland Maya Settlement Patterns,* ed. Wendy Ashmore, 371–382. Albuquerque: University of New Mexico Press.

Gibson, Eric C. 1986. "Diachronic Patterns of Lithic Production, Use, and Exchange in the Southern Maya Lowlands." PhD dissertation, Harvard University, Cambridge, MA.

Gibson, Eric C. 1989. "The Organization of Late Preclassic Maya Lithic Economy in the Eastern Lowlands." In *Prehistoric Maya Economies of Belize*, ed. Patricia A. McAnany and Barry L. Isaac, 115–138. Research in Economic Anthropology Supplement 4. Greenwich, CT: JAI.

Graham, Elizabeth. 2002. "Perspectives on Economy and Theory." In *Ancient Maya Political Economies*, ed. Marilyn A. Masson and David A. Freidel, 398–418. Walnut Creek, CA: Altamira.

Hagstrum, Melissa B. 2001. "Household Production in Chaco Canyon Society." *American Antiquity* 66 (1): 47–55.

Hammond, Norman. 1973. "Models for Maya Trade." In *The Explanation of Culture Change*, ed. Colin Renfrew, 501–607. Pittsburgh: University of Pittsburgh Press.

Hammond, Norman. 1975. "Maya Settlement Hierarchy in Northern Belize." In *Studies in Ancient Mesoamerica II*, ed. John A. Graham, 40–55. Contributions of the University of California Archaeological Research Facility 27. Berkeley: University of California.

Hammond, Norman. 1982. "Colha in Context." In *Archaeology at Colha, Belize: The 1981 Interim Report*, ed. Thomas R. Hester, Harry J. Shafer, and Jack D. Eaton, 65–74. San Antonio: Center for Archaeological Research, University of Texas.

Hammond, Norman. 1991. "Inside the Black Box: Defining Maya Polity." In *Classic Maya Political History*, ed. T. Patrick Culbert, 253–284. Cambridge: Cambridge University Press.

Hester, Thomas R. 1976. "Belize Lithics: Forms and Functions." In *Maya Lithic Studies: Papers from the 1976 Belize Field Symposium*, ed. Thomas R. Hester and Norman Hammond, 11–19. San Antonio: Center for Archaeological Research, University of Texas.

Hester, Thomas R. 1985. "The Maya Lithic Sequence in Northern Belize." In *Stone Tool Analysis: Essays in Honor of Don E. Crabtree*, ed. Mark G. Plew, James C. Woods, and Max G. Pavesic, 187–210. Albuquerque: University of New Mexico Press.

Hester, Thomas R., and Harry J. Shafer. 1984. "Exploitation of Chert Resources by the Ancient Maya at Colha, Belize." *World Archaeology* 16 (2): 157–173.

Hester, Thomas R., and Harry J. Shafer. 1994. "The Ancient Maya Craft Community at Colha, Belize, and Its External Relationships." In *Archaeological Views from the Countryside: Village Communities in Early Complex Societies*, ed. Glenn M. Schwartz and Steven E. Falconer, 48–63. Washington, DC: Smithsonian Institution Press.

Hirth, Kenneth G. 2006. "Households and Plazas: The Contexts of Obsidian Craft Production at Xochicalco." In *Obsidian Craft Production in Ancient Central Mexico*, ed. Kenneth G. Hirth and Ronald Webb, 18–62. Salt Lake City: University of Utah Press.

Hirth, Kenneth G. 2009. "Craft Production, Household Diversification, and Domestic Economy in Prehispanic Mesoamerica." *Archaeological Papers of the American Anthropological Association* 19 (1): 13–32.

Hruby, Zachary X. 2006. "The Organization of Chipped-Stone Economies at Piedras Negras, Guatemala." PhD dissertation, University of California, Riverside.

Inomata, Takeshi. 2001a. "The Power and Ideology of Artistic Creation: Elite Craft Specialists in Classic Maya Society." *Current Anthropology* 42 (3): 321–349.

Kidder, Alfred V. 1947. *The Artifacts of Uaxactun, Guatemala.* Publication 576. Washington, DC: Carnegie Institution of Washington.

King, Eleanor. 2000. "The Organization of Late Classic Lithic Production at the Prehistoric Maya Site of Colha, Belize: A Study in Complexity and Heterarchy." PhD dissertation, University of Pennsylvania, Philadelphia.

King, Eleanor, and Daniel Potter. 1994. "Small Sites in Prehistoric Maya Socioeconomic Organization." In *Archaeological Views from the Countryside: Village Communities in Early Complex Societies,* ed. Glenn M. Schwartz and Steven E. Falconer, 64–90. Washington, DC: Smithsonian Institution Press.

Kovacevich, Brigitte. 2006. "Reconstructing Classic Maya Economic Systems: Production and Exchange at Cancuen, Guatemala." PhD dissertation, Vanderbilt University, Nashville, TN.

Levi, Laura J. 1996. "Sustained Production and Residential Variation: A Historical Perspective on Lowland Maya Domestic Economy." In *Managed Mosaic: Ancient Maya Agriculture and Resource Use,* ed. Scott L. Fedick, 92–106. Salt Lake City: University of Utah Press.

Levi, Laura J. 2002. "An Institutional Perspective on Prehispanic Maya Residential Variation: Settlement and Community at San Estevan, Belize." *Journal of Anthropological Archaeology* 21: 120–141.

Lewenstein, Suzanne M. 1987. *Stone Tool Use at Cerros.* Austin: University of Texas Press.

Lewis, Brandon. 1995. "The Role of Specialized Production in the Development of Sociopolitical Complexity: A Test Case for the Late Classic Maya." PhD dissertation, University of California, Los Angeles.

Lewis, Brandon. 1996. "The Role of Attached and Independent Specialization in the Development of Sociopolitical Complexity." In *Research in Economic Anthropology,* vol. 17, ed. Barry L. Isaac, 357–388. Greenwich, CT: JAI.

Lewis, Brandon. 2003. "Environmental Heterogeneity and Occupational Specialization: An Examination of Lithic Production in the Three Rivers Region of the Northeastern Petén." In *Heterarchy, Political Economy, and the Ancient Maya,* ed. Vernon L. Scarborough, Fred Valdez Jr. and Nicholas Dunning, 122–135. Tucson: University of Arizona Pres.

Masson, Marilyn A. 1989. "Lithic Production Changes in Late Classic Maya Workshops at Colha, Belize: A Study of Debitage Variation." MA thesis, Florida State University, Gainesville.

Masson, Marilyn A. 2000. "The Economic Organization of Late and Terminal Classic Period Maya Stone Tool Craft Specialist Workshops at Colha, Belize." *Lithic Technology* 26: 29–49.

Masson, Marilyn A. 2001. "The Economic Organization of Late and Terminal Classic Period Maya Stone Tool Craft Specialist Workshops at Colha, Belize." *Lithic Technology* 26 (1): 29–49.

Masson, Marilyn A. 2002. "Introduction." In *Ancient Maya Political Economies*, ed. Marilyn A. Masson and David A. Freidel, 1–30. Walnut Creek, CA: Altamira.

McAnany, Patricia A. 1986. "Lithic Technology and Exchange among Wetland Farmers of the Eastern Maya Lowlands." PhD dissertation, University of New Mexico, Albuquerque.

McAnany, Patricia A. 1989. "Stone Tool Production and Exchange in the Eastern Maya Lowlands: The Consumer Perspective from Pulltrouser Swamp, Belize." *American Antiquity* 54: 332–346.

McAnany, Patricia A. 1992. "A Theoretical Perspective on Elites and the Economic Transformation of Classic Period Maya Households." In *Understanding Economic Process: Monographs in Economic Anthropology*, ed. Sutti Ortiz, 85–103. Lanham, MD: University of the Americas.

McAnany, Patricia A. 1993. "The Economics of Social Power and Wealth among Eighth-Century Maya Households." In *Lowland Maya Civilization in the Eighth Century AD*, ed. Jeremy A. Sabloff and John S. Henderson, 65–90. Washington, DC: Dumbarton Oaks Research Library.

McAnany, Patricia A. 1995. *Living with the Ancestors: Kinship and Kingship in Ancient Maya Society*. Austin: University of Texas Press.

McAnany, Patricia A. 2004a. "Appropriative Economics: Labor Obligations and Luxury Goods in Ancient Maya Societies." In *Archaeological Perspectives on Political Economies*, ed. Gary M. Feinman and Linda M. Nicholas, 145–166. Salt Lake City: University of Utah Press.

McAnany, Patricia A., ed. 2004b. *K'axob: Ritual, Work, and Family in an Ancient Maya Village*. Los Angeles: Cotsen Institute of Archaeology, University of California.

McAnany, Patricia A., and Polly A. Peterson. 2004. "Tools of the Trade: Acquisition, Use, and Recycling of Chipped Stone." In *K'axob: Ritual, Work, and Family in an Ancient Maya Village*, ed. Patricia A. McAnany, 279–305. Monumenta Archaeologica 22. Los Angeles: Cotsen Institute of Archaeology, University of California.

McAnany, Patricia A., Ben S. Thomas, Steven Morandi, Polly A. Peterson, and Eleanor Harrison. 2002. "Praise the Ajaw and Pass the Kakaw: Xibun Maya and the Political Economy of Cacao." In *Ancient Maya Political Economies*, ed. Marilyn A. Masson and David A. Freidel, 123–139. Walnut Creek, CA: Altamira.

McSwain, Rebecca. 1991a. "Chert and Chalcedony Tools." In *Cuello: An Early Maya Community*, ed. Norman Hammond, 160–169. Cambridge: Cambridge University Press.

McSwain, Rebecca. 1991b. "A Comparative Evaluation of the Producer-Consumer Model for Lithic Exchange in Northern Belize, Central America." *Latin American Antiquity* 2 (4): 337–351.

Michaels, George H. 1989. "A Description and Analysis of Early Postclassic Lithic Technology at Colha, Belize." Master's thesis, Texas A&M University, College Station.

Mitchum, Beverly A. 1986. "Chipped Stone Artifacts." In *Archaeology at Cerros, Belize, Central America*, vol. 1, ed. Robin A. Robertson and David A. Freidel, 105–115. Dallas: Southern Methodist University Press.

Mitchum, Beverly A. 1991. "Lithic Artifacts from Cerros, Belize: Production, Consumption, and Trade." In *Maya Stone Tools: Selected Papers from the Second Maya Lithic Conference*, ed. Thomas R. Hester and Harry J. Shafer, 45–54. Monographs in World Archaeology 1. Madison, WI: Prehistory Press.

Mitchum, Beverly A. 1994. "Lithic Artifacts from Cerros, Belize: Production, Consumption, and Trade." PhD dissertation, Southern Methodist University, Dallas, TX.

Moholy-Nagy, Hattula. 1991. "The Flaked Chert Industry of Tikal, Guatemala." In *Maya Stone Tools: Selected Papers from the Second Maya Lithic Conference*, ed. Thomas R. Hester and Harry J. Shafer, 189–202. Monographs in World Archaeology 1. Madison, WI: Prehistory Press.

Moholy-Nagy, Hattula. 1994. "Tikal Material Culture: Artifacts and Social Structure at a Classic Lowland Maya City." PhD dissertation, University of Michigan, Ann Arbor.

Moholy-Nagy, Hattula. 1997. "Middens, Construction Fill, and Offerings: Evidence for the Organization of Classic Period Craft Production at Tikal, Guatemala." *Journal of Field Archaeology* 24 (3): 293–313.

Moholy-Nagy, Hattula. 2003. *The Artifacts of Tikal: Utilitarian Artifacts and Unworked Material*. Tikal Report 27, Part B. Philadelphia: University of Pennsylvania Museum.

Murata, Satoru. 2010. "Maya Salters, Maya Potters: The Archaeology of Multicrafting on Non-Residential Mounds at Wits Cah Ak'al, Belize." PhD dissertation. Boston University, Boston, MA.

Muto, Guy R. 1971. "A Technological Analysis of the Early Stages of Manufacture of Lithic Artifacts." Master's thesis, Washington State University, Pullman.

Paling, Jason S.R. 2009. "Excavaciones en Groupo 4 residencial de K'o." In "Investigaciones Arqueologicas en la Region de Holmul, Petén: Holmul, Cival, La Sufricaya y K'o," ed. Francisco Estrada-Belli, 102–124. Report submitted to Instituto de Antropología e Historia, Guatemala City, Guatemala.

Paling, Jason S.R. 2016. "Leaving No Stone Unturned: Investigating Preclassic Lithic Production, Consumption, and Exchange at San Estevan, Belize, and K'o and Hamontún, Guatemala." PhD dissertation, State University of New York, Albany.

Paling, Jason S.R., Basile Sophet, Renee Morgan, Martin Rangel, Patty Mah, Marcia Chacón, Antolin Velasquez, Mauricio Diaz, Pedro Aragon, Sandra Ventura, Caitlin Taylor, Athena Abrams, and Joel Lopez. 2009. "Excavaciones Residencial de Hamontún." In "Investigaciones Arqueologicas en la Region de Holmul, Petén: Holmul, Cival, La Sufricaya, K'o y Hamontún," ed. Francisco Estrada-Belli, 119–129. Report submitted to Instituto de Antropología e Historia, Guatemala City, Guatemala.

Paris, Elizabeth H. 2007. "The Lithic Tools and Debitage of San Estevan, 2005." In *The San Estevan Project, 2005*, ed. Robert M. Rosenswig, 75–92. Institute of Mesoamerican Studies Publication 14. Albany: State University of New York.

Paris, Elizabeth H. 2012. "Cohesion and Diversity in Preclassic Period Maya Lithic Tools and Techniques." *Lithic Technology* 37 (2): 111–140.

Peregrine, Peter N. 1991. "Some Political Aspects of Craft Specialization." *World Archaeology* 23 (1): 1–11.

Peterson, Polly. 2001. "Testing the Producer-Consumer Model for Lithic Exchange: A View from K'axob, Belize." M.A. Thesis, Boston University, Department of Archaeology, Boston, MA.

Potter, Daniel R. 1991. "A Descriptive Taxonomy of Middle Preclassic Chert Tools at Colha, Belize." In *Maya Stone Tools: Selected Papers from the Second Maya Lithic Conference*, ed. Thomas R. Hester and Harry J. Shafer, 21–29. Monographs in World Archaeology 1. Madison, WI: Prehistory Press.

Potter, Daniel R., and Eleanor M. King. 1995. "A Heterarchical Approach to Lowland Maya Socioeconomies." *Archaeological Papers of the American Anthropological Association* 6 (1): 17–32.

Rands, Robert, and Ronald L. Bishop. 1980. "Resource Procurement Zones and Patterns of Ceramic Exchange in the Palenque Region, Mexico." In *Models and Methods in Regional Exchange*, ed. Robert E. Fry, 19–46. Society for American Archaeology Papers 1. Washington, DC: Society for American Archaeology.

Rangel, Marin. 2009. "Excavaciones en el Grupo 15 de K'o." In "Proyecto Arqueologico Holmul, Informe Temporada 2008," ed. Francisco Estrada-Belli, 125–154.

Report submitted to the Instituto de Antropología e Historia de Guatemala, Guatemala City, Guatemala.

Reents-Budet, Dorie. 1998. "Elite Maya Pottery and Artisans as Social Indicators." *Archaeological Papers of the American Anthropological Association* 8 (1): 71–89.

Rice, Prudence M. 1987. "Economic Change in the Lowland Maya Late Classic Period." In *Specialization, Exchange, and Complex Societies*, ed. Elizabeth M. Brumfiel and Timothy K. Earle, 76–85. Cambridge: Cambridge University Press.

Robb, John E. 1999. "Secret Agents: Culture, Economy, and Social Reproduction." In *Material Symbols: Culture and Economy in Prehistory*, ed. John E. Robb, 3–15. Center for Archaeological Investigations, Occasional Paper 26. Carbondale: Southern Illinois University Press.

Roemer, Erwin J. 1984. "Late Classic Maya Lithic Workshop at Colha, Belize." Master's thesis, Texas A&M University, College Station.

Roemer, Erwin J. 1991. "A Late Classic Workshop at Colha, Belize." In *Maya Stone Tools: Selected Papers from the Second Maya Lithic Conference*, ed. Thomas R. Hester and Harry J. Shafer, 55–66. Monographs in World Archaeology 1. Madison, WI: Prehistory Press.

Romney, D. H., ed. 1959. *Land in British Honduras*. Colonial Research Publication 24. London: Her Majesty's Stationery Office.

Rosenswig, Robert M. 2007. *The San Estevan Project, 2005*. Institute of Mesoamerican Studies, Occasional Publication 14. Albany: State University of New York.

Rosenswig, Robert M., and Douglas J. Kennett. 2007. "Reassessing San Estevan's Role in the Late Preclassic Political Landscape of Northern Belize." *Latin American Antiquity* 19: 124–146.

Rovner, Irwin, and Suzanne M. Lewenstein. 1997. *Maya Stone Tools of Dzibilchaltún, Yucatán, and Becán and Chicanná, Campeche*. Middle American Research Institute Publication 65. New Orleans: Middle American Research Institute, Tulane University.

Scarborough, Vernon L. 1991. *Archaeology at Cerros, Belize, Central America*, vol. 3: *The Settlement in a Late Preclassic Maya Community*. Dallas: Southern Methodist University Press.

Service, Elman. 1962. *Primitive Social Organization: An Evolutionary Perspective*. New York: Random House.

Shafer, Harry J. 1979. "Belize Lithics: Orange Peel Flakes and Adze Manufacture." In *Maya Lithic Studies: Papers from the 1976 Belize Field Symposium*, ed. Thomas R. Hester and Norman Hammond, 21–34. Special Report 4. San Antonio: Center for Archaeological Research, University of Texas.

Shafer, Harry J. 1982. "A Preliminary Report on the Lithic Technology at Kichpanha, Northern Belize." In *Archaeology at Colha, Belize: The 1981 Interim Report*, ed. Thomas R. Hester, Harry J. Shafer, and Jack D. Eaton, 167–181. San Antonio: Center for Archaeological Research, University of Texas.

Shafer, Harry J. 1983. "The Lithic Artifacts of the Pulltrouser Area: Settlement and Fields." In *Pulltrouser Swamp: Ancient Maya Habitat, Agriculture, and Settlement in Northern Belize*, ed. B. L. Turner II and Peter D. Harrison, 212–245. Austin: University of Texas Press.

Shafer, Harry J. 1990. "The Puleston Axe: A Late Preclassic Hafted Tool from Northern Belize." In *Ancient Maya Wetland Agriculture*, ed. Mary D. Pohl, 279–294. Boulder: Westview.

Shafer, Harry J. 1991. "Late Preclassic Formal Stone Tool Production at Colha, Belize." In *Maya Stone Tools: Selected Papers from the Second Maya Lithic Conference*, ed. Thomas R. Hester and Harry J. Shafer, 31–44. Monographs in World Archaeology 1. Madison, WI: Prehistory Press.

Shafer, Harry J. 1994. "A Late Preclassic Household Lithic Assemblage at Colha: Operation 2011 Midden." In *Continuing Archaeology at Colha, Belize*, ed. Thomas R. Hester, Harry J. Shafer, and Jack. R. Eaton, 137–154. Studies in Archaeology 16. Austin: Texas Archaeological Research Laboratory, University of Texas.

Shafer, Harry J., and Thomas R. Hester. 1983. "Ancient Maya Chert Workshops in Northern Belize, Central America." *American Antiquity* 48 (3): 519–543.

Shafer, Harry J., and Thomas R. Hester. 1986. "Maya Stone-Tool Craft Specialization and Production at Colha, Belize: Reply to Mallory." *American Antiquity* 51: 148–166.

Shafer, Harry J., and Thomas R. Hester. 1991. "Lithic Craft Specialization and Product Distribution at the Maya Site of Colha." *World Archaeology* 23 (1): 79–97.

Sheets, Payson D. 1979a. "Environmental and Cultural Effects of the Ilopango Eruption in Central America." In *Volcanic Activity and Human Ecology*, ed. Payson D. Sheets and Donald K. Grayson, 525–564. New York: Academic.

Sheets, Payson D. 1979b. "Maya Recovery from Volcanic Disasters Ilopango and Cerén." *Archaeology* 32: 32–44.

Sheets, Payson D. 2000. "Provisioning the Cerén Household: The Political Economy, the Village Economy, and the Household Economy in the Southeastern Maya Periphery." *Ancient Mesoamerica* 11: 217–230.

Smith, Augustus L. 1950. *Uaxactun, Guatemala: Excavations of 1931–1937*. Publication 436 (5). Washington, DC: Carnegie Institution of Washington.

Smith, Michael E. 2004. "The Archaeology of Ancient State Economies." *Annual Review of Anthropology* 33: 73–102.

Speal, C. Scott. 2005. "A Conjunctive Approach to Ancient Maya Economic Structure: Levels of Integration, Modes of Exchange, and the Lithic Assemblage from Cabbage Ridge, Belize." Master's thesis, State University of New York, Albany.

Speal, C. Scott. 2006. "Regional Economic Interaction in the Coastal Maya Lowlands: The Lithic Assemblage of Saktunha, Belize." *Lithic Technology* 31 (1): 3–26.
Stoltman, James B. 1978. *Lithic Artifacts from a Complex Society: The Chipped-Stone Tools of Becán, Campeche, Mexico*. Occasional Paper 2. New Orleans: Middle American Research Institute, Tulane University.
Thompson, Marc. 1991. "Flaked Celt Production at Becan, Campeche, Mexico." In *Maya Stone Tools: Selected Papers from the Second Maya Lithic Conference*, ed. Thomas R. Hester and Harry J. Shafer, 143–154. Monographs in World Archaeology 1. Madison, WI: Prehistory Press.
Tobey, Mark H. 1986. *Trace Element Investigations of Maya Chert from Belize*. Papers of the Colha Project, vol. 1. San Antonio: Center for Archaeological Research, University of Texas.
Tobey, Mark H., Harry J. Shafer, and Marvin W. Rowe. 1994. "Trace Element Investigations of Chert from Northern Belize." In *Continuing Archaeology at Colha, Belize*, ed. Thomas R. Hester, Harry J. Shafer, and Jack D. Eaton, 267–276. Austin: Texas Archaeological Research Laboratory, University of Texas.
Tomasic, John J. 2008. "Excavaciones Arqueológicas en K'o 2007." In "Archaeological Investigations in the Holmul Region, Petén, Guatemala: Results of the Seventh Season," ed. Francisco Estrada-Belli, 16–20. Report submitted to Instituto de Antropología Historia, Guatemala City, Guatemala.
Tomasic, John. J. 2006. "Investigaciones Arqueológicas en K'o de 2005." In "Investigaciones arqueológicas en la region de Holmul, Petén, Guatemala: Informe preliminar de la temporada 2005," ed. Francisco Estrada-Belli, 121–152. Vanderbilt University, Vanderbilt, TN. http://www.bu.edu/holmul/.
Tomasic, John J. 2009a. "Excavaciones Arqueológicas en K'o 2008." In "Archaeological Investigations in the Holmul Region, Petén, Guatemala: Results of the Eighth Season," ed. Francisco Estrada-Belli, 64–70. Report submitted to Instituto de Antropología e Historia, Guatemala City, Guatemala.
Tomasic, John J. 2009b. "Investigating Terminal Preclassic and Classic Period Power and Wealth at K'o, Guatemala." PhD dissertation. Vanderbilt University, Nashville, TN.
Tomasic, John J., Melvin Rodrigo Guzmán, Jason Paling, and Martín Rangel. 2008. "Mapeo en K'o y resumen de excavaciones del 2007." In "Proyecto Arqueológico Holmul, Informe Temporada 2007," ed. Francisco Estrada-Belli, 68–70. Report submitted to Instituto de Antropología e Historia de Guatemala, Guatemala City, Guatemala.
Tomasic, John J., Jason Paling, and Martín Rangel. 2009a. "Excavaciones en el Grupo 25 de K'o." In "Proyecto Arqueológico Holmul, Informe Temporada 2008," ed.

Francisco Estrada-Belli, 155–170. Report submitted to Instituto de Antropología e Historia de Guatemala, Guatemala City, Guatemala.

Tomasic, John J., Jason Paling, and Martín Rangel. 2009b. "Investigaciones en las trincheras de saqueo de K'o." In "Proyecto Arqueológico Holmul, Informe Temporada 2008," ed. Francisco Estrada-Belli, 71–101. Report submitted to Instituto de Antropología e Historia de Guatemala, Guatemala City, Guatemala.

Tomasic, John J., and Francisco Estrada-Belli. 2008. "Ancient Maya Settlement at K'o, Petén Guatemala and the Transition from the Preclassic to the Classic Period." Paper presented at the Society for American Archaeology meetings, Vancouver, British Columbia, Canada, March 26–30.

West, Georgia. 2002. "Ceramic Exchange in the Late Classic and Postclassic Maya Lowlands: A Diachronic Approach." In *Ancient Maya Political Economies*, ed. Marilyn A. Masson and David A. Freidel, 140–196. New York: Altamira.

Whittaker, John C. 1994. *Flintknapping: Making and Understanding Stone Tools*. Austin: University of Texas Press.

Widmer, Randolph. 2009. "Elite Household Multicrafting Specialization at 9N8, Patio H, Copan." *Archaeological Papers of the American Anthropological Association* 19: 174–204.

Wilk, Richard. 1977. "Macroscopic Analysis of Chipped Stone Tools from Barton Ramie, British Honduras." *Estudios de la Cultura Maya* 10: 53–68.

Willey, Gordon R. 1965. "Artifacts." In *Prehistoric Maya Settlements in the Belize Valley*, ed. Gordon R. Willey. 391–449. Papers of the Peabody Museum of Archaeology and Ethnology 54. Cambridge: Harvard University.

Willey, Gordon R. 1972. *The Artifacts of Altar de Sacrificios*. Papers of the Peabody Museum 64 (1). Cambridge: Harvard University.

Willey, Gordon R., William R. Bullard Jr., John B. Glass, and James C. Gifford. 1965. *Prehispanic Maya Settlements in the Belize Valley*. Papers of the Peabody Museum Number 54. Cambridge: Harvard University.

Willey, Gordon R., T. Patrick Culbert, and Richard E.W. Adams. 1967. "Maya Lowland Ceramics: A Report from the 1965 Guatemala City Conference." *American Antiquity* 32: 289–315.

5

The Economic Organization of the Extraction and Production of Utilitarian Chert Tools in the Mopan Valley, Belize

Rachel A. Horowitz

A common thread in the study of lithic technology in sedentary societies is the interaction between lithic production and economic organization. In the Maya area, economic organization is an issue of much debate, including top-down economic strategies, with political leaders collecting and redistributing economic goods; bottom-up strategies focused on production, exchange, and interaction among householders; and economic schema that incorporate both extremes, suggesting that various goods operated through different systems (i.e., Aoyama 1996; Braswell 2010; Golitko and Feinman 2015; Masson and Friedel 2012; McKillop 2002; Pohl 1994; Santone 1993; Scarborough and Valdez 2009, 2014; Shaw 2012). The technological organization of material production provides an avenue through which we can elucidate the ways specific goods operated in past economic systems. This chapter focuses on utilitarian tools produced from locally available materials to examine the role of such items in the economic system of the Late to Terminal Classic Maya (600–890 CE); that is, was utilitarian tool production using locally available raw materials managed by political leaders, householders, or some combination of the two? By examining these materials, we can refine our understanding of the management of past economic systems that tended to rely on more easily sourced commodities, such as those exchanged over long distances and prestige items. A focus on long-distance trade and prestige items leads to a focus on top-down models centered around the

DOI: 10.5876/9781607328926.c005

economic practices of political leaders (Demarest et al. 2014; Freidel et al. 2002; Hammond et al. 1977; Kovacevich 2014; Meadows 2001; Taube 2005). By examining materials that were locally obtained and modified, a different perspective can be provided. Furthermore, the focus on lithic technology allows an opportunity to examine a reductive technology that has greater potential to be tracked through multiple stages of production because of the presence of production debris, permitting a better understanding of lithic production and its role in past economies.

Lithic materials, specifically chert, provide a particularly important window into past economic systems, as they preserve well and were used by all sectors of society—mostly for quotidian activities—thus allowing chert materials to serve as a proxy for locally produced items that cannot be preserved in the archaeological record, such as foodstuffs and other perishable goods. Many models of economic organization are based on archaeologically invisible materials, so examining other artifacts with distributions that are potentially similar to these archaeologically invisible materials provides a window into the potential importance of these resources.

Furthermore, the reductive nature of the lithic production process provides important data about lithic extraction, production, distribution, and use, as all steps of the production and use of lithic materials are easily identifiable from the archaeological record. The extensive quantity of lithic artifacts permits detailed analyses of lithic economies in ways that are not possible with non-reductive technologies. As such, lithic materials provide a proxy by which to examine the economic importance of locally available raw materials and to understand the social and political connections involved in lithic economies.

The study of items produced with locally available raw materials, such as chert, provides a different view of economic organization than studies that focus on items produced from non-local raw materials. Many Maya lithic studies focus on obsidian tool production, the raw material for which is found only in the Guatemalan and Mexican highlands (e.g., Braswell 1996; Charlton 1978; Daras 1999; Gaxiola Gonzalez and Guevara 1989; Healan 1997, 2002, 2003; Pastrana 1998, 2002). The production and distribution of obsidian is generally thought to be controlled and managed by political leaders, in part because of the restricted source locations of such items (Aoyama 1996, 2001, 2008; Clark 1997; Spence 1981; but see Braswell and Glascock 2002; Cap 2015; Keller 2006). In contrast, materials produced of locally available raw materials might indicate variation within the ancient Maya economic system as a result of the additional complexities in managing access to locally available raw materials. To fully understand the variation present in ancient Maya

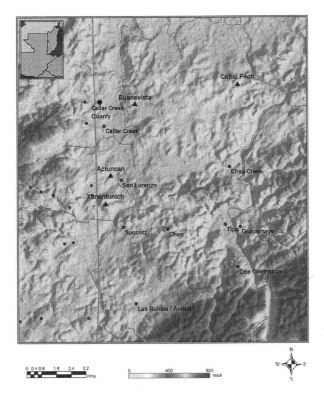

FIGURE 5.1. *Map showing the location of research*

economic systems, we must examine a broader range of materials than only those that arrived through long-distance exchange.

Here I present evidence from three chert source and production areas in the upper Belize River valley (UBRV), located in the lowland region of the Maya area: Callar Creek Quarry, Succotz, and San Lorenzo (figure 5.1). The UBRV is an area of extensive past archaeological investigations, which examined the region's economic and political organization (see Chase and Garber 2004; Helmke and Awe 2008; Houk 2015; LeCount and Yaeger 2010; Willey 2004 for overviews of investigations in the region). Evidence indicates occupation in the UBRV from the Preclassic through the Postclassic, although the focus of this chapter is the Late/Terminal Classic period.

In particular, I examine the organization of extraction and production of chert raw materials at three chert extraction and production sites in the Mopan Valley. Through an examination of these three sites, we can better understand the importance of lithic raw material resources and their management and economic role among the Late to Terminal Classic period Maya. Chert is unevenly distributed across the landscape throughout the UBRV, as the surface geology consists of chert-bearing limestones from the Paleogene (Cornec 2004). Today, extant chert deposits include subsurface bedded deposits, eroded cobbles located across the surface, and piles redeposited by floodwaters along the banks of the Mopan River, indicating that a plethora of chert resources exist to this day. In addition to the uneven distribution of materials, the quality of chert raw materials in the region is highly variable, particularly in contrast to some of the other regions of Belize such as the Northern Belize Chert-bearing Zone (NBCBZ) (see Hester and Shafer 1984, 1991; Shafer and Hester 1983), where uniformly high-quality chert is common. The uneven distribution of chert from similar geologic formations, the presence of secondary deposits of chert materials, and the presence of intra-source variation make chemical sourcing and thus studies of distribution of chert sources in the Mopan Valley difficult. Despite this drawback, the uneven distribution of chert resources may lead to unique economic roles for these source areas, as the localness and abundance of chert resources changes the ability and purpose of restricting access to source areas.

Previous studies of economic organization during the Late/Terminal Classic period in the UBRV point to the presence of marketplaces at the sites of Xunantunich and Buenavista del Cayo (hereafter Buenavista) (Cap 2015; Keller 2006) and close relationships between producers and consumers (Ashmore 2010; Yaeger 2010). Small-scale chert production within the UBRV occurred in households throughout the region (Connell 2000; Robin 1999; VandenBosch 1999; Yaeger 2000) and more intensively in specialized household contexts (Hearth 2012; VandenBosch 1999; Yaeger 2000) and in public spaces, such as the marketplaces at Buenavista and Xunantunich (Cap 2015; Keller 2006; see also Whittaker et al. 2009). These previous studies demonstrate that local householders produced lithic materials, particularly chert, and that some types of lithic tools were distributed through marketplace exchange.

The lithic analyses and their implications for broader trends are based on an organizational framework. Technological organization, a framework for integrating measurable characteristics of past technologies with broader social structures, provides a link between material culture and past behaviors through examinations of the ways past behaviors influenced tool shape, production activities, and material distribution (Carr 1994a, 1994b; Carr et al. 2012; Cowan 1999; Kuhn 1994; Lothrop 1989; McCall 2015; Nelson 1991; Shott 1989; Torrence 1989). The use of an organizational framework, integrated with a detailed attribute analysis, permits an examination of the nuances of lithic extraction and reduction and the ways they articulate with past economic activities. Such an approach, which includes an analysis of all detritus from the reduction process, including cores and debitage as well as formal and informal tools, provides a more holistic picture of past production processes than the exclusive examination of formal tools or modified objects—the focus of many studies of lithic technology, particularly in sedentary societies. Organizational approaches, although based on studies of hunter-gatherer societies, have utility in the examination of sedentary societies, as the difference in understanding past behaviors among mobile and sedentary peoples is an issue of scale rather than of substantive differences; the principles utilized to understand past behaviors in mobile groups also apply to sedentary groups (see Druart 2010; McDonald 1991; Parry and Kelly 1987; Rosen 2010; Sorensen 2010; Teltser 1991; Torrence 1984, 1986).

CHERT PRODUCTION AREAS IN THE MOPAN VALLEY

The three sites that are the focus of this chapter are Callar Creek Quarry, San Lorenzo, and Succotz (see figure 5.1). In total, the distance between these three sites is about 4 kilometers at its greatest extent, the distance from Callar Creek Quarry to Succotz (see figure 5.1). While all three of these sites were utilized for longer periods of time, the focus of this chapter is the Late to Terminal Classic period, during which time extraction and production occurred at all three sites and their utilization was at its greatest. This chapter traces evidence for the extraction, production, and, when possible, distribution of materials from the three sites and examines the evidence for management of lithic extraction, production, and distribution by political leaders and other individuals.

Comparisons among these three extraction and production contexts highlight the variability in contexts of lithic production and extraction. Some care must be taken, however, when evaluating the comparisons, as the lithic analysis from the three sites was performed by three different individuals; inter-observer error has been shown to be problematic in comparisons of lithic materials (e.g., Gnaden and Holdaway 2000; Lyman and VanPool 2009). I performed the attribute analysis on the Callar Creek Quarry materials, while the information from San Lorenzo and Succotz comes from published accounts of the excavations. The sample size analyzed also limits statistical comparisons among the three sites, which limits the conclusions that can be drawn about variability in production sequences and processes. As discussed further below, far more materials from Callar Creek Quarry were analyzed, leading to some limitations in the ability to compare these three contexts.

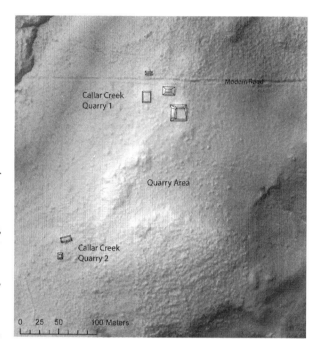

FIGURE 5.2. *Map of Callar Creek Quarry illustrating the layout of the quarry, production area, and household area. Base map by Bernadette Cap, courtesy of the Mopan Valley Archaeological Project.*

Callar Creek Quarry is a chert quarry located in the Callar Creek hinterlands on the Belize-Guatemala border (Horowitz 2017, 2018). I directed investigations at the quarry and adjacent habitation areas under the auspices of the Mopan Valley Archaeological Project (MVAP). The quarry is located between two household groups, a patio group to the northeast and an L-shaped group to the southwest of the main quarry and production areas (figure 5.2). The construction and occupation of the household groups is contemporaneous with the most intensive period of use and extraction of the quarry area, the Late/Terminal Classic, although the residential group to the northeast was first inhabited in the Middle Preclassic (1200–400 BCE), with major construction episodes in the Early Classic (200–600 CE) and the Late Classic II (670–780 CE) periods.

The chert deposits at Callar Creek Quarry consist of in situ bedded chert from chert formations in the limestone bedrock and large nodules on the surface, some as large as 1 meter in diameter. The chert quality ranges from high-quality small-grained cherts with minimal inclusions to larger-grained lower-quality cherts. Chert of varying qualities co-occurs in the same nodule, indicating its production was part of the same formation processes.

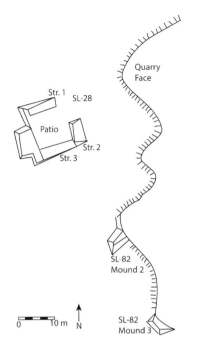

FIGURE 5.3. *Map of San Lorenzo, SL-28, illustrating the layout of the quarry, production area, and household area. Redrawn from Yaeger 2000.*

San Lorenzo, investigated by Yaeger (2000), is a small residential settlement located to the northeast of Xunantunich and is interpreted as having had links to the Xunantunich social, economic, and political sphere in the Late Classic. The settlement contains a quarry and production area, as represented by a debitage mound, within its bounds. They are located in the western part of the settlement zone near household SL-28, a lithic-producing household (figure 5.3).

San Lorenzo chert consists of redeposited chert cobbles from the Mopan River, where these materials washed out of bedrock and were deposited during flooding events. These flooding episodes resulted in deposits of chert cobbles that were buried by subsequent geologic processes and hence were extracted through digging into the hillside to remove the chert beds; the secondary chert deposits exploited by the Maya at San Lorenzo were deposited long before the site was occupied, and the households near the area of resource extraction sit on top of additional subsurface deposits (Yaeger 2000). The San Lorenzo deposit predominantly contains rounded cobbles, which were deposited by riverine activity; the riverine nature of the deposition is illustrated by the smoothing of the cortex of cobbles and the rounded nature of most of

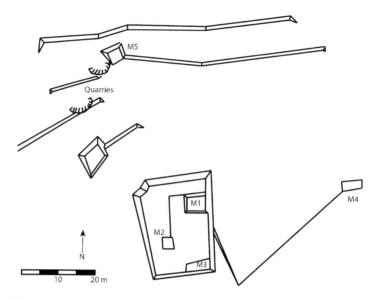

FIGURE 5.4. *Map of Succotz, TA2-001, illustrating the layout of the quarry, production area, and household area. Redrawn from VandenBosch 1999.*

the materials. The color and quality of the chert from these deposits varied greatly as well. The quality ranges from high-quality to low-quality raw materials, with evidence of the testing of raw materials for quality occurring near the extraction point (Yaeger 2000).

Succotz, investigated by VandenBosch (1999), is a small settlement located across the river from Xunantunich and found within the modern village of San Jose Succotz. The quarry and production area are located adjacent to two household groups, TA1-2 and TA1-3, within the settlement cluster. The household groups contain debitage mounds as well as evidence of chert extraction (figure 5.4). Succotz contains in situ bedded chert from chert formations in the limestone bedrock. The chert from deposits at Succotz is of the highest quality and is the most uniform of the three (VandenBosch 1999).

Extraction of chert materials occurred at all three sites through excavation of a quarry face, where materials were extracted by digging into a hillside to remove such materials. Extraction in this manner results in a scalloped pattern identifiable as a quarry cut; the scalloping results when certain sections of the hillside are more intensively utilized than others, leading to an indented area in the hillside that shows extraction patterns (figure 5.5). At Callar Creek Quarry, extraction also occurred through the removal of cobbles visible on the

FIGURE 5.5. *Photograph of the quarry cut from Callar Creek Quarry*

surface and the extraction of lithic materials from other areas of the quarry in addition to the quarry face (see Horowitz 2017).

The production goal at the three sites differed slightly. At Callar Creek Quarry, production focused on generalized core and flake tool manufacture, based on analysis of approximately 36,000 items. Evidence of generalized core production comes from a detailed attribute analysis of both core and flake qualities. The majority of cores (71.7%) recovered from Callar Creek Quarry are multi-directional. Of the remainder, most are unidirectional cores, illustrating the testing of cobbles and the discard of raw materials as a result of poor raw material quality or internal flaws not evident prior to knapping (table 5.1). Debitage analysis also indicates generalized core reduction through the low number of dorsal flake scars (average = 1.67), the low number of platform facets (average = 1.04), and the lack of platform preparation on flakes throughout the assemblage (99.7% of flakes showed no evidence of platform preparation). Evidence for flake tool production, as indicated by the presence of retouch, was minimal, including only 0.6 percent (n = 1,724) of flakes from the quarry (figure 5.6). The few tools produced

TABLE 5.1. Frequency of core types at Callar Creek Quarry

Core Type	Frequency
Discoidal	1 (0.6%)
Multi-directional	114 (71.7%)
Unidirectional	25 (15.7%)
Core fragments	8 (5%)
Other	11 (6.9%)

were probably generalized, multifunctional tools used for subsistence and craft production activities.

Chert production at San Lorenzo focused on generalized lithics, particularly of flake tools, as well as biface production and finishing at two households, SL-31 and SL-28, located near the quarry face. Yaeger (2000: 1062) identified biface production at SL-31 based on the high density of bifacial thinning flakes and the presence of 10 bifacial pre-forms. SL-31 contained a total of 649 flakes, of which just over 50 percent are secondary flakes (Yaeger 2000: 1086–1087). Evidence for generalized production at SL-28, another household group near the quarry cut, comes from the higher densities of lithic materials compared with other households at San Lorenzo and the attributes of chert, which indicate generalized production techniques; Yaeger (2000: 1086–1087) recorded a total of 303 flakes, of which 67 percent are secondary flakes. Again, these tools were probably used for multifunctional purposes, include subsistence activities and craft production.

Chert production at Succotz demonstrates an exclusive focus on formal tool production, with the goal of producing General Utility Bifaces (GUBs), at two households, TA1-2 and TA1-3. Evidence for the prevalence of biface production comes from the presence of high densities of chert debitage, including bifacial thinning flakes and broken bifaces. VandenBosch's (1999; VandenBosch et al. 2010: 276) excavation of debitage deposits revealed lithic densities between 900,000 and 2 million flakes per cubic meter and an average of 13.9 bifaces per cubic meter. Recovered bifaces included biface pre-forms and utilized and discarded bifaces (VandenBosch 1999: 254). Although VandenBosch did not record the presence of bifacial thinning flakes, the presence of bifaces

FIGURE 5.6. *Photographs of typical cores and flakes from Callar Creek Quarry*

broken in production indicates that biface production occurred within the area. GUBs are thought to have been multifunctional tools used for heavy-duty tasks including farming, chopping, and quarrying.

Production in all three locations occurred on a small scale compared to the village-level specialization at Colha, but these locations represent some of the most intensive extraction and production locales in the Mopan Valley. In all cases, production occurred on a scale greater than that required for the household level, but quantitatively, the amount of production does not indicate full-time specialization but rather part-time production such as intermittent or seasonal crafting. At Callar Creek Quarry, production intensity is difficult to determine because of the generalized reduction sequences, but I use the lower than expected frequency of cores in comparison to flake counts as an indication of production scale. Over 99 percent of materials recovered from Callar Creek Quarry excavations were debitage, with only 152 cores as opposed to approximately 36,000 pieces of debitage. Using estimates developed by Montet-White (1988) and Ohnuma (1995), I estimate that 600–1,800 cores would have been necessary to produce the amount of debitage recovered from the quarry. Although such estimates are problematic because of the variation in raw material size, the amount of reduction that occurred, and the nature of reduction sequences—all of which affect the number of flakes that can be removed from a core—the range of cores necessary to produce the total number of flakes at Callar Creek Quarry is so much greater than the number of cores recovered from the quarry that these estimates are taken as an indication that cores were removed from the quarry for use elsewhere.

Production estimates for San Lorenzo are similarly difficult because of a lack of concrete products with which to measure reduction. Although it is clear that some households at San Lorenzo were engaged in chert production, Yaeger (2000) states that all households produced chert tools and suggests that chert tools and chert raw material were exchanged within the community. I suggest that the production that occurred at San Lorenzo was small-scale, part-time production at a much smaller scale than at Callar Creek Quarry or Succotz.

The production intensity at Succotz was much greater than that at the other two sites; the density of flakes per cubic meter, 2 million (VandenBosch et al. 2010), is more comparable to large-scale production such as at Colha, where the average density of lithic production contexts is 5 million flakes per cubic meter (Roemer 1991). The density of materials at Succotz indicates part-time production of materials as well, given the lengthy occupation of the households in which production occurred and the nature of lithic production, biface production, and finishing, all of which result in large amounts of debitage.

Production at the three sites can be considered intermittent crafting, or the discontinuous or periodic production of goods in a domestic context (Hirth 2009) and a common method of risk reduction (Brumfiel and Nichols 2009; Hirth 2009). Intermittent crafting is a manner of integrating craft production into the household economy without disrupting other household economic activities. The craft production may be seasonal so as not to interrupt agricultural production, or it may be performed by individuals not involved in other aspects of the domestic economy (Hirth 2009). The intermittent nature of these activities stems from the scale of production; not enough materials were produced for full-time specialization. Furthermore, intermittent crafting helps explain how residents of the three contexts benefited from lithic production activities; these activities not only provide economic benefits but also serve as mechanisms for risk reduction by providing a more diverse set of economic activities and creating networks through which individuals can obtain goods (see Hirth 2009 for an expanded discussion of crafting and risk reduction).

The nature of the extraction of chert materials here provides additional support for the presence of intermittent crafting and distribution beyond the household level. As chert is abundantly available throughout the UBRV, including along the riverbed (in summer 2015 I was able to collect large quantities of medium-quality chert from walking along the modern river course), the additional effort the residents of these three sites expended on lithic extraction through quarrying would not have been advantageous unless residents profited from the extraction and production of chert materials. Quarrying itself serves as an indication of the profitability of chert extraction and production, as other, more easily obtained lithic materials could also have been exploited.

The intensity of production and whether it is greater than the household need can tell us something about how materials may have been distributed. As discussed above, the extent of chert production and the general lack of cores at Callar Creek Quarry support the exportation of cores away from the main body of the quarry, although the location and extent of such distribution are unknown. Consumers may have visited the quarry to obtain chert materials or cores, or quarry residents may have transported materials to the local community, similar to the itinerant merchants discussed elsewhere in the Maya area (see McAnany 2010; Tokovinine and Beliaev 2013), or transported them to other lithic producers in the region for production and distribution in marketplaces such as Buenavista, where evidence of biface production exists (Cap 2015).

Most households in San Lorenzo show evidence of small-scale lithic production at a scale commensurate with household use (Yaeger 2000). Although the two households adjacent to the quarry area show greater involvement in the lithic production industry than do other households, no evidence indicates that materials were removed from the community.

In the Succotz household workshops, the amount of biface production is greater than that necessary for a single household, indicating distribution of these materials beyond the household level. The density of production is far greater than would be necessary for household production and is similar to Colha (Roemer 1991). While we cannot trace the exact distribution of these materials, it seems likely that they circulated within the immediate region. As further discussed below, the presence of biface production at the site implies that residents in the area around Succotz procured bifaces from Succotz producers. The acquisition of these materials could have occurred in a centralized marketplace area, such as those seen at Xunantunich and Buenavista (Cap 2015; Keller 2006); in local settings, such as the settlement surrounding the site; or from visits to the production location. As a result of the difficulty in tracing chert sources, the exact nature of the distribution of these materials is hard to trace.

As this discussion of these three chert extraction and production sites illustrates, variability exists in the mechanisms and manners in which chert was extracted and produced within the UBRV. These differences permit an examination of a wider range of material production and the role of individuals of varying sociopolitical status in such production. Similarities in the economic role of these sites in the regional economy point to similar roles for locally produced and available resources, such as chert, in Maya economic organization.

SOCIOPOLITICAL STATUS AND CHERT PRODUCTION

One avenue for addressing the role of chert extraction and production areas in the producers' economic activity is to examine the role of chert production and its economic importance in integrating lithic producers into and insulating them from regional sociopolitical phenomena. Here I use the example of Callar Creek Quarry's relationship with the economic and political developments of the Mopan Valley to illustrate the ways the economic benefit of lithic production both integrated residents into regional sociopolitical networks and insulated them against changes to these same networks.

Evidence from excavations at the Callar Creek Quarry households points to clear political connections between the Buenavista political sphere and Callar Creek Quarry, in the form of polychrome ceramics with glyphs, pseudo-glyphs, Buenavista-style ceramics, and a sherd with a representation of the Buenavista device (see Ball and Taschek 2004 for a discussion of the Buenavista device). Buenavista, a major political power in the UBRV in the Early Classic period, and Xunantunich vied for power during the Late Classic I period (600–670 CE), while in the Late Classic II period (670–780 CE) Xunantunich became the preeminent site in the region (see LeCount and Yaeger 2010). The neighboring site of Callar Creek, also in the Buenavista sphere, was abandoned in the Terminal Classic period, with evidence of desicratory terminations throughout the site (Kurnick 2013) (figures 5.7, 5.8).

Despite the political connections between Callar Creek Quarry and Buenavista, Callar Creek Quarry's location between Buenavista and Xunantunich, and the region's changing political dynamics, occupation and use of the quarry remained stable throughout the Late to Terminal Classic periods, when political cycling and conflict occurred in the Mopan Valley. The evidence from excavations at Callar Creek Quarry indicates that the quarry and household were used and occupied during this period of increased turbulence (see Horowitz 2017). Thus the residents of Callar Creek Quarry seem to have been insulated from the broader political dynamics in the region, despite their connection to those dynamics through participation in the Buenavista political community.

This continuity in the face of changing political patterns could be related to Callar Creek Quarry residents' access to a necessary resource—chert materials. Their access to this resource seems to have provided a buffer against political

FIGURE 5.7. *Image of the sherd with the Buenavista device fragment*

FIGURE 5.8. *Drawing of the Buenavista device (after Ball and Taschek 2003)*

changes, suggesting that access to chert materials was a mechanism of risk reduction. The role of lithic resources in this continuity could be seen through access to these resources, which gave Callar Creek Quarry residents some economic power. The households' continuity during the corresponding political changes suggests some level of independence of Callar Creek Quarry producers in the extraction and production of raw materials. Although Callar Creek Quarry residents may have extracted materials for exchange in elite-managed marketplaces or as taxation or tribute, they had sufficient autonomy concerning the extraction and distribution of the lithic materials that they were not negatively impacted by the political unrest in the region during the Late Classic II and Terminal Classic periods. The continuity of residence and production at Callar Creek Quarry highlights the residents' economic autonomy; although they were dependent on others in the Mopan Valley for certain goods, they maintained enough economic independence to weather political changes.

Callar Creek Quarry residents' connections to and independence from regional political centers point to their economic independence. This independence can be taken as an indication that lithic production served as a beneficial economic activity that both integrated and insulated producers from changing political landscapes. The production of these materials by local occupants points to economies as spaces in which individuals of varying sociopolitical backgrounds negotiated status, power, and identity.

DISCUSSION AND CONCLUSIONS

I argue that the Callar Creek Quarry, San Lorenzo, and Succotz examples demonstrate that utilitarian tools, such as generalized cores, flake tools, and bifaces, manufactured with locally available materials were produced by local residents in the Late to Terminal Classic in the UBRV. The production of these tools both integrated residents into regional political communities and insulated them from regional political changes through their economic importance to local residents.

An additional facet of the regional chert economy in the UBRV is the extent to which householders in the valley relied on specialized producers or independently produced chert tools. Specialized production contexts for bifaces, such as the final-stage finishing for chert bifaces at the Buenavista marketplace, suggest that specialized producers fashioned some bifaces and that householders could obtain bifaces through a marketplace or by visiting specialized household workshops (Cap 2015). Concentrations of biface production debris at households in Succotz (VandenBosch 1999) and Chan (Hearth 2012) indicate that limited numbers of householders produced bifaces, as within those communities a single household produced bifaces, indicating that other residents obtained bifaces from those producers.

The production of other types of tools, such as utilitarian chert implements, appears to have been more widespread. While areas of chert production exist, such as Callar Creek Quarry and San Lorenzo, regional household excavations (i.e., Connell 2000; Robin 1999, 2012, 2013; VandenBosch 1999; VandenBosch et al. 2010; Yaeger 2000) have found that all households in the upper Belize River valley contained lithic materials, indicative of some lithic production at the household level (table 5.2). The variability present in chert production areas and the distribution of production activities illustrate the varied economic role of chert tools in the Late/Terminal Classic Maya economy.

TABLE 5.2. Table showing lithic density (by excavation area/volume) for households from the upper Belize River valley including Chan (CN), Chaa Creek (CC), and San Lorenzo (SL)

Location	Debitage Density (debitage/m²)	Lithic Density (all lithics/m²)	Source
SL-13	3.5	4.1	Yaeger 2000: 1087–1088, table III:13
SL-22	0.4	0.6	Yaeger 2000: 1087–1088, table III:13
SL-31	19.7	20.3	Yaeger 2000: 1087–1088, table III:13

	Lithic Count	Density (all lithics/m³)	
CC 1	409	110.84	Connell 2000: 553, table 9.80
CC 15	60	240.00	Connell 2000: 553, table 9.80
CC 17	40	111.11	Connell 2000: 553, table 9.80
CC 18	571	220.46	Connell 2000: 553, table 9.80
CC 19	189	136.96	Connell 2000: 553, table 9.80
CC 2	37	38.14	Connell 2000: 553, table 9.80
CC 25	1,123	1,369.51	Connell 2000: 553, table 9.80
CC 27	492	305.59	Connell 2000: 553, table 9.80
CC 3	573	295.38	Connell 2000: 553, table 9.80
CC 30	1,799	1,799.00	Connell 2000: 553, table 9.80
CC 33	116	99.15	Connell 2000: 553, table 9.80
CC 4	535	247.69	Connell 2000: 553, table 9.80
CC 5	197	59.70	Connell 2000: 553, table 9.80
CC 63	33	37.08	Connell 2000: 553, table 9.80
CC 64	423	919.57	Connell 2000: 553, table 9.80
CN 1	2,479	209.70	Robin 1999: 272, table 14
CN 4	435	85.90	Robin 1999: 272, table 14
CN 5	329	99.60	Robin 1999: 272, table 14
CN 6	346	185.00	Robin 1999: 272, table 14
CN 7	1,404	253.70	Robin 1999: 272, table 14

The role of local residents in the lithic production and distribution process in the UBRV indicates that these actors had an important role in the ancient Maya economy, particularly concerning utilitarian goods. The case studies presented here represent one way in which the Classic Maya organized chert production and do not exclude the possibility of political leaders' involvement in chert economies either in the UBRV, through indirect control, or in other areas of the Maya lowlands. In the UBRV, however, political power seems not to have been based on the management of the production and distribution of tools necessary for subsistence.

This chapter not only illustrates variation and the importance of individuals of varying sociopolitical status in the operation of the Late to Terminal Classic Maya economy, it also emphasizes the importance of chert analysis in the Maya area. Lithics in the Maya area are generally understudied, and the focus of such analysis is generally on obsidian rather than chert (see Gaxiola Gonzalez and Clark 1989; Hester 1978; Hirth 2003, 2006; Hirth and Andrews 2002; Levine and Carballo 2014 for an idea of Maya studies' emphasis on obsidian). More broadly, both within the Maya area and in other sedentary societies, the investigation of utilitarian chert implements provides a window through which to view past economic organization. For a truly comprehensive understanding of past economic practices and the role of lithic technology in those practices, scholars of sedentary societies must focus more attention on lithic technology to develop a comprehensive dataset of lithic materials for broader comparisons of production activities. The systematic application of rigorous lithic analysis, such as detailed attribute analysis and understandings of production sequences, would allow more in-depth comparisons—including statistical analyses—to evaluate micro-regional and regional variability in lithic production systems and the causes of that variability, such as raw material availability and quality, economic organization, and the role of various actors in production systems.

ACKNOWLEDGMENTS

Funding for the Callar Creek Quarry excavations was provided by a National Geographic Young Explorer Grant (#9089-12), a National Science Foundation Doctoral Dissertation Improvement Grant (#1416212), and the School of Liberal Arts at Tulane University. Many thanks to Jason Yaeger and the staff of the Mopan Valley Archaeological Project (MVAP) for their support of this project, and thanks to Jason Yaeger, Marcello Canuto, Phil Carr, Bernadette Cap, and Lisa Fontes who provided comments on earlier versions of this chapter.

REFERENCES

Aoyama, Kazuo. 1996. "Exchange, Craft Specialization, and Ancient Maya State Formation: A Study of Chipped Stone Artifacts from the Southern Maya Lowlands." PhD dissertation, University of Pittsburgh, PA.

Aoyama, Kazuo. 2001. "Classic Maya State, Urbanism, and Exchange: Chipped Stone Evidence of the Copán Valley and Its Hinterland." *American Anthropologist* 103 (2): 346–360.

Aoyama, Kazuo. 2008. "Preclassic and Classic Maya Obsidian Exchange, Artistic and Craft Production, and Weapons in the Aguateca Region and Seibal, Guatemala." *Mexicon* 30 (4): 78–86.

Ashmore, Wendy. 2010. "Antecedents, Allies, Antagonists: Xunantunich and Its Neighbors." In *Classic Maya Provincial Polities: Xunantunich and Its Hinterlands*, ed. Lisa J. LeCount and Jason Yaeger, 46–65. Tucson: University of Arizona Press.

Ball, Joseph W., and Jennifer T. Taschek. 2004 "Buenavista del Cayo: A Short Outline of the Occupational and Cultural History of an Upper Belize Valley Regal Ritual Center." In *Ancient Maya of the Belize Valley: Half a Century of Archaeological Research*, ed. James F. Garber, 149–167. Gainesville: University Press of Florida.

Braswell, Geoffrey E. 1996. "A Maya Obsidian Source: The Geoarchaeology, Settlement History, and Ancient Economy of San Martin Jilotepeque, Guatemala." PhD dissertation, Tulane University, New Orleans, LA.

Braswell, Geoffrey E. 2010. "The Rise and Fall of Market Exchange: A Dynamic Approach to Ancient Maya Economy." In *Archaeological Approaches to Market Exchange in Ancient Societies*, ed. Christopher P. Garraty and Barbara L. Stark, 127–140. Boulder: University Press of Colorado.

Braswell, Geoffrey E., and Michael D. Glascock. 2002. "The Emergence of Market Economies in the Ancient Maya World: Obsidian Exchange in Terminal Classic Yucatan, Mexico." In *Geochemical Evidence for Long Distance Exchange*, ed. Michael D. Glascock, 33–52. Westport, CT: Bergin and Garvey.

Brumfiel, Elizabeth M., and Deborah L. Nichols. 2009. "Bitumen, Blades, and Beads: Prehispanic Craft Reproduction and the Domestic Economy." *Archaeological Papers of the American Anthropological Association* 19 (1): 239–251.

Cap, Bernadette. 2015. "Classic Maya Economies: Identification of a Marketplace at Buenavista del Cayo, Belize." PhD dissertation, University of Wisconsin, Madison.

Carr, Philip J. 1994a. "The Organization of Technology: Impact and Potential." In *The Organization of North American Prehistoric Chipped Stone Tool Technologies*, ed. Philip J. Carr, 1–8. Archaeological Series 7. Ann Arbor: International Monographs in Prehistory.

Carr, Philip J. 1994b. "Technological Organization and Prehistoric Hunter-Gatherer Mobility: Examination of the Hayes Site." In *The Organization of North American Prehistoric Chipped Stone Tool Technologies*, ed. Philip J. Carr, 35–44. Archaeological Series 7. Ann Arbor: International Monographs in Prehistory.

Carr, Philip J., Andrew P. Bradbury, and Sarah E. Price. 2012. "Lithic Studies in the Southeast: Retrospective and Future Potential." In *Contemporary Lithic Analysis in the Southeast: Problems, Solutions, and Interpretations*, ed. Philip J. Carr, Andrew P. Bradbury, and Sarah E. Price, 1–12. Tuscaloosa: University of Alabama Press.

Charlton, Thomas H. 1978. "Teotihuacán, Tepeapulco, and Obsidian Exploitation." *Science* 200 (4347): 1227–1236.

Chase, Arlene F., and James F. Garber. 2004. "The Archaeology of the Belize Valley in Historical Perspectives." In *Ancient Maya of the Belize Valley: Half a Century of Archaeological Research*, ed. James F. Garber, 1–14. Gainesville: University Press of Florida.

Clark, John E. 1997. "Prismatic Blademaking, Craftsmanship, and Production: An Analysis of Obsidian Refuse from Ojo de Agua, Chiapas, Mexico." *Ancient Mesoamerica* 8: 137–159.

Connell, Samuel V. 2000. "Were They Well Connected? An Exploration of Ancient Maya Regional Integration from the Middle Level Perspective of Chaa Creek, Belize." PhD dissertation, University of California, Los Angeles.

Cornec, Jean H. 2004. Geology Map of Belize. http://med.gov.bz/wp-content/uploads/2017/01/Geology-Map-of-Belize.pdf.

Cowan, Frank L. 1999. "Making Sense of Flake Scatters: Lithic Technology Strategies and Mobility." *American Antiquity* 64 (4): 593–607.

Daras, Veronique. 1999. *Technologicas prehispanicas de la obsidiana: Los centros de porduccion de la region de zinaparo—Prieto, Michoacan*. Mexico City: Centre Francais de etudes mexicaines et centroamericanes.

Demarast, Arthur A., Chloé Andrieu, Paola Torres, Mélanie Forné, Tomás Barrientos, and Marc Wolf. 2014. "Economy, Exchange, and Power: New Evidence from the Late Classic Maya Port City of Cancuen." *Ancient Mesoamerica* 25 (1): 187–219.

Druart, Chloe. 2010. "Production and Function of Stone Arrowheads in the Mycenean Civilization: A Technomorphological and Functional Approach." In *Lithic Technology in Metal Using Societies—Proceedings of a UISPP Workshop, Lisbon, September 2006*, ed. Bert Valentin Eriksen, 143–155. Hogbjerg, Denmark: Jutland Archaeological Society.

Freidel, David A., Kathryn Reese-Taylor, and David Mora-Marin. 2002. "The Origins of Maya Civilization: The Old Shell Game, Commodity, Treasure, and Kingship." In *Ancient Maya Political Economies*, ed. Marilyn A. Masson and David A. Freidel, 41–86. Walnut Creek, CA: Altamira.

Gaxiola Gonzalez, Margarita, and John E. Clark, eds. 1989. *La obsidiana en Mesoamerica*. Mexico City: Instituto Nacional de Antropología e Historia.

Gaxiola Gonzalez, Margarita, and Jorge Guevara. 1989. "Un conjunto habitacional en Huapalcalco, Hidalgo, especializado en la talla de obsidiana." In *La obsidiana en Mesoamérica*, ed. Margarita Gaxiola Gonzalez and John E. Clark, 227–242. Mexico City: Instituto Nacional de Antropología e Historia.

Gnaden, Denis, and Simon Holdaway. 2000. "Understanding Observer Variation when Recording Stone Artifacts." *American Antiquity* 65 (4): 739–747.

Golitko, Mark, and Gary M. Feinman. 2015. "Procurement and Distribution of Pre-Hispanic Mesoamerican Obsidian 900 BC–AD 1520: A Social Network Analysis." *Journal of Archaeological Method and Theory* 22: 206–247.

Hammond, Morman, Arnold Aspinall, Stuard Feather, John Hazelden, Trevor Gazard, and Stuart Agnell. 1977. "Maya Jade: Source Location and Analysis." In *Exchange Systems in Prehistory*, ed. Timothy K. Earle and Jonathon E. Ericson, 35–67. New York: Academic.

Healan, Dan M. 1997. "Pre-Hispanic Quarrying in the Ucareo-Zinapecuaro Obsidian Source Area." *Ancient Mesoamerica* 8: 77–100.

Healan, Dan M. 2002. "Producer versus Consumer: Prismatic Core-Blade Technology at Epiclassic/Early Postclassic Tula and Ucareo." In *Pathways to Prismatic Blades: A Study in Mesoamercian Obsidian Core-Blade Technology*, ed. Kenneth G. Hirth and Bradford Andrews, 27–35. Los Angeles: Cotsen Institute of Archaeology, University of California.

Healan, Dan M. 2003. "From the Quarry Pit to the Trash Pit: Comparative Core-Blade Technology at Tula, Hidalgo, and the Ucareo Obsidian Source Region." In *Mesoamerican Lithic Technology: Experimentation and Interpretation*, ed. Kenneth G. Hirth, 153–169. Salt Lake City: University of Utah Press.

Hearth, Nicholas F. 2012. "Organization of Chert Tool Economy during Late and Terminal Classic Periods at Chan: Preliminary Thoughts Based upon Debitage Analyses." In *Chan: An Ancient Maya Farming Community*, ed. Cynthia Robin, 192–206. Gainesville: University of Florida Press.

Helmke, Christophe, and Jaime Awe. 2008. "Organización territorial de los antiguos mayas de Belice Central: confluencia de datos arqueológicos y epigráficos." *Mayab* 20: 65–91.

Hester, Thomas R., ed. 1978. *Archaeological Studies of Mesoamerican Obsidian*. Socorro, NM: Ballena.

Hester, Thomas R., and Harry J. Shafer. 1984. "Exploitation of Chert Resources by the Ancient Maya of Northern Belize, Central America." *World Archaeology* 16 (2): 157–173.

Hester, Thomas R., and Harry J. Shafer. 1991. "Lithics of the Early Postclassic at Colha, Belize." In *Maya Stone Tools: Selected Papers from the Second Maya Lithic Conference*, ed. Thomas R. Hester and Harry J. Shafer, 155–162. Madison, WI: Prehistory Press.

Hirth, Kenneth G., ed. 2003. *Mesoamerican Lithic Technology: Experimentation and Interpretation*. Salt Lake City: University of Utah Press.

Hirth, Kenneth G., ed. 2006. *Obsidian Craft Production in Ancient Central Mexico*. Salt Lake City: University of Utah Press.

Hirth, Kenneth G. 2009. "Craft Production, Household Diversification, and Domestic Economy in Prehispanic Mesoamerica." *Archaeological Papers of the American Anthropological Association* 19 (1): 13–32.

Hirth, Kenneth G., and Bradford Andrews, eds. 2002. *Pathways to Prismatic Blades: A Study in Mesoamerican Obsidian Core Blade Technology*. Los Angeles: Cotsen Institute of Archaeology, University of California.

Horowitz, Rachel A. 2017. "Understanding Ancient Maya Economic Variability: Lithic Technological Organization in the Mopan Valley, Belize." PhD dissertation, Tulane University, New Orleans, LA.

Horowitz, Rachel A. 2018. "Uneven Lithic Landscapes: Raw Material Procurement and Economic Organization among the Late/Terminal Classic Maya in Western Belize." *Journal of Archaeological Sciences: Reports* 19: 949–957.

Houk, Brett A. 2015. *Ancient Maya Cities of the Eastern Lowlands*. Gainesville: University Press of Florida.

Keller, Angela H. 2006. "Roads to the Center: The Design, Use, and Meaning of the Roads of Xunantunich, Belize." PhD dissertation, University of Pennsylvania, Philadelphia.

Kovacevich, Brigitte. 2014. "The Inalienability of Jades in Mesoamerica." *Archaeological Papers of the American Anthropological Association* 23 (1): 95–111.

Kuhn, Steven L. 1994. "A Formal Approach to the Design and Assembly of Mobile Toolkits." *American Antiquity* 59 (3): 426–442.

Kurnick, Sarah J. 2013. "Negotiating the Contradictions of Political Authority: An Archaeological Case Study from Callar Creek, Belize." PhD dissertation, University of Pennsylvania, Philadelphia.

LeCount, Lisa J., and Jason Yaeger. 2010. "Provincial Politics and Current Models of the Maya State." In *Classic Maya Provincial Polities: Xunantunich and Its Hinterlands*, ed. Lisa J. LeCount and Jason Yaeger, 20–45. Tucson: University of Arizona Press.

Levine, Marc N., and David M. Carballo, eds. 2014. *Obsidian Reflections: Symbolic Dimensions of Obsidian in Mesoamerica*. Boulder: University Press of Colorado.

Lothrop, Jonathan C. 1989. "The Organization of Paleoindian Lithic Technology at the Potts Site." In *Eastern Paleoindian Lithic Resource Use*, ed. Christopher J. Ellis and Jonathan C. Lothrop, 99–137. Boulder: Westview.

Lyman, R. Lee, and Todd L. VanPool. 2009. "Metric Data in Archaeology: A Study of Intra-Analyst and Inter-Analyst Variability." *American Antiquity* 74 (3): 485–504.

Masson, Marilyn A., and David A. Friedel. 2012. "An Argument for Classic Era Maya Market Exchange." *Journal of Anthropological Archaeology* 31 (4): 455–484.

McAnany, Patricia A. 2010. *Ancestral Maya Economies in Archaeological Perspective*. Cambridge: Cambridge University Press.

McCall, Grant. 2015. *Before Modern Humans: New Perspectives on the African Stone Age*. Walnut Creek, CA: Left Coast Press.

McDonald, Mary M.A. 1991. "Technological Organization and Sedentism in the Epipaleolithic of Dakhleh Oasis, Egypt." *African Archaeological Review* 9: 81–109.

McKillop, Heather. 2002. *Salt: White Gold of the Ancient Maya*. Gainesville: University Press of Florida.

Meadows, Richard K. 2001. "Crafting K'awil: A Comparative Analysis of Maya Symbolic Flaked Stone Assemblages from Three Sites in Northern Belize." PhD dissertation, University of Texas, Austin.

Montet-White, Anta. 1988. "Raw Material Economy among Medium Sized Late Paleolithic Campsites of Central Europe." In *Upper Pleistocene Prehistory of Western Eurasia*, ed. Harold L. Dibble and Anta Montet-White, 361–374. Monograph 54. Philadelphia: University Museum, University of Pennsylvania.

Nelson, Margaret C. 1991. "The Study of Technological Organization." In *Archaeological Method and Theory*, vol. 3, ed. Michael B. Schiffer, 57–100. Tucson: University of Arizona Press.

Ohnuma, Katsuhiko. 1995. "Analysis of Debitage Pieces from Experimentally Reduced 'Classical Levallois' and 'Discoidal' Cores." In *The Definition and Interpretation of Levallois Technology*, ed. Harold L. Dibble and Ofer Bar-Yosef, 257–266. Monographs in World Archaeology 23. Madison, WI: Prehistory Press.

Parry, William J., and Robert L. Kelly. 1987. "Expedient Core Technology and Sedentism." In *The Organization of Core Technology*, ed. Jay K. Johnson and Carol A. Morrow, 285–304. Boulder: Westview.

Pastrana, Alejandro. 1998. *La explotación Azteca de la obsidiana en la Sierra de las Navajas*. Mexico City: Colección Científica, Instituto Nacional de Antropología e Historia.

Pastrana, Alejandro. 2002. "Variation at the Source: Obsidian Exploitation at Sierra de Las Navajas, Mexico." In *Pathways to Prismatic Blades: A Study in Mesoamerican Obsidian Core Blade Technology*, ed. Kenneth G. Hirth and Bradford Andrews, 15–26. Los Angeles: Cotsen Institute of Archaeology, University of California.

Pohl, Mary D. 1994. "The Economic Politics of Maya Meat Eating." In *The Economic Anthropology of the State*, ed. Elizabeth M. Brumfiel, 119–148. Monographs in Economic Anthropology 11. Lanham, MD: University Press of the Americas.

Robin, Cynthia. 1999. "Towards an Archaeology of Everyday Life: Maya Farmers of Chan Noohol and Dos Chambitos Cik'in, Belize." PhD dissertation, University of Pennsylvania, Philadelphia.

Robin, Cynthia, ed. 2012. *Chan: An Ancient Maya Farming Community*. Gainesville: University Press of Florida.

Robin, Cynthia. 2013. *Everyday Life Matters: Maya Farmers at Chan*. Gainesville: University Press of Florida.

Roemer, Erwin. 1991. "A Late Classic Workshop at Colha, Belize." In *Maya Stone Tools: Selected Papers from the Second Maya Lithic Conference*, ed. Thomas R. Hester and Harry J. Shafer, 55–66. Madison, WI: Prehistory Press.

Rosen, Steven A. 2010. "The Desert and the Sown: A Lithic Perspective." In *Lithic Technology in Metal Using Societies—Proceedings of a UISPP Workshop, Lisbon, September 2006*, ed. Bert Valentin Eriksen, 203–219. Hojbjerg, Denmark: Jutland Archaeological Society.

Santone, Leonore. 1993. "Interregional Exchange: Aspects of the Prehistoric Lithic Economy of Northern Belize." PhD dissertation, University of Texas, Austin.

Scarborough, Vernon L., and Fred Valdez Jr. 2009. "An Alternative Order: The Dualistic Economies of the Ancient Maya." *Latin American Antiquity* 20 (1): 207–227.

Scarborough, Vernon L., and Fred Valdez Jr. 2014. "The Alternative Economy: Resilience in the Face of Complexity from the Eastern Lowlands." *Archaeological Papers of the American Anthropological Association* 24: 124–141.

Shafer, Harry J., and Thomas R. Hester. 1983. "Ancient Maya Chert Workshops in Northern Belize, Central America." *American Antiquity* 48 (3): 519–543.

Shaw, Leslie C. 2012. "The Elusive Maya Marketplace: An Archaeological Consideration of the Evidence." *Journal of Archaeological Research* 20 (2): 117–155.

Shott, Michael J. 1989. "Technological Organization in Great Lakes Paleoindian Assemblages." In *Eastern Paleoindian Lithic Resource Use*, ed. Christopher J. Ellis and Jonathan C. Lothrop, 221–237. Boulder: Westview.

Sorensen, Lasse. 2010. "Obsidian from the Final Neolithic Site of Pangali in Western Greece: Development of Exchange Patterns in the Aegean." In *Lithic Technology in Metal Using Societies—Proceedings of a UISPP Workshop, Lisbon, September 2006*, ed. Bert Valentin Eriksen, 183–202. Hojbjerg, Denmark: Jutland Archaeological Society.

Spence, Michael W. 1981. "Obsidian Production and the State at Teotihuacan." *American Antiquity* 46 (4): 769–788.

Taube, Karl A. 2005. "The Symbolism of Jade in Classic Maya Religion." *Ancient Mesoamerica* 16: 23–50.

Teltser, Patrice A. 1991. "Generalized Core Technology and Tool Use: A Mississippian Example." *Journal of Field Archaeology* 18 (3): 363–375.

Tokovinine, Alexandre, and Dmitri Beliaev. 2013. "People of the Road: Traders and Travelers in Ancient Maya Words and Images." In *Merchants, Markets, and Exchange in the Pre-Columbian World*, ed. Kenneth G. Hirth and Joanne Pillsbury, 169–200. Washington, DC: Dumbarton Oaks Research Library and Collection.

Torrence, Robin. 1984. "Monopoloy or Direct Access? Industrial Organization at the Melos Obsidian Quarries." In *Prehistoric Quarries and Lithic Production*, ed. Jonathon E. Ericson and Barbara A. Purdy, 49–64. Cambridge: Cambridge University Press.

Torrence, Robin. 1986. *Production and Exchange of Stone Tools: Prehistoric Obsidian in the Aegean*. Cambridge: Cambridge University Press.

Torrence, Robin. 1989. "Retooling: Toward a Behavioral Theory of Stone Tools." In *Time, Energy, and Stone Tools*, ed. Robin Torrence, 57–66. Cambridge: Cambridge University Press.

VandenBosch, Jon C. 1999. "Lithic Economy and Household Interdependence among the Late Classic Maya of Belize." PhD dissertation, University of Pittsburgh, PA.

VandenBosch, Jon C., Lisa J. LeCount, and Jason Yaeger. 2010. "Integration and Interdependence: The Domestic Chipped Stone Economy of the Xunantunich Polity." In *Classic Maya Provincial Polities: Xunantunich and Its Hinterlands*, ed. Lisa J. LeCount and Jason Yaeger, 272–294. Tucson: University of Arizona Press.

Whittaker, John C., Kathryn A. Kamp, Anabel Ford, Rafael Guerra, Peter Brands, Jose Guerra, Kim McLean, Alex Woods, Melissa Badillo, Jennifer Thornton, and Zerifeh Eiley. 2009. "Lithic Industry in a Maya Center: An Axe Workshop at el Pilar, Belize." *Latin American Antiquity* 20 (1): 134–156.

Willey, Gordon R. 2004. "Retrospective." In *Ancient Maya of the Belize Valley: Half a Century of Archaeological Research*, ed. James F. Garber, 15–24. Gainesville: University Press of Florida.

Yaeger, Jason. 2000. "Changing Patterns of Social Organization: The Late and Terminal Classic Communities at San Lorenzo, Cayo District, Belize." PhD dissertation, University of Pennsylvania, Philadelphia.

Yaeger, Jason. 2010. "Commodities, Brands, and Village Economies in the Classic Maya Lowlands." In *Cultures of Commodity Branding*, ed. Andrew Bevan and David Wengrow, 167–195. Walnut Creek, CA: Left Coast Press.

6

Chert at Chalcatzingo

Implications of Knapping Strategies and Technological Organization for Formative Economics

GRANT S. MCCALL, RACHEL A. HOROWITZ, AND DAN M. HEALAN

It is little secret that with the exception of some key instances of highly specialized craft production of obsidian blades and chert bifaces, the study of lithic technology in Mesoamerican prehistory has received short shrift. There are some obvious (if not good) reasons for this. Outside of these specialized contexts, the production of lithic technology across the complex societies of Mesoamerica tended to be "expedient" or "informal," in the sense of having very few formal retouched tools and generally unremarkable core reduction strategies. In most cases, local lithic raw materials (usually chert) were reduced without making use of the complex knapping techniques associated with blade production or bifacial thinning, and the resulting debris was apparently used on an ad hoc basis for immediate domestic purposes. Thus studies aimed at understanding knapping activities under such circumstances were not widely viewed as articulating with any pressing theoretical questions concerning issues such as craft specialization, elite control of craft production, exchange, or inter-polity interaction; to be even more blunt, they have not been viewed as all that interesting otherwise.

Indeed, when viewed solely from the perspective of *production*, expedient lithic technologies of this kind really do not seem to have much to offer to our understanding of prehistory. Further, it is clear that much of our field has embraced production as its particular pinhole through which to view technology in terms

DOI: 10.5876/9781607328926.c006

of many theoretical issues, ranging from agency and practice to the microeconomics of households. Yet we hold that lithic technology has vastly more to contribute to our understanding of the past than what can be gleaned simply from the technical procedures through which stone tools were made. For expedient lithic technologies, the processes of production were indeed quite banal. Yet we feel strongly that all lithic technologies, from the initial collection of raw materials to the discard of exhausted tools and waste products, were intimately intertwined with other aspects of the lives of the people who made them. Even when the techniques of stone tool production were not particularly interesting, the lives of the prehistoric people who made them were. Therefore, for us, the grand challenge for the archaeology of stone tools is to develop analytical approaches for making inferences about the broader lives of prehistoric peoples on the basis of the stone tool technology they left behind. Furthermore, we see this grand challenge as exactly the same no matter whether one is concerned with the most formally striking lithic technologies requiring tremendous skill to produce, such as blades, bifaces, and eccentrics, or the oft-ignored expedient flake production that typified the bulk of complex societies in ancient Mesoamerica. Therefore, we believe that an exclusive focus on production without a broader concern for technological organization does little to meet the grand challenge facing the archaeology of stone tools.

In this chapter we present an analysis of the chert lithic technology from the Formative period site of Chalcatzingo (Morelos, Mexico). Between 900 and 500 BCE, Chalcatzingo was a major population center with clear cultural and economic connections to the burgeoning Olmec world of the Gulf Coast (Grove 1984, 1987, 2014; figure 6.1). In addition to its Olmec-style art, Chalcatzingo is also famous for its specialized production of obsidian blades in elite-controlled craft workshops (Burton 1987; De León et al. 2009; Hirth 2012). Along with greenstone and some other local resources, Chalcatzingo exported obsidian blades to the growing urban centers of the Olmec heartland. Its obsidian blades, therefore, constituted a major economic commodity. Lesser known, however, is the massive accumulation of chert lithic debris at Chalcatzingo generally found within residential compounds (Burton 1987). As a classic example of the expedient knapping of locally available raw material, the production of chert lithics at Chalcatzingo has received relatively little attention. Yet in this chapter we show that the expedient chert industry present at this site holds important clues about the economic contexts in which the residents of Chalcatzingo lived.

FIGURE 6.1. *Location of Chalcatzingo in Morelos, Mexico*

Most prominently, our analysis of the chert artifacts from Chalcatzingo suggests that there was a surprising degree of raw material stress, given the prevalence of expedient knapping strategies. While no specialized knapping strategies were present and formal retouched tools were rare, several lines of evidence suggest a concern for raw material economization and the exhaustive reduction of cores. In general, the characteristics of the chert assemblage from Chalcatzingo contradict widespread views concerning the link between raw material abundance and expedient knapping strategies in sedentary residential contexts (e.g., Parry and Kelly 1987). Instead, other organizational factors seem to have fostered these observed patterns in terms of the economic contexts in which raw materials were collected, the constellation of the tasks for which stone tools were used, and the circumstances under which stone tool use occurred. In considering these issues, we make use of some ethnoarchaeological studies of stone tool production among sedentary peoples and propose a generalized model to help explain our observed dynamics (see also McCall 2012). Finally, we briefly consider the implications of the contrasting dynamics of obsidian and chert stone tool production at Chalcatzingo.

If nothing else, our study demonstrates some of the ways the chert lithic assemblage from Chalcatzingo reflects important aspects of the economic life ways of its thrifty residents. In concluding, however, we go further in proposing some ways variability within and between the expedient stone tool assemblages of ancient Mesoamerica might be used to assess both modes of lithic technological organization and the broader economic contexts in which stone tool production occurred. In this respect, we offer some potential directions for future research and even go so far as to offer predictions about the characteristics of assemblages produced under various sets of conditions.

MATERIALS AND METHODS

The chert assemblage analyzed in this study was collected during excavations directed by David Grove at Chalcatzingo during field seasons conducted in the period 1995–1998. Although these excavations were aimed in part at examining potential differences between elite and non-elite residential contexts, we consider the entire chert lithic assemblage as a single entity. We did so in part because on the basis of our preliminary statistical analyses, we failed to find any significant differences between any residential compounds, as did Burton (1987) in an earlier analysis. In addition, the bulk of the chert lithic assemblage was recovered from non-elite contexts. Furthermore, at this stage our analysis has lacked the resolution with which to tackle issues of potential change over time, although we consider this a promising avenue for future investigation. For now, we feel that the Chalcatzingo chert assemblage reflects a general set of overlapping economic contexts in which tools were produced; therefore, it can plausibly be treated in terms of variability within a single class of phenomena.

In terms of analytical methods, we decided to conduct an attribute analysis of the majority of the assemblage available for study: 9,935 lithic artifacts. We began by classifying them into the categories of cores, core fragments, whole flakes, broken flakes, flake fragments, shatter, projectile points, scrapers, notches, denticulates, drills, other retouched tools, bipolar pieces, and hammerstone spalls. For all artifacts, we recorded various measurements of size (length, width, thickness, and mass). For flakes with intact platforms, we recorded platform faceting and width. Though fairly basic, recording this information for each individual lithic artifact offered an approach for documenting variability in terms of the size and shape characteristics of those artifacts, as well as the knapping techniques and sequential dynamics involved in their production. Furthermore, while somewhat labor-intensive, this approach to studying a fairly large sample of lithic artifacts resulted in the identification of some particularly detailed forms of patterning that other forms of bulk analysis might miss, in particular having to do with the general impressions of this type of chert lithic industry as expedient. Thus the value of detailed analysis and the attribute analysis approach is apparent and constitutes a major point of our conclusions in conducting this research.

RESULTS

Our analysis of the Chalcatzingo chert lithic assemblage resulted in some provocative findings. We begin by offering some basic characteristics of the lithic raw materials exploited and the knapping techniques used in their reduction. We then proceed to a more detailed description of the characteristics of the chert lithic assemblage and implications for issues pertaining to both positioning within sequences of reduction and broader patterns of technological organization. In general, the results of our study contradict some long-held notions about the nature of the expedient knapping of locally available raw materials in sedentary farming societies and, more specifically, throughout ancient Mesoamerica.

The chert lithic raw materials at Chalcatzingo were apparently available in the form of tabular blocks occurring in secondary alluvial and colluvial contexts. Although examination of the dorsal surfaces of flakes and the unmodified surfaces of cores made it clear to us that some geological transport and weathering had occurred, the lithic raw materials were generally blocky and lacked significant rounding on their edges. In addition, although we recorded the color of all pieces, we quickly realized that color varied immensely within individual blocks of chert and therefore held little significance in terms of the identification of material source and similar factors. In general, we propose that chert raw materials were collected locally in the alluvial and colluvial margins of Chalcatzingo, having eroded out of a common primary source in the nearby uplands. We also feel that chert procurement may well have been embedded within the clearing of fields for farming and other similar local economic activities, given the erosional distribution of chert from its upland primary sources. We discuss these dynamics further in the next section.

The vast majority of the flake assemblage is composed of unretouched flakes and debris resulting from the reduction of informal cores (figures 6.2 and 6.3). We found that retouched tools comprised around only 3.5 percent of the total lithic assemblage, almost exactly the same as the frequency found by Burton (1987) in her earlier work on the Chalcatzingo chert assemblage. Even within the retouched tool assemblage, we found little systematic formal patterning (figure 6.4). Instead, most retouched tools tended to be relatively large flakes with a single edge modified through retouch into a spectrum of scraper,

TABLE 6.1. Count by tool type of items from the Chalcatzingo assemblage

	Type	Frequency	Percent	Valid Percent	Cumulative Percent
Valid	Whole flake	1,885	19.0	19.0	19.0
	Broken flake	817	8.2	8.2	27.2
	Flake fragment	3,856	38.8	38.8	66.0
	Shatter	2,787	28.0	28.1	94.1
	Core	69	0.7	0.7	94.8
	Core fragment	152	1.5	1.5	96.3
	Projectile point	8	0.1	0.1	96.4
	Drill	39	0.4	0.4	96.8
	Scraper	46	0.5	0.5	97.2
	Notch	54	0.5	0.5	97.8
	Denticulate	25	0.3	0.3	98.0
	Bipolar piece	42	0.4	0.4	98.4
	Other tool	128	1.3	1.3	99.7
	Hammerstone spall	11	0.1	0.1	99.8
	Other tool fragment	16	0.2	0.2	100.0
	Subtotal	9,935	99.9	100.0	
Missing	Unknown	7	0.1		
Total		**9,942**	**100.0**		

notch, and denticulate forms (table 6.1). Of the retouched tool assemblage, drills were the most distinctive and systematic formal type but accounted for only around 0.4 percent of the total assemblage. In addition, we found only 8 projectile points from the whole assemblage, accounting for less than 0.1 percent of the total assemblage. Clearly, retouched tools were fairly unimportant in comparison with the use of expedient unmodified flakes, which formed the vast majority of the assemblage.

The core assemblage also showed little in terms of the use of systematic reduction strategies but rather was characterized by informal knapping procedures. Virtually all of the cores were polyhedral and lacked any recognizable axis or clear horizon of orientation. Furthermore, there were no core bifaces or other distinctive core reduction strategies, and virtually all of the specimens were consistent with what we are comfortable calling an expedient core strategy. Instead, the most distinctive feature of the core assemblage was the mean size of cores and

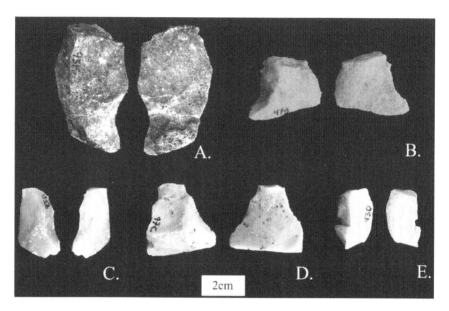

FIGURE 6.2. *Sample of representative flakes from Chalcatzingo chert assemblage*

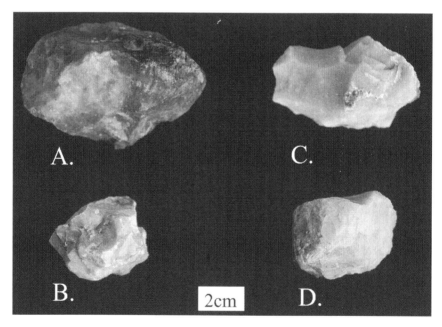

FIGURE 6.3. *Representative sample of cores from Chalcatzingo chert assemblage*

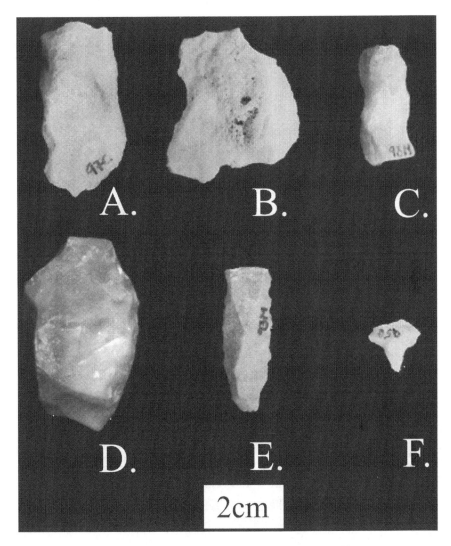

FIGURE 6.4. *Sample of retouched tools from Chalcatzingo chert assemblage*

the distribution of size range ranges. Figures 6.5 and 6.6 show histograms of the distributions of longest core dimensions and core masses for the Chalcatzingo chert assemblage. Obviously, the mean size of cores in this assemblage is rather small, and a great many of the cores are almost shockingly diminutive. In addition, we also observed that a very high proportion of cores were recycled into battered hammering tools, with most exhibiting some form of pitting on their

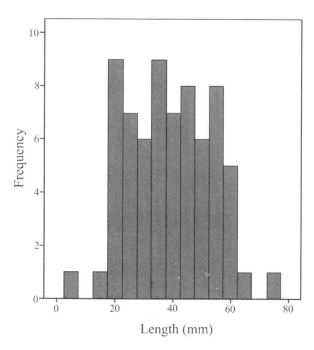

FIGURE 6.5.
Histogram showing longest linear dimensions of whole cores

surfaces and rounding of flake scar edges (see figure 6.3). In short, cores were reduced until they were too small to produce any more usable flakes, and then they were often recycled into hammers. In addition, the Chalcatzingo chert assemblage has a very high ratio of flakes to cores, with 39.2 flakes for each core present (calculated as [whole flakes + broken flakes] / cores). This again suggests the extreme exhaustion of cores at the time of their discard.

The flake assemblage showed similar patterning in terms of size and other characteristics likely related to raw material economy. As figures 6.7 and 6.8 show, the distributions of whole flake lengths and masses center on rather small values and are also strongly right skewed. In fact, 50.8 percent of the entire flake assemblage is less than 2 cm in length, and 67.0 percent is less than 5 g in mass. Although there are some large outliers, the bulk of the flake assemblage is obviously fairly small. As with the core assemblage, we believe this pattern indicates that knappers continued to reduce cores until they were thoroughly exhausted. In addition, there is also evidence that large flakes, which would have been most useful, were commonly and fairly intensively recycled through retouch. Retouched flakes were on average 6.9 mm (35.5%) longer (F = 16.918; p < 0.001) and 3.4 g (91.3%) heavier (F = 22.569; p < 0.001)

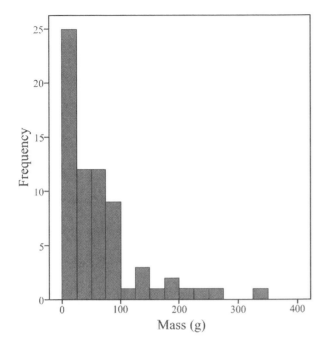

FIGURE 6.6. *Histogram showing the masses of whole cores*

than their unretouched counterparts (table 6.2),[1] in spite of the fact that mass and, normally, length were lost through the process of retouch. Again, this reflects preferential recycling of the larger, more useful, and therefore more valuable chert flakes.

We also examined the characteristics of striking platforms as a way of elucidating salient knapping dynamics. Of the total assemblage, 77.1 percent of the striking platforms had one facet or were cortical, while 22.9 percent were multifaceted (figure 6.9). Under the circumstances, we actually take this to be a fairly high frequency of multifaceted platforms. We feel that this value is high in comparison with those resulting from expedient knapping described elsewhere in Mesoamerica (and beyond) and considering that more complicated strategies of core reduction were not employed here, which might have given rise to higher frequencies of multifaceted platforms. In addition, platform sizes were fairly small and once again showed a strongly right skewed distribution (figure 6.10). Here, 37.3 percent of striking platforms are 3 mm wide or less and 88.0 percent are 10 mm wide or less. Likewise, in the total absence of any non-expedient knapping strategies that might lead to small platform sizes (i.e., bifacial

TABLE 6.2. Descriptive statistics for length and mass of materials

		Group Statistics			
		N	*Mean*	*Std. Deviation*	*Std. Error Mean*
Length	Unretouched	1,885	19.47	10.072	0.232
	Retouched	172	26.50	12.183	0.929
Mass	Unretouched	1,885	3.68	8.921	0.205
	Retouched	171	6.04	9.717	0.743

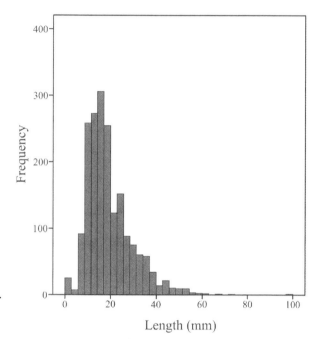

FIGURE 6.7. *Histogram showing lengths of whole flakes*

thinning or blade production), this clearly points to a great deal of raw material economizing and stress.

In summary, the chert lithic assemblage from Chalcatzingo shows strong evidence for (1) informal or expedient knapping strategies and (2) the intensive reduction of cores to the point of exhaustion, which resulted in (3) high frequencies of very small flakes and cores. Retouching of flakes was rare and seems to have been aimed mostly at the recycling of particularly nice flakes through relatively informal scraper retouch, notching, and denticulation. Thus while there was no concomitant specialization in core reduction

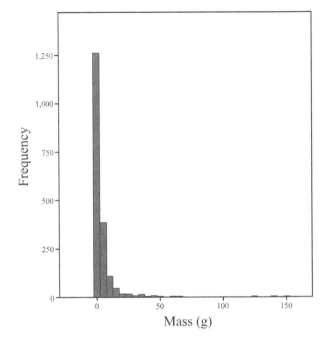

FIGURE 6.8. *Histogram showing masses of whole flakes*

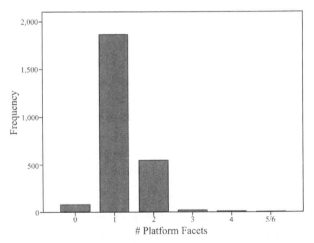

FIGURE 6.9. *Bar chart showing frequencies of striking platform facet patterns*

strategies, there is clear and perhaps surprising evidence of raw material stress and economizing of lithic raw materials. As we discuss further below, these findings contradict many suppositions about the nature of expedient knapping in sedentary and complex societies.

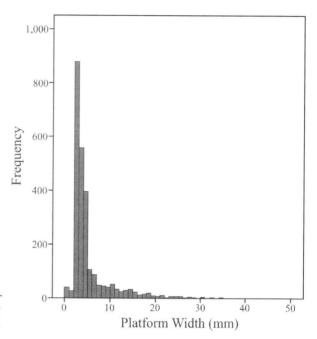

FIGURE 6.10. *Histogram showing striking platform widths*

DISCUSSION

Some time ago, Parry and Kelly (1987) provided a seminal viewpoint on expedient knapping in sedentary societies. Their paper has largely framed discussion on this topic since its publication. In very basic outline, Parry and Kelly argued that expedient or informal knapping strategies predominated in sedentary societies (in contrast to mobile hunter-gatherers), since knappers could collect lithic raw materials from nearby sources and stockpile them in their residential contexts. Thus a supply of lithic raw material would always have been present, and more complex knapping strategies aimed at economizing lithic raw materials or special design properties anticipating future use (e.g., bifacial projectile points) were obviated. In this way, Parry and Kelly made a variety of organizational arguments that offered a broad and powerful explanation of the observed patterning among lithic assemblages across North America and over time, with implications for other sedentary societies. Without a doubt, this perspective has contributed enormously to our views of lithic assemblage variability among mobile and sedentary peoples in prehistory.

In more recent years, however, some scholars have begun to find flaws with the Parry and Kelly (1987) model, and our findings here seem to constitute another somewhat contradictory case. In short, it seems that while the Parry and Kelly model seems to be right about a great deal, it perhaps misses some important nuances. Specifically, while we absolutely agree with broad generalizations at the heart of the Parry and Kelly model, there appear to be some problems with issues related to the availability of lithic raw materials and the phenomenon of stockpiling at residential sites. In the case of the chert at Chalcatzingo, the many signatures of lithic raw material stress and dynamics of economization seem to contradict the broadly expected conditions of the Parry and Kelly model in terms of abundant locally available lithic material as well as its stockpiling in residential contexts.

In a recent survey of ethnoarchaeological studies of modern stone tool production, McCall (2012) identified many cases in which knappers acquired lithic raw materials from local contexts during the conduct of various economic activities and knapped them expediently in residential contexts. Subsequently, useful flakes were selected on an ad hoc basis for the resolution of immediate technical problems, used expediently, and then discarded. In fact, of the scant few remaining cases of modern stone tool production, most fit this general description (see McCall 2012 for a more painfully detailed review). In the case of Chalcatzingo, we find it likely that knappers acquired stone in the course of daily economic activities, such as the clearing of agricultural fields or during short trips to exploit other local economic resources, which brought them into contact with knappable lithic raw materials in one way or another. Then, resulting blocks of lithic raw material were knapped expediently within residential units and used for various domestic activities, perhaps especially the manufacture and repair of other tool components (mostly made from wood). Most flakes were likely discarded just as expediently as they were made and used; the best flakes were sometimes recycled through quick and informal retouch.

Hence, our results suggest a picture of the residents of Chalcatzingo acquiring chert during the course of their daily economic lives and reducing that material surprisingly intensively, likely as one aspect of a broader pattern of quotidian frugality. By itself, this phenomenon may not seem that interesting to those without a deep interest in lithics, who are likely to focus more on its implications for the Parry and Kelly (1987) model. However, two broader implications for the lives of Chalcatzingoans are worth considering relative to broader theoretical issues. First, we find it likely that this pattern of chert economization has noteworthy organizational relationships with other aspects of household economies. Just as Chalcatzingo knappers got every possible bit of utility out of their chert blocks, there is good evidence that the residents of Chalcatzingo expended great effort in maximizing the utility of all of their economic commodities.

These inferred patterns of chert core reduction are not the static (and boring) endpoint in a study aimed at elucidating lithic production processes but are indeed rather more interesting in what they have to say about the broader economic conditions under which Chalcatzingo residents lived their lives. The residents of Chalcatzingo were tough, resourceful, and frugal (as are most peasants in small-scale farming societies); and their exploitation of local chert resources reflects this. Furthermore, these results add depth to other aspects of household economy that have been more thoroughly studied, offering avenues for future investigation and theory building by integrating lithic data.

Second and perhaps more important, the contrast between chert and obsidian production highlights some dynamics of social inequality and likely the elite control of craft production at Chalcatzingo. At the same time that non-elite residential compounds show evidence for the intensive reduction of what must be considered relatively low-quality chert almost to the point of absurdity, highly specialized obsidian blade production occurred nearby in residential units presumably populated by attached craft specialists. It is telling that so many non-elite residential compounds focused so much effort on the reduction of chert in a settlement in which high-quality obsidian blades were being mass-produced (a bit like Detroit factory workers taking the bus to work to go assemble cars).

It is clear that the obsidian blade production economy was organized in radically different ways than was its chert counterpart, with high-quality obsidian acquired at considerable cost from more distant sources (e.g., Charlton et al. 1978) and resulting blades exchanged with various far-flung Olmec trading partners along the Gulf Coast (e.g., Hirth 1978). It is evident that the organization of obsidian blade production was controlled by political-economic elites and that blade core reduction techniques emerged as a strategy for optimizing obsidian as an economic commodity within the context of long-distance raw material acquisition and final product exchange. It is also telling that despite the presence of perhaps tons of (apparently) unused obsidian waste debris in blade production workshops, very little ever found its way into non-elite residences. Not only did elites control the distribution of finished obsidian blades, which were far more valuable as exchange commodities than as tools for local use, they also even (apparently) controlled the distribution of garbage from the production of blades. Contrasting obsidian blade production in craft workshops with the everyday expedient reduction of chert in non-elite residences helps bring into focus some salient aspects of social inequality and of the control of trade as an elite strategy for acquiring wealth and maintaining political power.

Indeed, while this is perhaps an extreme case, it is certainly not unique to Chalcatzingo. There are many instances across Mesoamerica of what we would call *closed system* lithic production in which local, usually relatively low-quality lithic raw material resources were exploited by the residents of adjacent population centers. This class of phenomenon is usually characterized by informal or expedient knapping strategies, and under such circumstances, variability in lithic assemblage characteristics may indeed be manifested most obviously in terms of the intensity of core reduction and result in various archaeological signatures of raw material economization. In such situations, longer site occupations and larger residential populations will depress the availability of local lithic raw material more quickly, resulting in more extreme signatures of raw material stress, such as those apparent in the chert assemblage at Chalcatzingo (figure 6.11). Thus as the occupation of a population center continues and, under most circumstances, its population increases, local lithic raw materials will become scarcer, and the modal size and quality of blocks will decrease as larger and higher-quality pieces are exploited first. These are all predictions we would make for *closed system* cases, and we hope further investigations of the Chalcatzingo chert test these predictions in the future.

In contrast, instances in which high-quality lithic raw materials were acquired from more distant sources and then exchanged further afield are what we would call *open systems*. In most such cases, raw materials are extracted from their sources in very large quantities, and these sources can usually be considered effectively infinite with respect to their abundance of lithic raw material. On the one hand, this creates a situation in which variability in lithic production dynamics depends on the distance of the high-quality raw material source from the craft center in which it is knapped and also the quality of the lithic raw material itself (although clearly these two variables will usually be strongly tied to one another). More distant raw material sources offer greater opportunities for elite control, since this increases their cost and requires more specialized economic pathways in terms of raw material acquisition. On the other hand, dynamics of knapping under such *open system* conditions also depend on the nature of external dynamics and especially external demand. Circumstances in which there is great external demand, such as that from population centers located in regions with little direct access to lithic raw materials, tend to increase the exchange value of stone tool commodities and promote dynamics of elite control.

Situations in which high-quality lithic raw materials are distant and there is great external demand for lithic resources foster increased elite control of production and therefore complex knapping strategies aimed at optimizing lithic raw material commodities relative to their exchange. While this seems

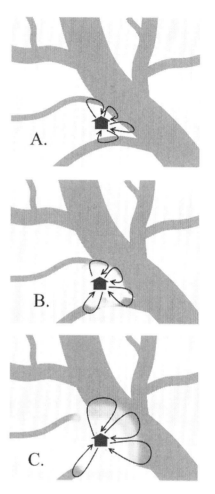

FIGURE 6.11. *Closed system lithic raw material acquisition dynamics at Chalcatzingo. Gray coloring shows the availability of chert. At the time of settlement (A), chert is common in secondary deposits in fluvial features. As chert is removed from these deposits during everyday economic activities and is knapped in residential contexts, it becomes rarer (B). Eventually, chert becomes relatively scarce in nearby locations, and dynamics of raw material stress/ economization become the norm (C).*

to have been the case with obsidian blade production at Chalcatzingo, there is great variability within the *open system* category; further, there are many instances (including some discussed elsewhere in this book) in which lithic raw materials were closer to population centers and there was less external demand, less elite control of lithic raw material circulation, and less specialized knapping practices. Thus variability across such *open system* cases clearly has organizational relationships with broader economic and political dynamics having to do with craft production, consumption, exchange, and political control of various economic resources. But then, this is probably not news to most of the readers of this volume.

Finally, the comparison and contrast of *closed system* and *open system* cases holds great value in reconstructing prehistoric political economy in Mesoamerica and beyond. There are a great many cases in which both system states existed side by side, with each affecting the other in subtle and often oblique ways. In particular, while most lithic analysis in the region has focused on the highly specialized and technically impressive lithic production in *open system* cases, this may only be part of the picture. While *closed system* lithic production is usually much less impressive from a technical standpoint, it has much to offer in terms of elucidating the everyday lives of individuals in household economies, as well as bringing into sharper focus the nature of specialized lithic production as an element of the larger political economy.

METHODOLOGICAL AFTERTHOUGHTS

In closing, we briefly consider some analytical implications of our findings concerning the Chalcatzingo chert assemblage. At the outset, some may have questioned the wisdom of conducting a detailed attribute analysis of an assemblage of nearly 10,000 individual lithic pieces, the vast majority of which seemed (at least superficially) to be fairly uninteresting pieces of debris resulting from expedient core reduction. Indeed, there were moments when we questioned this ourselves. However, it is evident that this detailed analysis yielded subtle aspects of assemblage patterning that turned out to be the key to a deeper understanding of knapping practices and therefore of broader economic dynamics.

It has been most common in previous examinations of these sorts of *closed system* contexts for researchers to report the frequencies of various core, debitage, and retouched tool types (if, in fact, anything beyond the simple presence of lithic debris was reported at all). This is even true of previous analyses of the Chalcatzingo chert assemblage (Burton 1987). However, the signals of raw material stress and economization that we see as so surprising and important were only detectable using finer-grained analytical approaches. If we had been satisfied to state that around 97 percent of the assemblage was composed of debris resulting from expedient flaking and the rest consisted of expedient retouch, then it would seem to be very much a confirmation of Parry and Kelly's (1987) model. This case shows fairly clearly that it is worth the trouble to make this level of fine-grained observation even on assemblages that do not superficially seem very interesting. Going forward, it is not hard to imagine analytical tactics involving an attribute analysis of a sample of what are frequently impossibly large assemblages in combination with other forms of aggregate analysis as a way of characterizing entire assemblages, especially their size distributions as well as their variability between spatial contexts and over time.

Finally, once we "got in the groove," our attribute analysis did not take that long. Horowitz and McCall did the majority of the analysis (approximately 8,000 pieces) during a week of spring break, constituting at most 100 person-hours. Relative to the time spent on other aspects of fieldwork and analysis, this constitutes a fairly negligible time investment, one which resulted in some information that provides depth concerning certain aspects of the economic systems in place at Chalcatzingo. We suspect that this is another case in which this form of analysis seems as though it is more tedious or time-consuming than it actually is. Therefore we close by making the case for wider-spread application of this analytical approach to Mesoamerican lithic assemblages as well as to those from similar contexts further afield.

CONCLUSION

Like many Mesoamerican sites, Chalcatzingo has a large chert lithic assemblage characterized by informal or expedient knapping strategies and made of locally available raw materials. In contrast with obsidian blade production, which occurred using highly specialized knapping techniques, exploited distant raw material resources, and was controlled by elites for the purposes of trade with distant Gulf Coast polities, the knapping of chert was a frugal quotidian activity, occurring pervasively across non-elite residential compounds. Furthermore, our fine-grained analysis of the chert assemblage has shown that it contradicts some long-held notions about the nature of expedient knapping in sedentary societies, as well as its likely causes.

We argue that the residents of Chalcatzingo used informal knapping strategies in reducing cores not because raw materials were unlimited on the landscape or stockpiled in limitless stores but rather because of the local nature of raw material procurement in reliable combination with a predictable set of domestic activities. Perhaps more important, we have shown that careful attention to these sorts of informal lithic industries in places like Mesoamerica has a great deal to offer the field, especially in moving beyond its current focus on production. While certain lithic industries may have employed more complex knapping strategies than others, no lithic industry is inherently more interesting or important in terms of what it can say about the broader patterns of human economic behavior in which it was produced.

NOTE

1. When considering the results of these T tests, never mind that we just showed that these distributions are right skewed and therefore not normal/befitting the expectations of parametric tests of probability. Take our word for it: the retouched flakes are significantly bigger than the unretouched ones.

REFERENCES

Burton, Susan S. 1987. "Obsidian Blade Manufacturing Debris on Terrace 37." In *Ancient Chalcatzingo*, ed. David C. Grove, 321–328. Austin: University of Texas Press.

Charlton, Thomas H., David C. Grove, and Philip K. Hopke. 1978. "The Paredon, Mexico, Obsidian Source and Early Formative Exchange." *Science* 201 (4358): 807–809.

De León, Jason P., Kenneth G. Hirth, and David M. Carballo. 2009. "Exploring Formative Period Obsidian Blade Trade: Three Distribution Models." *Ancient Mesoamerica* 20 (1): 113–128.

Grove, David C. 1984. *Chalcatzingo: Excavations on the Olmec Frontier*. New York: Thames and Hudson.

Grove, David C., ed. 1987. *Ancient Chalcatzingo*. Austin: University of Texas Press.

Grove, David C. 2014. *Discovering the Olmecs: An Unconventional History*. Austin: University of Texas Press.

Hirth, Kenneth G. 1978. "Inter-regional Trade and the Formation of Prehistoric Gateway Communities." *American Antiquity* 43 (1): 35–45.

Hirth, Kenneth G. 2012. "The Organizational Structures of Mesoamerican Obsidian Prismatic Blade Technology." In *The Emergence of Pressure Blade Making*, ed. Pierre M. Desrosiers, 401–415. New York: Springer.

McCall, Grant S. 2012. "Ethnoarchaeology and the Organization of Lithic Technology." *Journal of Archaeological Research* 20 (2): 157–203.

Parry, William J., and Robert L. Kelly. 1987. "Expedient Core Technology and Sedentism." In *The Organization of Core Technology*, ed. Jay K. Johnson and Carol A. Morrow, 285–304. Carbondale: Southern Illinois University Press.

7

Unraveling Sociopolitical Organization using Lithic Data

A Case Study from an Agricultural Society in the American Southwest

Fumiyasu Arakawa

Few lithic studies that intend to reconstruct and understand sociopolitical organization in agricultural societies have been conducted (e.g., Anderson 1992; Kardulias and Yerkes 1996). This can be explained by four factors. First, archaeologists who research agricultural societies have developed a remarkable level of pottery analysis that allows for the reconstruction of some aspects of sociopolitical organization in Neolithic Age societies in both the Old and New Worlds (e.g., Abbott 2009; Arnold 1985; Crown 2000; Glowacki 2015; Mills and Crown 1995). Pottery remains and typological data from these societies are extensive and generally offer information related to trade, social interaction, and gender. Based on ceramic attribute analysis, ceramic seriation can help us expose the temporal occupation of a particular site. The results of the temporal seriation allow us to explore topics related to gender, ceramic specialization, and trade simply using pottery data.

No comprehensive debitage analysis technique has been developed that allows for the understanding of sociopolitical organization using lithic data. In agricultural societies, archaeologists generally deal with massive quantities of debris collections and stone tools (e.g., modified flakes and utilized flakes). For example, at one of the largest ancestral Pueblo villages at Yellow Jacket Pueblo in the central Mesa Verde region (Arakawa 2000), over 13,000 pieces of debitage were recovered from the site. Analysis of the

DOI: 10.5876/9781607328926.c007

collection was laborious, as it took approximately 1 hour to analyze 100 to 150 pieces of debitage using metric analysis. With this as a rough guide, one would need to spend at least 130 hours to complete the analysis of about 13,000 pieces of debitage. To analyze such large collections, archaeologists need to find a more thorough, expedient, and efficient debitage analysis technique. Indeed, lithic analysts have employed two different methods of examining debitage: mass versus metric analysis (Ahler 1989; Andrefsky 2006; Patterson 1990). Mass analysis is an approach that records basic attributes of debitage, including raw material type, size-grade, absence or presence of cortex, and weight. Since this analysis does not focus on an individual flake or angular shatter, lithic analysts spend much less time doing this analysis compared with metric analyses (e.g., using personal experience, it takes approximately 1 hour to analyze more than 500 pieces of debitage using mass analysis). As Ahler (1989) notes, the mass analysis technique allows us to deal with massive lithic assemblages efficiently and conveniently. In contrast, metric analysis records several attributes such as length, width, thickness, weight, material type, and amount of cortex. Metric analysis allows us to examine reduction activities and resolves problems related to the mixed or multiple reduction activities at a site (Andrefsky 2007). Unlike mass analysis, lithic analysts who use metric analysis spend vast amounts of time analyzing a single debitage assemblage. In this chapter I demonstrate an efficient way of using both mass and metric analyses on agrarian debitage collections. I argue that using the results of both types of debitage analysis allows us to employ another method by which we can recognize different aspect of sociopolitical organization in prehistoric agricultural societies.

Archaeologists who research prehistoric agricultural societies generally find it difficult to apply the well-established lithic reduction sequence approach originally developed to understand technological dynamics in foraging societies (Bleed 1986; Bradley 1976). The lithic reduction sequence approach focuses on trajectories of stone tool production based on stone tool replications and middle-range experiments (Bordes and Crabtree 1969; Bradley 1975; Crabtree 1972; Flenniken and Raymond 1986; Flenniken and Wilke 1989; Frison 1968; Kuhn 1991; Shott 1994). On the basis of these studies we have inferred that prehistoric flintknappers went through stages of a reduction sequence, beginning with the core and moving through the flake, biface, pre-form, and finally the projectile point (Andrefsky 2007; Bradley 1975; Whittaker 1994). When analyzing a lithic assemblage, the focus is geared toward the stages of lithic reduction. This approach is valuable because reconstructing the reduction sequences allows us to infer what kind of work activities people conducted at a site, which in turn allows us to examine topics related to subsistence patterns, lithic technology, and trade. However, the majority of stone tools recovered from prehistoric agricultural society contexts appear to have been expediently manufactured. Thus these stone tools and their debitage rarely show patterns of lithic reduction sequences similar to those from non-agricultural, foraging sites.

In agricultural societies, it appears that the majority of expedient tools were manufactured from proximal flakes or even angular shatter. After prehistoric flintknappers conducted a core or bipolar reduction, they used the pressure flaking technique to retouch and modify edges of the flake. To improve our methodological approach regarding lithic materials recovered from these contexts, I examine debitage from the perspective of both formal (projectile points and bifacial tools) and expedient tools and use the results to reconstruct tool-stone procurement patterns.

In addition to methodological weaknesses, archaeologists have not fruitfully developed research questions with respect to sociopolitical organization that uses lithic data. A variety of topics have been addressed using lithic data sets from prehistoric agricultural societies, including use-wear and residue analysis of flake and bifacial tools (Eisele et al. 1995; Feidel 1996; Hyland et al. 1990; Kimura et al. 2001; Vaughn 1985), retouch tools (Andrefsky 2006; Clarkson 2002; Kuhn 1990; Shott and Sillitoe 2005), and tool-stone procurement patterns (Arakawa 2012; Harro 1997; Walsh 1998). There has been some success investigating the functions of stone tools; however, tool-stone procurement patterns can be further explored by addressing sociopolitical organization from the perspective of tool manufacturing.

This research attempts to demonstrate how tool-stone procurement patterns from lithic data can unravel sociopolitical organization using a case study from the central Mesa Verde region of the American Southwest (figure 7.1). To achieve the goal, this chapter focuses on three spatial scales: residential, community, and region. Here, a residential site is the smallest unit of scale, with the Yellow Jacket Pueblo site (YJP) representing that unit. The YJP is the largest Pueblo III component site in the central Mesa Verde region, containing approximately 700 rooms with an isolated tower complex located in the northeast portion of the site (Varien and Wilshusen 2002). A community is defined here as many households that regularly engage in face-to-face interaction and share social and natural resources; communities ordinarily include multiple sites (Kolb and Snead 1997; Murdock 1949; Varien 1999: 19). The region is the largest scale used, and here it encompasses all areas of the central Mesa Verde region (figure 7.1). I argue that tool-stone procurement patterns in

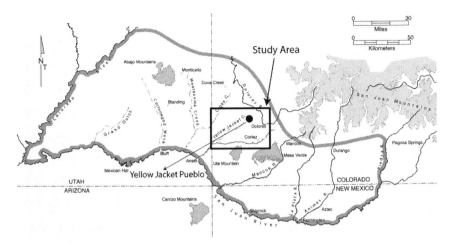

FIGURE 7.1. *Study area of the central Mesa Verde region (adapted by permission of the Crow Canyon Archaeological Center)*

conjunction with residential-, community-, and regional-level scales of analyses allow us to unravel sociopolitical organization, particularly gendered lithics, territoriality, and the earliest stage of the migration process.

METHODS

Both mass and metric debitage analyses are used to address sociopolitical organization. This analysis began using mass analysis and recording raw material type, size-grade, absence or presence of cortex, and weight. Subsequently, a metric analysis was conducted that recorded maximum length, width, thickness, weight, and amount of cortex for debitage recovered from well-recorded contexts (i.e., floors and middens) (see Arakawa 2006 for more detailed information regarding methods of debitage analysis).

For the projectile point analysis, this study focuses on two attributes. One attribute analysis focuses on raw material type, and the other involves the typology of each projectile point. On the basis of the Crow Canyon Archaeological Center lithic classification scheme (Ortman et al. 2005: 8-2), twenty-five different raw material types are used for the manufacture of projectile points in the central Mesa Verde region. These different raw material types can be further classified into local, semi-local, and non-local materials (Arakawa 2000). After raw material type was identified, the typology of each projectile point was assigned. Since the majority of projectile points recovered from the central Mesa Verde region are manufactured expediently and appear to be small side- or corner-notched points dating to 900–1300 CE, I only used these side- and corner-notched points as the representation of stone tools manufactured and used by agriculturalists in the region.

CASE STUDY
Gendered Procurement

One line of inquiry that uses lithic assemblages to examine sociopolitical organization is how men and women were involved in the acquisition of stone tools in ancestral Pueblo society. Beginning at the residential level, I examine lithic assemblages recovered from Yellow Jacket Pueblo from 1050 to 1300 CE (Arakawa 2000, 2013; Varien and Wilshusen 2002) to show that there were gendered differences in acquisition of stone tools. To support this hypothesis, I review ethnographic documents and evaluate how these observations are applicable to lithic data from YJP. This includes a discussion of Pueblo cultural geography and how space is conceived as gendered. I compare lithic data from YJP to the ethnographic model to show how tool-stone procurement was a gendered activity. I argue that tool-stone procurement of specific types of raw materials reflects different acquisition patterns by men and women. This is illustrated by examining raw material types used for manufacturing projectile points and food-processing tools, which includes manos and metates for grinding food and peckingstones that were used to roughen the surfaces of these grinding tools (Adams 2002: 152–153).

Ethnographic Record

In the modern Pueblo world, all human and non-human beings are defined and represented by a central place (Ortiz 1969, 1972: 142). Ortiz (1969) explains the cardinal dimensions of the Tewa world and suggests that the world near the village, with the fields, crops, and houses, is the feminine world, whereas the world at the edges, with the mountains, snowpack, rain clouds, and game animals, is the masculine world (figure 7.2). Some ethnographic data examine this concept of landscape in greater detail. For example, the pueblo of Ohkay Owingeh classifies its physical world into three concentric spheres. The first sphere (the village, farmlands, and other lowlands near the village) is defined and occupied by women; women know and control the knowledge of important family practices within this sphere. The second sphere lies beyond the first and is the domain of both men and

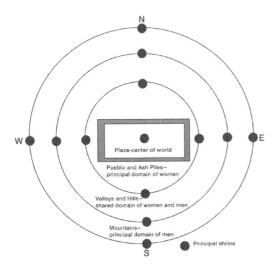

FIGURE 7.2. *The Tewa world (adapted from Anschuetz et al. 2002; Ortiz 1969). From Arakawa 2013. Reprinted by permission of the publisher (Taylor and Francis Ltd., http://www.tandfonline.com).*

women who share knowledge of the hills, mesas, and washes. The outermost, third sphere is composed of distant hunting-and-gathering areas that are purely the domain of men (figure 7.2; Anschuetz et al. 2002). In the Santa Clara Pueblo, Arnon and Hill (1979: 303) noted that while farming was done mostly by men, with women's assistance in communal tasks, women primarily worked in the household—caring for children, preparing food, and making pottery. Hill (1982: 162–164) found Santa Clara men engaged in tasks mostly in the field and Santa Clara women in and around the home. In sum, these ethnographies reveal distinct men's and women's domains and their differential use of space.

Lowell (1991) compiled information about the organization of men's and women's labor at Hopi and Zuni from early Spanish documents and from ethnographies that date to the late nineteenth and early twentieth centuries. Lowell found a difference in the ways men and women used dwellings, kivas, and the village. Women conducted most food preparation activities in dwellings, including food storage, corn grinding, cooking, and serving. The domestic dwellings were effectively the women's domain (Beaglehole 1937; Bunzel 1929; Cushing 1920, 1979; Eggan 1950; Hammond and Rey 1940; Hough 1915; James 1919; Lowell 1991: 452; Powell 1972; Stephen 1936; Stevenson 1904; Titiev 1992 [1944]). In contrast, men generally brought food, stone, and wood to the dwellings (Beaglehole 1937; Benedict 1934; Eggan 1950; Hough 1915; James 1919; Mindeleff 1891; Parsons 1917; Simmons 1942; Titiev 1992 [1944]). According to Lowell (1991: 452), "Their [men's] primary loci of economic activities are outside of the village proper, in the corn field, woods, and quarries." At Hopi and Zuni Pueblo, men spent far more time in activities outside the village proper than did women (Beaglehole 1937; Bunzel 1929; Eggan 1950; Hough 1915; James 1919; Lowell 1991: 459; Mindeleff 1891; Simmons 1942; Stevenson 1904; Titiev 1992 [1944]). Men's activity areas inside the village were limited and tended to occur in specific spaces.

These ethnographic accounts bring several points to bear. First and not surprising, these studies detail how Pueblo people conceptualized space in gendered terms, such that the area within the village was female and areas distant from the village were male. In addition, these studies indicate that there was a gendered division of labor. Women were in charge of food processing activities, most of which occurred inside the residential site. In contrast, hunting large game was mostly done by men at locations outside the village.

Tool-Stone Procurement in the Residential Scale

To address gendered differences in the production and use of stone tools at YJP, I investigate the abundance of two different raw materials—Morrison rocks (figure 7.3; Arakawa 2000, 2013) and Cretaceous Dakota/Burro Canyon silicified sandstone (Kdb SS; figure 7.4). Over 40 percent of projectile points were manufactured from Kdb SS, while more than 90 percent of peckingstones were made of Morrison rocks. I focus on projectile points made of Kdb SS as a reliable indicator of men's activities, while peckingstones made of Morrison rocks serve as an indicator of women's activities and space. Several archaeologists (Hruby 1988: 354–356; Lightfoot and Etzkorn 1993; Stevenson 1984) have asserted that lithic raw materials in the central Mesa Verde region are distributed ubiquitously across this landscape. To determine the validity of this statement, I conducted a survey of 16 km² in the upper portion of Yellow Jacket Canyon to investigate the lithology and distribution of raw materials (figure 7.3; Arakawa 2000). During this survey, I examined all exposures of the Morrison Formation to identify raw materials suitable for stone tool manufacture. Raw materials that were suitable for knapping were examined with a hand lens; and color, mineral composition, and texture were recorded. I also recorded the presence of culturally modified materials, including proximal and angular shatter flakes, cores, and other artifacts.

MORRISON FORMATION RAW MATERIALS (KJM AND KJC)

The geology of Yellow Jacket Canyon is typical of many other canyons in the Four Corners area. The distribution of knappable Morrison Formation rocks is illustrated in figure 7.3, which shows that the rocks are widely distributed in

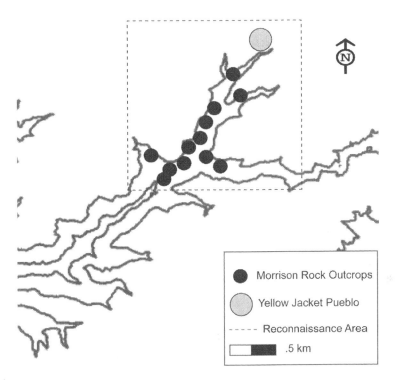

FIGURE 7.3. *Map showing the reconnaissance in the upper portions of Yellow Jacket Canyon, including Morrison rock only around Yellow Jacket Pueblo. From Arakawa 2013. Reprinted by permission of the publisher (Taylor and Francis Ltd., http://www.tandfonline.com).*

the canyon. Artifacts such as cores, hammerstones, and pottery were present at some but not all of the areas where suitable material occurred.

Raw material from the Morrison Formation is the most abundant lithic resource at sites in the region. At YJP, more than 90 percent of the cores and 80 percent of peckingstones were made of Morrison Formation materials. More than 90 percent of the debitage was from Morrison Formation rocks. Wide availability was documented in the portion of Yellow Jacket Canyon that I surveyed, and this ubiquitous distribution appears to be typical of other canyons in which the Morrison Formation is exposed. The results of this lithic raw material survey indicate that Morrison Formation lithic materials were directly procured from areas nearby most occupied sites in the region (e.g., within 2 km). Thus raw materials for peckingstones came from local, easily accessible sources.

DAKOTA/BURRO CANYON SILICIFIED SANDSTONE (KDB SS)

Cretaceous Dakota/Burro Canyon silicified sandstone (Kdb SS) raw materials are not nearly as ubiquitous as Morrison Formation raw materials; however, the Kdb SS material was prized for stone tool manufacture. Kdb SS material was the most popular raw material for the manufacture of projectile points in the region and was the raw material most readily available. More than 40 percent of projectile points were made of this material; other raw materials used to produce projectile points include silicified sandstone, agate/chalcedony, Burro Canyon chert, Morrison chert, obsidian, unknown chert or siltstone, and non-local chert (Arakawa 2015). Morrison chert is the only material that was easily accessible; all other local raw materials used for projectile points were scarce in the central Mesa Verde region, and many of the raw materials were non-local and were transported from a great distance. It is likely that residents of villages in the central Mesa Verde region traveled long distances to obtain high-quality raw materials to make projectile points.

To establish the abundance of material types, I conducted a lithic source survey to locate ninety-four sources of Kdb SS. Fifty-three of the ninety-four quarries (56%) contained the Kdb SS material (Arakawa 2006: 360–365). Figure 7.4 shows the distribution of Kdb SS quarries in this study area. At most of the quarries I observed debitage, cores, tested cobbles, and bifacial thinning flakes—all evidence that ancestral Pueblo people knew of these quarries, tested the raw material, and obtained raw material from them by direct or indirect procurement.

Figure 7.4 shows that the Kdb SS resources were not only fewer in number than Morrison rocks but also unevenly distributed. To procure Kdb SS materials, Pueblo people had to travel beyond the immediate proximity of the settlement. For most residential sites, people would have had to have traveled more than 7 km to obtain these materials; this corresponds roughly to the 7 km and 18 km catchment zones discussed by Varien (1999: 153–155) where people gathered most of their wild food and non-food resources. This contrasts with the procurement pattern for Morrison Formation materials discussed above, which could be found in the immediate vicinity of most settlements.

On the basis of the results of tool-stone procurement patterns and surveys of local quarries, the different strategies for procuring high-quality (Kdb SS) versus low-quality (Morrison rocks) materials are evident. The use of different raw material types is also related to different tool types, such as projectile points and peckingstones. Because of the extent to which tool-stone procurement patterns corresponded to men's and women's tool manufacture and use, the study of those patterns enables us to address the topic of gender using lithic data.

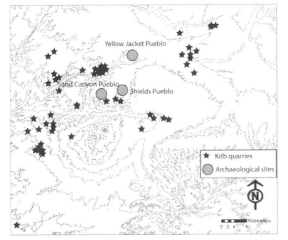

FIGURE 7.4. *Map showing all three pueblos and outcrops/quarries of Kdb SS. From Arakawa 2013. Reprinted by permission of the publisher (Taylor and Francis Ltd., http://www.tandfonline.com).*

Territoriality

Territoriality is inferred through social, economic, or ecological restrictions on resource use that are imposed by individuals or groups on other individuals and groups. But what might lithic raw material procurement patterns in the central Mesa Verde region indicate about territoriality from 600 to 1300 CE? To understand how territoriality changed through time, I reanalyzed debitage from seventy excavated sites in the central Mesa Verde region from the years 600 to 1280 CE to focus on the community-level scale (Arakawa 2006, 2012). As discussed in the previous section, results from ninety-four recorded quarry sites in this region were used to understand how far people traveled to obtain lithic raw material types in each community.

To reconstruct and interpret the development of territoriality through time, I used Renfrew's (1977) distance-decay model to investigate the use of debitage data in the study area. On the basis of that model, the proportional presence of certain objects decreases when the distance from the source increases. Renfrew (1977) used two zones (contact and fall-off) to describe the distance-decay model. The contact zone is within about a 200 km radius, while outside of that radius the proportion of raw materials exponentially decreases. In the central Mesa Verde region, almost all lithic raw materials were procured close to habitation sites. Thus I expect that tool-stone procurement behaviors in this region were within the contact zone (200 km). In the distance-decay model, two analyses, regression analysis and R-squares, were used to understand the development of territoriality through time. I hypothesize that people who live closer to a quarry should use a larger proportion of that raw material. Thus a regression line with the proportion of that raw material on the y-axis and the cost-distance on the x-axis should show a negative slope when these valuables are regressed for a number of sites. When there is a strong negative slope, this means people have a strong tendency to use a raw material close to their residence. The size of the R-square indicates variability in tool-stone procurement patterns across the landscape. In other words, a high R-square value indicates that within the region, people behaved differently in regard to their stone tool procurement practices. When everyone is similarly sensitive to the cost-distance relationship, the R-square value tends to be high because all sites fall near the regression line. If this is not the case, then a high degree of trade, interactions, or frequent mobility must be inferred.

To reconstruct how far people actually traveled to obtain their raw materials, I used a cost-distance (energy-expenditure) and cost-weight analysis in ArcGIS 10.0 with Spatial Analyst. The cost-distance analysis calculates a proxy for how much energy one needs to expend to procure certain raw material types. A cost-weight analysis calculates approximate energy-expenditure values by knowing the minimum distance from point X to point Y. A major advantage of using the energy-expenditure values (or cost-distances) is that they may better reflect walking costs in this mesa and canyon landscape rather than Euclidian straight-line distances.

The calculation of minimum energy expended between a habitation site and the nearest quarry was conducted using the cost-weight procedure. Although there is a shortest-path function in spatial analysis, it does not calculate and identify which quarry site is closest to a habitation. In the cost-weight analysis, each habitation site was selected, and I ran the cost-weight function for all seventy existing excavated site collections. Next, all habitation and quarry sites were entered into the model as a beginning point and destination. To identify the nearest quarry from a habitation site, the Extract Values to Point function was used. Then the habitation point features were input, as were all quarry sites for each raw material; next, the habitation sites were input as a raster layer. Extracted values represent the minimum accumulated energy value (energy-expenditure value) for the quarry sites and for each raw material type.

The results of this analysis are shown in table 7.1. They indicate that the early Pueblo III (EPIII) period shows high standard deviation (standard slope estimates [stb]) with strong R-square values compared to the results from other periods. This suggests that ancestral Pueblo people in each community expended less energy for tool-stone procurement from 1140 to 1225 CE (EPIII). During the early 1200s CE, approximately 15,000–25,000

TABLE 7.1. Summary of the stb (standardized slope estimates) from the Basketmaker III (BMIII) to late Pueblo III periods. Stb values with correlation coefficients (r2) > 0.3 are shown in bold. The results from the early Pueblo III (EPIII) period (underlined) indicate high stb with strong r2 values, compared to the results of other periods.

Material Types CE	BMIII (Basketmaker III) 600–725	PI (Pueblo I) 725–920	EPII (Early Pueblo II) 920–1060	LPII (Late Pueblo II) 1060–1140	EPIII (Early Pueblo III) 1140–1225	LPIII (Late Pueblo III) 1225–1280
Chalcedony	−0.244	−0.233	−0.223	−0.279	<u>−0.374</u>	−0.226
Kdbq (Cretaceous Dakota/Burro Canyon quartzite)	−0.255	−0.068	**−0.418**	−0.176	<u>−0.523</u>	**−0.415**
Kbc (Cretaceous Burro Canyon chert)	**−0.608**	−0.323	−0.232	**−0.426**	<u>−0.328</u>	−0.263
Morrison	**−0.424**	−0.292	**−0.816**	**−0.765**	<u>−0.900</u>	**−0.360**
Jmbc (Jurassic Morrison Brushy Basin chert)	**0.475**	−0.207	−0.262	**0.456**	<u>0.441</u>	**0.567**
Igneous	**−0.861**	**−0.661**	**−0.954**	**−0.860**	−0.765	**−0.795**

people are thought to have inhabited this portion of the central Mesa Verde region (Schwindt et al. 2016; Varien et al. 2007). Consequently, the population exceeded 20,000 people between 1225 and 1260 CE; then the population size declined to approximately 10,000 after 1260 CE (Schwindt et al. 2016; Varien et al. 2007). The early 1200s constituted the period when the ancestral Pueblo people began to aggregate, living in a large village with more than 200–700 rooms. The tool-stone procurement patterns indicate that the ancestral Pueblo people also experienced constrained or restricted territories around the early 1200s CE. The development of territoriality or land-tenure systems around the early 1200s CE is a unique phenomenon in both human prehistory and history worldwide because population size increased exponentially during this period (Varien et al. 2007), although ancestral Pueblo people's mobility declined. As this study of territoriality using debitage data demonstrates, tool-stone procurement patterns through time allow us to tackle the topic of sociopolitical organization, particularly a sense of territoriality at the community-level scale of analysis.

Migration Process

In a regional-scale analysis, I focus on the period just prior to depopulation in the central Mesa Verde region, from 1225 to 1280 CE. During the late 1200s CE, approximately 10,000 people would have migrated out from this study area to other areas in the American Southwest (Ortman et al. 2007; Schwindt et al. 2016; Varien et al. 2007). These include areas in Hopi, Zuni, Acoma, Laguna, and the northern Rio Grande region. Archaeologists have identified and argued for various destination areas. For example, Ortman (2012) argues that many of the central Mesa Verde residents migrated into the northern Rio Grande region based on his studies of linguistic evidence, human cranium analysis, and other archaeological evidence.

To understand the migration process during this period, I focused on obsidian procurement patterns using the results of X-ray fluorescence (XRF) analysis (Arakawa et al. 2011). Shackley (2005a) has identified more than twenty obsidian sources using XRF analysis in the American Southwest. XRF is a nondestructive method of chemical analysis based on the use of high-energy X-rays. On the basis of his study, ancestral Pueblo people in the central Mesa Verde region procured obsidian from three major areas: San Francisco Peak (Government Mountains) in Arizona, Mount Taylor, and the Jemez Mountains in New Mexico; there are no obsidian quarries in the central Mesa Verde region.

I compiled obsidian samples from twenty different assemblages and sent them to the University of California, Berkeley, for XRF analysis (Shackley

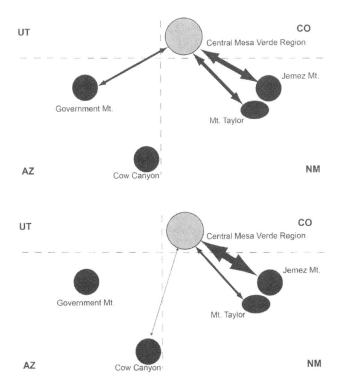

FIGURE 7.5. *Interaction and exchange systems for obsidian connecting the central Mesa Verde region to other portions of the Southwest. Width of lines suggests degree of interaction (Arakawa et al. 2011). Reprinted by permission of Cambridge University Press.*

1995, 1998, 2005b, 2008). In my dataset, 274 pieces of obsidian were analyzed. Eighty-eight items were tools, such as modified flakes, projectile points, and bifaces; the remainder were small pieces of debitage. The XRF analyses showed that 245 of the 274 (89.4 percent) obsidian items in our dataset were derived from Jemez Mountain sources.

To interpret the obsidian data, I separated a roughly 700-year interval (600–1280 CE) into two broad sub-periods—600–1020 CE and 1020–1280 CE—on the basis of the rise and fall of two population cycles (small villages and large, aggregated villages). The top panel of figure 7.5 shows interaction and exchange from various areas, including Government Mountain, Mount Taylor, and the Jemez Mountains, with the majority of obsidian originating from the Jemez Mountains during the years 600–1020 CE. The bottom panel of figure

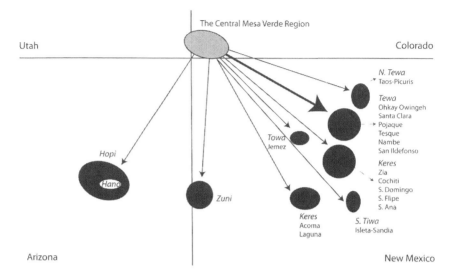

FIGURE 7.6. *Possible destination areas by the ancestral Pueblo people in the central Mesa Verde region. The thickness indicates the most likely destinations based on the results of obsidian studies. Reprinted by permission of Cambridge University Press.*

7.5 shows use of a single source in the Jemez Mountains (about 99 percent) for the period 1020–1280 CE.

How do these results inform us about migration processes? Figure 7.6 shows the possible destination areas of ancestral Pueblo people in the central Mesa Verde region after 1280 CE. These circles also indicate modern Pueblo groups based on historical and language diversity. After 1280 CE, residents of the central Mesa Verde region depopulated the area. Many archaeologists have argued that people in the Mesa Verde region migrated to a number of different areas. However, as discussed in the previous section, Ortman (2012) argues that many people emigrated to the northern Rio Grande region. The result of the obsidian study supports his claim, since about 99 percent of obsidian tools and debitage can be traced back to the Jemez Mountains from 1020 to 1280 CE.

To interpret the results of obsidian studies I use migration theory, focusing on the earliest stages of the migration process. In his long-distance migration theory, Anthony (1990) defines four important terms—scouting, return migration, migration streams, and leapfrogging—used in a sequence that can be employed to reconstruct migration processes. Scouting refers to people traveling and obtaining important information about a destination area. Return

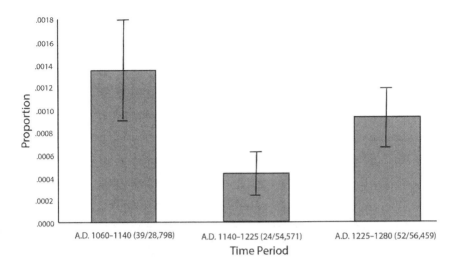

FIGURE 7.7. *Frequency of obsidian artifacts in total chipped stone assemblages, by time period (Arakawa et al. 2011). Error bars represent two standard errors of the proportion (> 95% confidence intervals). Sample data are the number of obsidian artifacts divided by the total number of chipped stone artifacts assigned to a raw material category in the Crow Canyon Archaeological Center database (January 2009). Reprinted by permission of Cambridge University Press.*

migration refers to scouts bringing back important information related to migration. Migration streams relate to the number of people who move from one place to another by way of a very specific route, and leapfrogging is migration not as a direct movement but rather by people jumping over one place to settle in another.

I hypothesize that if scouts bring back information about the local environment, climate, and people in a destination area, then we would expect to see an increased flow of certain objects between the two areas, possibly taken as tokens of the destination's attractiveness. Figure 7.7 illustrates obsidian importation patterns from 1060 to 1280 CE. It shows that the proportion of obsidian was very high during the Chaco period (1060–1140 CE). This is expected because when Chaco Canyon flourished from 900 to 1140 CE, frequent trade and interaction were common. Another interesting pattern seen from this analysis is that although the proportion of obsidian decreased during the years 1140 to 1250 CE, the proportion of obsidian increased just prior to depopulation of the area (1225–1280 CE). In addition, when we compare

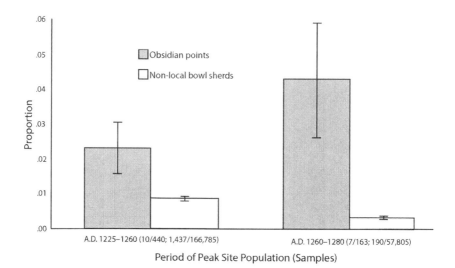

FIGURE 7.8. *Proportion of obsidian points and non-local bowl sherds through time (Arakawa et al. 2011). Error bars represent one standard error of the proportion (> 68% confidence intervals). Sites and obsidian data sources for each group are 1225–1260 CE: Shields Pueblo (Till et al. 2015), Yellow Jacket Pueblo (Ortman 2003b: table 28), Albert Porter Pueblo (CCAC Research Database, January 2009); 1260–1280 CE: Sand Canyon Pueblo (Till and Ortman 2007: table 61), Castle Rock Pueblo (Ortman 2000: table 25), Woods Canyon Pueblo (Ortman 2003a: table 37); bowl sherd data from these sites from the Crow Canyon Archaeological Center database (January 2009). Local bowl sherds are of Mesa Verde White Ware; non-local bowl sherds are of San Juan Red Ware, Tsegi Organge Ware, White Mountain Red Ware, Cibola White Ware, Tusayan White Ware, and Chuska White Ware. Reprinted by permission of Cambridge University Press.*

the post-Chaco period and the period just prior to depopulation in the central Mesa Verde region, we can see that the proportion of obsidian imported increased during the latter period (figure 7.7). Figure 7.8 compares proportions of non-local pottery and obsidian in two time periods (1225–1260 CE and 1260–1280 CE) from three large aggregated sites: Yellow Jacket, Shields, and Woods Canyon Pueblos (www.crowcanyon.org) during the late Pueblo III period. Interestingly, during the period of aggregation and increasing population (1225–1250 CE), a relatively low frequency of non-local pottery and obsidian was imported into this region compared to the subsequent period (just prior to depopulation of the region). When we compare these two time periods, it is obvious that the proportion of obsidian as finished tools increased in the period just prior to depopulation of the region.

These obsidian studies indicate an increased flow of obsidian artifacts just prior to depopulation in the central Mesa Verde region. Obsidian procurement patterns reflect interaction between and migration of residents of the central Mesa Verde and northern Rio Grande regions, and the increased flow of obsidian artifacts indicates the earliest stages in the migration process. Obsidian tool-stone procurement pattern studies allow us to investigate how people in two different regions interacted, traded, and moved and also to address sociopolitical organization at a regional scale.

CONCLUSION

On the basis of these three case studies in a Neolithic agricultural society in the central Mesa Verde region, archaeologists can use the material record, particularly lithic data, to contribute information regarding sociopolitical organization at multiple spatial scales (e.g., resident, community, and region). The study of tool-stone procurement patterns is indeed one effective way to address this. I recommend that archaeologists consider the following: (1) lithic data, particularly debitage collections, can be massive in agricultural societies, and the combination of mass and metric analyses can offer a thorough and efficient way of addressing topics related to sociopolitical organization; (2) tool-stone procurement patterns of both local and non-local materials can reveal how people structured their landscape and behaviors and can minimize the constraints of applying well-established lithic reduction approaches to the debitage dataset; and (3) archaeologists can further develop research questions regarding sociopolitical organization using lithic data, such as gendered lithics, territoriality, and migration processes.

REFERENCES

Abbott, David R. 2009. "Extensive and Long-Term Specialization: Hohokam Ceramic Production in the Phoenix Basin, Arizona." *American Antiquity* 74: 531–557.

Adams, Jenny L. 2002. *Ground Stone Analysis: A Technological Approach*. Salt Lake City: University of Utah Press.

Ahler, Stanley A. 1989. "Mass Analysis of Flaking Debris: Studying the Forest Rather than the Trees." In *Alternative Approaches to Lithic Analysis*, ed. Donald O. Henry, and George H. Odell, 85–118. Archaeological Papers of the American

Anthropological Association 1. Washington, DC: American Anthropological Association.

Anderson, Patricia C. 1992. "Experimental Cultivation, Harvest, and Threshing of Wild Cereals and Their Relevance for Interpreting the Use of Epipaleolithic and Neolithic Artefacts." In *Prehisoire de l'agriculture: Nouvelles Approches Experimentals et Ethnographiques*, ed. Patricia C. Anderson. Monographie du CRA 6. Paris: Editions du CNRS.

Andrefsky, William, Jr. 2006. *Lithics: Macroscopic Approaches to Analysis*. 2nd ed. Cambridge: Cambridge University Press.

Andrefsky, William, Jr. 2007. "The Application and Misapplication of Mass Analysis in Lithic Debitage Studies." *Journal of Archaeological Science* 34: 392–402.

Anschuetz, Kurt F., T. J. Ferguson, Harris Francis, Klara B. Kelley, and Cherie L. Scheick. 2002. *That Place People Talk About: The Petroglyph National Monument Ethnographic Landscape Report*. Albuquerque, NM: Petroglyph National Monument, National Park Service.

Anthony, David W. 1990. "Migration in Archaeology: The Baby and the Bathwater." *American Anthropologist* 92: 895–914.

Arakawa, Fumiyasu. 2000. "Lithic Analysis of Yellow Jacket Pueblo as a Tool for Understanding and Visualizing Women's Roles in Procuring, Utilizing, and Making Stone Tools." Master's thesis, University of Idaho, Moscow.

Arakawa, Fumiyasu. 2006. "Lithic Raw Material Procurement and the Social Landscape in the Central Mesa Verde Region, AD 600–1300." PhD dissertation, Washington State University, Pullman.

Arakawa, Fumiyasu. 2012. "Tool-Stone Procurement in the Mesa Verde Core Region through Time." In *Emergence and Collapse of Early Villages Models of Central Mesa Verde Archaeology*, ed. Timothy A. Kohler and Mark D. Varien. Berkeley: University of California Press.

Arakawa, Fumiyasu. 2013. "Gendered Analysis of Lithics from the Central Mesa Verde Region." *Kiva* 78: 279–312.

Arakawa, Fumiyasu. 2015. "Artifact Chapters." In *Albert Porter Pueblo Site Report*, ed. Susan Ryan, 120–282. Cortez, CO: Crow Canyon Archaeological Center. Accessed July 31, 2018. http://crowcanyon.org/ResearchReports/AlbertPorter/Albert_Porter_Pueblo_Final.pdf.

Arakawa, Fumiyasu, Scott G. Ortman, M. Steve Shackley, and Andrew Duff. 2011. "Obsidian Evidence of Interaction and Migration from the Mesa Verde Region, Southwest Colorado." *American Antiquity* 76: 773–795.

Arnold, Dean E. 1985. *Ceramic Theory and Cultural Process*. Cambridge: Cambridge University Press.

Arnon, N. S., and W. W. Hill. 1979. "Santa Clara Pueblo." In *Handbook of North American Indians*, vol. 9: *Southwest*, ed. A. Ortiz, 296–307. Washington, DC: Smithsonian Institution.

Beaglehole, Ernest. 1937. "Notes on Hopi Economic Life." *Yale University Publications in Anthropology* 15: 1–88.

Benedict, Ruth. 1934. *Patterns of Culture*. Boston: Houghton Mifflin.

Bleed, Peter. 1986. "The Optimal Design of Hunting Weapons: Maintainability or Reliability." *American Antiquity* 51 (4): 737–747.

Bordes, Francois, and Don E. Crabtree. 1969. "The Corbiac Blade Technique and Other Experiments." *Tebiwa* 12: 1–21.

Bradley, Bruce A. 1975. "Lithic Reduction Sequences: A Glossary and Discussion." In *Lithic Technology: Making and Using Stone Tools*, ed. Earl Swanson, 5–14. The Hague: Mouton.

Bradley, Bruce A. 1976. "Experimental Lithic Technology, with Special Reference to the Middle Paleolithic." PhD dissertation, University of Cambridge, UK.

Bunzel, Ruth L. 1929. "Introduction to Zuni Ceremonialism." *Bureau of American Ethnology Annual Report* 47: 467–544.

Clarkson, Chris. 2002. "An Index of Invasiveness for the Measurement of Unifacial and Bifacial Retouch: A Theoretical, Experimental, and Archaeological Verification." *Journal of Archaeological Science* 29: 65–75.

Crabtree, Don E. 1972. *An Introduction to Flintknapping*. Occasional Papers 28. Pocatello: Idaho State Museum.

Crown, Patricia L. 2000. *Women and Men in the Prehispanic Southwest: Labor, Power, and Prestige*. Santa Fe, NM: School of American Research Press.

Cushing, F. H. 1920. *Zuni Breadstuff*. Indian Notes and Monographs 8. New York: Museum of the American Indian Heye Foundation.

Cushing, Frank H. 1979. *Zuni: Selected Writings of Frank Hamilton Cushing*, ed. J. Green. Lincoln: University of Nebraska Press.

Eggan, F. 1950. *Social Organization of the Western Pueblos*. Chicago: University of Chicago Press.

Eisele, J. A., D. D. Fowler, G. Haynes, and R. A. Lewis. 1995. "Survival and Detection of Blood Residues on Stone Tools." *Antiquity* 69: 36–46.

Feidel, Stuart J. 1996. "Blood from Stones? Some Methodological and Interpretive Problems in Blood Residue Analysis." *Journal of Archaeological Science* 23: 139–147.

Flenniken, J. Jeffery, and Anan W. Raymond. 1986. "Morphological Projectile Point Typology: Replication Experimentation and Technological Analysis." *American Antiquity* 51: 603–614.

Flenniken, J. Jeffery, and Philip J. Wilke. 1989. "Typology, Technology, and Chronology of Great Basin Dart Points." *American Anthropologist* 91: 603–614.

Frison, George C. 1968. "A Functional Analysis of Certain Chipped Stone Tools." *American Antiquity* 33: 149–158.

Glowacki, Donna. 2015. *Living and Leaving: A Social History of Regional Depopulation in Thirteenth-Century Mesa Verde*. Tucson: University of Arizona Press.

Hammond, George P., and Agapito Rey. 1940. *Narratives of the Coronado Expedition 1540–1542*. Albuquerque: University of New Mexico Press.

Harro, Douglas R. 1997. "Patterns of Lithic Raw Material Procurement on the Pajarito Plateau, New Mexico." MA thesis, Washington State University, Pullman.

Hill, W. W. 1982. *An Ethnography of Santa Clara Pueblo New Mexico*. Albuquerque: University of New Mexico Press.

Hough, W. 1915. *The Hopi Indians*. Cedar Rapids, IA: Torch Press.

Hruby, T. H. 1988. "Dolores Anasazi Household and Interhousehold Cluster Toolkits: Technological Organization in the Transition from Hamlets to Villages." In *Dolores Archaeological Program, Supporting Studies: Additive and Reductive Technologies*, ed. Eric Blinman, Carl J. Phagan, and Richard H. Wilshusen, 283–362. Denver: Engineering and Research Center, Bureau of Reclamation, US Department of the Interior.

Hyland, D. C., J. M. Tersak, J. M. Adovasio, and M. I. Siegel. 1990. "Identification of the Species of Origin of Residual Blood on Lithic Material." *American Antiquity* 55 (1): 104–112.

James, George W. 1919. *The Indians of the Painted Desert Region, Wallapais, Havasupais*. Boston: Little, Brown.

Kardulias, P. N., and R. W. Yerkes. 1996. "Microwear and Metric Analysis of Threshing Sledge Flints from Greece and Cyprus." *Journal of Archaeological Science* 23: 657–666.

Kimura, Birgitta, Steven A. Brandt, Bruce L. Hardy, and William W. Hauswirth. 2001. "Analysis of DNA from Ethnoarchaeological Stone Scrapers." *Journal of Archaeological Science* 28: 45–53.

Kolb, Michael J., and James E. Snead. 1997. "It's a Small World After All: Comparative Analyses of Community Organization in Archaeology." *American Antiquity* 62: 609–628.

Kuhn, Steven L. 1990. "A Geometric Index of Reduction for Unifacial Stone Tools." *Journal of Archaeological Science* 17: 585–593.

Kuhn, Steven L. 1991. "'Unpacking' Reduction: Lithic Raw Material Economy in the Mousterian of West-Central Italy." *Journal of Anthropological Archaeology* 10: 76–106.

Lightfoot, Ricky R., and Mary C. Etzkorn. 1993. *The Duckfoot Site: Descriptive Archaeology*. Occasional Paper 3. Cortez, CO: Crow Canyon Archaeological Center.

Lowell, J. C. 1991. "Reflections of Sex Roles in the Archaeological Record: Insights from Hopi and Zuni Ethnographic Data." In *The Archaeology of Gender*, ed. D. Wade and N. D. Willows, 452–461. Alberta: University of Calgary.

Mills, Barbara J., and Patricia L. Crown. 1995. *Ceramic Production in the American Southwest*. Tucson: University of Arizona Press.

Mindeleff, Victor. 1891. "A Study of Pueblo Architecture: Tusayan and Cibola." Eighth Annual Report of the Bureau of Ethnology to the Secretary of the Smithsonian Institution 1886–1887.

Murdock, George P. 1949. *Social Structure*. New York: Macmillan.

Ortiz, A. 1969. *The Tewa World: Space, Time, Being, and Becoming in a Pueblo Society*. Chicago: University of Chicago Press.

Ortiz, A. 1972. "Ritual Drama and the Pueblo World View." In *New Perspectives on the Pueblos*, ed. A. Ortiz, 135–161. Albuquerque: University of New Mexico Press.

Ortman, Scott G. 2000. "Castle Rock Artifacts." Crow Canyon Archaeological Center. Accessed February 2016. http://www.crowcanyon.org/research/research.asp.

Ortman, Scott G. 2003a. "Woods Canyon Pueblo Artifacts." Crow Canyon Archaeological Center. Accessed February 2016. http://www.crowcanyon.org/research/research.asp.

Ortman, Scott G. 2003b. "Yellow Jacket Pueblo Artifacts." Crow Canyon Archaeological Center. Accessed February 2016. http://www.crowcanyon.org/research/research.asp.

Ortman, Scott G. 2012. *Wind from the North: Tewa Origins and Historical Anthropology*. Salt Lake City: University of Utah Press.

Ortman, Scott G., Erin L. Baxter, Carole L. Graham, G. Robin Lyle, Lew W. Matis, Jamie A. Merewether, R. David Satterwhite, and Jonathan D. Till. 2005. "The Crow Canyon Archaeological Center Laboratory Manual, Version 1." Crow Canyon Archaeology Center. http://www.crowcanyon.org/researchreports/labmanual/laboratorymanual.pdf.

Ortman, Scott G., Mark D. Varien, and T. Lee Gripp. 2007. "Empirical Bayesian Methods for Archaeological Survey Data: An Application from the Mesa Verde Region." *American Antiquity* 72: 241–272.

Parsons, Elsie Clews. 1917. "Notes on Zuni." *American Anthropological Association Memoirs* 4 (1): 151–327.

Patterson, Leland W. 1990. "Characteristics of Bifacial-Reduction Flake-Size Distribution." *American Antiquity* 55: 550–558.

Powell, John W. 1972. *The Hopi Villages*. Palmer Lake, CO: Filter Press.

Renfrew, Colin. 1977. "Alternative Models for Exchange and Spatial Distribution." In *Exchange Systems in Prehistory*, ed. Timothy K. Earle and J. E. Ericson, 71–90. New York: Academic.

Schwindt, Dylan M., R. Kyle Bocinsky, Scott G. Ortman, Donna M. Glowacki, Mark D. Varien, and Timothy A. Kohler. 2016. "The Social Consequences of Climate Change in the Central Mesa Verde Region." *American Antiquity* 81 (1): 74–96.

Shackley, M. Steven. 1998. "Geochemical Differentiation and Prehistoric Procurement of Obsidian in the Mount Taylor Volcanic Field, Northwest New Mexico." *Journal of Archaeological Science* 25: 1073–1082.

Shackley, M. Steven. 2005a. *Obsidian: Geology and Archaeology in the North American Southwest*. Tucson: University of Arizona Press.

Shackley, M. Steven. 2005b. "Source Provenance of Obsidian Artifacts from Mesa Verde, Sand Canyon, Duckfoot, and Dolores Project Sites, Southwestern Colorado." Manuscript on file, Crow Canyon Archaeological Center, Cortez, CO.

Shackley, M. Steven. 2008. "Source Provenance of Obsidian Artifacts from Archaeological Sites from the Dolores Archaeological Project, Southwestern Colorado." Manuscript on file, Crow Canyon Archaeological Center, Cortez, CO.

Shott, Michael J. 1994. "Size and Form in the Analysis of Flake Debris: Review and Recent Approaches." *Journal of Archaeological Method and Theory* 1: 69–110.

Shott, Michael J., and Paul Sillitoe. 2005. "Use Life and Curation in New Guinea Experimental Used Flakes." *Journal of Archaeological Science* 32: 653–663.

Simmons, L. W. 1942. *Sun Chief: The Autobiography of a Hopi Indian*. New Haven, CT: Yale University Press.

Stephen, Alexander M. 1936. *Hopi Journal of Alexander M. Stephen*, ed. E. C. Parsons. New York: AMS Press.

Stevenson, Adalynn J. 1984. "Diachronic Analysis of Chipped Stone Materials from Site 5MT3, Yellow Jacket Pueblo." PhD dissertation, University of Colorado, Boulder.

Stevenson, Matilda Cox. 1904. "The Zuni Indians." *Bureau of American Ethnology, Annual Report* 23: 1–634.

Till, Jonathan, Jamie Merewether, Robin Lyle, and Scott G. Ortman. 2015. "Shields Pueblo Artifacts." Crow Canyon Archaeological Center. Accessed August 2018. http://www.crowcanyon.org/research/research.asp.

Till, Jonathan, and Scott G. Ortman. 2007. "Sand Canyon Pueblo Artifacts." Crow Canyon Archaeological Center. Accessed February 2016. http://www.crowcanyon.org/research/research.asp.

Titiev, Mischa. 1992 [1944]. *Old Oraibi: A Study of the Hopi Indians of Third Mesa*. Peabody Museum of Archaeology and Ethnology Papers 22 (1). Cambridge, MA: Peabody Museum of Archaeology and Ethnology.

Varien, Mark D. 1999. *Sedentism and Mobility in a Social Landscape*. Tucson: University of Arizona Press.

Varien, Mark D., Scott G. Ortman, Timothy A. Kohler, Donna M. Glowacki, and C. David Johnson. 2007. "Historical Ecology in the Mesa Verde Region: Results from the Village Project." *American Antiquity* 72: 273–299.

Varien, Mark D., and Richard Wilshusen. 2002. *Seeking the Center Place: Archaeology and Ancient Communities in the Mesa Verde Region*. Salt Lake City: University of Utah Press.

Vaughn, Patrick C. 1985. "Methodology." In *Use-Wear Analysis of Flaked Stone Tools*, by Patrick C. Vaughn, 9–46. Tucson: University of Arizona Press.

Walsh, Michael R. 1998. "Lines in the Sand: Competition and Stone Selection on the Pajarito Plateau, New Mexico." *American Antiquity* 63: 573–593.

Whittaker, John C. 1994. *Flintknapping: Making and Understanding Stone Tools*. Austin: University of Texas Press.

8

Using Portable X-Ray Fluorescence (pXRF) to Source Burlington Chert from the Carson Site, 22CO505, Coahoma County, Mississippi

Jayur Madhusudan Mehta,
Grant S. McCall,
Theodore Marks,
and James Enloe

Hierarchical, agricultural, and monument-building societies become commonplace in the Eastern Woodlands of North America after 1000 CE and are typically identified as Mississippian cultures in the archaeological literature (Pauketat 2004; Smith 1984, 1990). More recently, scholars have illustrated that local population histories in the discrete river valleys, plateaus, and floodplains of the mid-continental and southeastern United States demonstrate that local and unique cultural trajectories were both similar to and different from developmental sequences at early Mississippian monumental centers like Cahokia, Illinois (e.g., Rees 1997; Steponaitis 1991). Nevertheless, it must also be acknowledged that historical events and developments at Cahokia played a role in influencing cultural developments across the Southeast and that categorizing Mississippian as a historical phenomenon, as opposed to a cultural trait list, facilitates a conversation around *how* other monumental centers developed and the degree to which those developments were influenced by Cahokian communities and Cahokian émigrés who brought with them cultural practices typically associated with hierarchical, agricultural, and monument-building societies from the American Bottom (Pauketat 2007). Following the latter model, the acquisition of raw materials from the American Bottom to the Yazoo Basin and the manufacturing of specific toolkits using those lithic resources help scholars examine economic and political structures—especially the intersection of

DOI: 10.5876/9781607328926.c008

lithic trade and exchange, craft production, and Mississippian hierarchy—as well as providing a framework for evaluating the importance of foreign trade among similar societies across the globe. This study is an initial attempt to clarify the nature of trade and exchange in Burlington chert between Carson, Mississippi, and points north, including Cahokia.

Burlington chert microlithic artifacts recovered from elite and non-elite contexts at Carson (occupied from the thirteenth through seventeenth centuries; Mehta et al. 2016b, 2017) are remarkably similar in material and morphology to microlithic artifacts recovered at large Mississippian sites in the Central Mississippi Valley (CMV; McNutt 1996: 187; Yerkes 1983), including at Cahokia (occupied from roughly 1000 to 1350 CE; Emerson and Hedman 2015). Based on extensive research on Cahokia's microlithic industry and, more generally, microlithic technologies as manifest across the southeastern United States (Ensor 1991; Jackson 2003; Johnson 1987; Morse and Sierzchula 1977; Schnell et al. 1981; Yerkes 1983, 1989, 1991), it seemed likely that the source of Burlington chert for Carson's community of flintknappers and craft workers would have been located in the vicinity of Cahokia. Perhaps the community even acquired the chert directly from the Crescent Quarry, a geologic stone outcrop, access to which was controlled by Cahokia (Johnson 1987: 188, 1993; Koldehoff and Brennan 2010). Based on a visual analysis of Burlington chert microlithic tools, Johnson's (1987) research asserted that a point-to-point network of trade and exchange of Burlington chert linked Carson and Cahokia, drawing a direct link between sociocultural developments in the CMV and the Lower Mississippi Valley (LMV) (see Johnson 1987: 201; Smith 1984). Although microlithic technologies can be found across the southeastern United States (see Ensor 1991; Schnell et al. 1981), few microlithic industries are produced on Burlington chert outside of the CMV. Furthermore, geological sources of Burlington chert are quite expansive and can be accessed in outcrops in several areas of the mid-South adjacent to the Mississippi River Valley, from Iowa to Arkansas, and from Illinois to Kansas (figure 8.1). Given its widespread availability in regions to the north of Carson, it remains unclear if singular or multiple networks of exchange characterize lithic procurement strategies. Consequently, additional research was needed to directly link geological sources to archaeological finds at Carson.

This chapter reports on research directed toward identifying the geologic sources of archaeological Burlington chert identified and recovered at Carson. The site has been the focus of anthropological interest for over 100 years (C. Brown 1926; I. Brown 1978; Butz 2015; James 2010; Johnson 1987, 1993;

FIGURE 8.1. *The black polygons show the locations of Burlington chert outcrops in northern Arkansas and south-central Missouri. The gray-filled star marks the location of Crescent Quarry, and the white-filled star marks the location of chert sampled from the Ozark Mountains. Adapted from Mehta et al. 2017: 382; Ray 2007: 200. The Carson site is located in northwestern Mississippi and is marked by a black circle (see also figure 8.2).*

Lansdell 2009; McLeod 2015; Mehta 2015; Mehta et al. 2012, 2016a, 2016b; Phillips et al. 2003 [1951]; Settle 2012; Thomas 1891, 1894). Among many yet unknown components of prehistoric life at Carson, the point of origin (or origins) for the Burlington chert worked by prehistoric Mississippians at Carson is still unknown, although based on existing studies (Johnson 1987, 1993) we hypothesize that the source of knappable Burlington chert was the Crescent Quarry. Understanding the source of trade goods raises many questions and permits the analysis of how chert was obtained and used by ancient Mississippians at Carson. Furthermore, this research informs studies of Mississippian societies and their networks both upriver and downriver (Brown et al. 1990; Peregrine and Lekson 2012). Through pXRF analyses of Burlington chert from the Carson site and comparison with geological sources in the Ozark Buffalo River drainage and the Crescent Quarry near St. Louis, we found that an assemblage of Burlington chert from Carson exhibited a significant amount of geochemical variation in elemental iron (Fe); consequently, it appears that the assemblage did not come exclusively from either the Crescent Quarry or the Ozark source. Based on our analyses, only 9.7 percent of our archaeological sample is geochemically similar to the Crescent Quarry source; the remainder demonstrates significant variation, and while some of it is similar to the Ozark source, much of it exceeds the range of variation for both quarries. Consequently, it appears that Burlington chert at Carson represents a diverse array of geologic sources, likely from places outside of our current sampling area. The data reported here contribute new findings about the trade and exchange of lithic resources during the Mississippi period and demonstrate that lithic procurement strategies at Carson were varied, relying on a multitude of different sources. This study is a preliminary attempt at chert sourcing and provides an exciting starting point for future work in the analysis of lithic trade and exchange in the Central and Lower Mississippi Valleys.

GEOGRAPHICAL AND GEOLOGICAL BACKGROUND

The Carson site (22CO505) is a large monumental center composed of over 88 earthen mounds spanning 1.5 kilometers (figure 8.2). The site is located in northeastern Mississippi within the Yazoo Basin, a broad alluvial floodplain carved out by the Mississippi River over several thousand years (Fisk 1944; Gagliano and van Beek 1970; Saucier 1974, 1994). The Yazoo Basin is an active geomorphic environment largely devoid of any bedrock geology; the mounds and village at Carson were constructed on quaternary sedimentary deposits in a complex alluvial meander belt landscape with characteristic scroll bar and overbank deposits (Mehta et al. 2012, 2016b). An ancient course of the Mississippi River was located just west of the site and was actively flowing until sometime around the middle of the first millennium CE (Mehta et al. 2016b). This waterway was likely important to transportation and trade during the Mississippi period, and it was certainly documented as such during the Hernando de Soto expedition (Ethridge 2010; Hudson 1997).

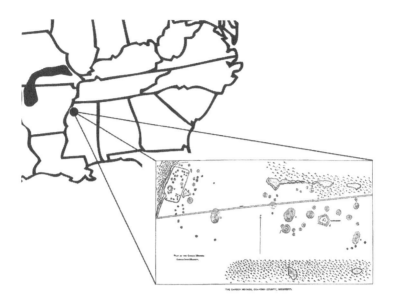

FIGURE 8.2. *Image showing the location of the Carson site relative to Burlington chert resources. The oblong black polygon shows the geology of available Burlington chert. Black circles in the inset image connote large earthen platform mounds. The light gray outline in the inset image shows the outline of a higher-elevation, overbank sediment deposit.*

As well as linking different Mississippian centers along its length, the Mississippi River and its tributaries eroded and exposed outcrops of stone that were important resources for prehistoric groups. Burlington chert appears within the Burlington-Keokuk Formation, a dolomitic limestone formation that outcrops throughout western Illinois, southeastern Iowa, and eastern and central Missouri (Ray 2007; Stuckey and Morrow 2013: 20; figure 8.1). Given its broad distribution across the landscape of the CMV and LMV, there is a significant amount of variation in the visual, chemical, and mechanical properties of Burlington chert (Stuckey and Morrow 2013: 20). Therefore, visual sourcing studies should be supplemented with geochemical analysis of both geologic and archaeological samples. Archaeologists have noted that Crescent Quarry Burlington chert sources tend to be fine-grained and of a uniform, milky-white color; these visual features may be part of the reason why the polity at Cahokia favored working with and perhaps monopolizing this raw material resource (Koldehoff and Brennan 2010).

ARCHAEOLOGICAL BACKGROUND

Burlington chert is a marker of early Mississippian interactions between the Central and Lower Mississippi Valley and between the Yazoo Basin and northern Arkansas (at the Zebree site; figure 8.1) and southern Missouri/Illinois (at the Cahokia site; Johnson 1987; Morse and Morse 1990; Phillips 1970; figure 8.1). Both Cahokia and Zebree are well-studied Mississippian culture sites with significant evidence of microlithic tools made on Burlington chert (Ensor 1991; Johnson 1987; Mason and Perino 1961; Pauketat 1997; Trubitt 2000, 2003; Yerkes 1983, 1989). Koldehoff and Brennan (2010: 138) found that in a sample of 6,908 lithic artifacts taken from the Figurehut Tract (11S34/7) at Cahokia, 90 percent were made on Crescent Quarry–sourced Burlington chert; another sample from Cahokia yielded 89.3 percent of materials from the same source. Cahokia was the dominant cultural entity in the American Bottom early in the second millennium CE (Pauketat 2007); the people of Cahokia, as well as outlying villages, almost exclusively (Mill Creek hoes aside) used Burlington chert for microlithic artifacts like microblades, microdrills, and gravers. In addition, outlying villages and hamlets also relied on Burlington chert, and it was a regionally important lithic resource (Fowke 1928: 535; Koldehoff and Brennan 2010: 139). At Labras Lake, an independent village 10–15 km southwest of Cahokia, three centrally located houses produced evidence of Burlington chert microlithic tools (Yerkes 1983: 514, 1987: 185, 189). Other village sites in the American Bottom, such as Lohmann, Turner, Mitchell, and BBB Motor, also have Burlington chert microlithic toolkits (Yerkes 1987: 184). These sites are almost all within 50 km of the Crescent Quarry source. Yerkes (1987: 184) has suggested that the rarity of microlithic toolkits, their limited distribution at sites, and their general confinement to elite contexts at sites points to an industry and scale of craft production limited to specialists and powerful elites. At Cahokia as at Labras Lake, microlithic toolkits are made on Burlington chert (Koldehoff and Brennan 2010) and are composed of drills, cores, and blades generally found in high-status or elite households (Yerkes 1983: 514).

The Zebree site is located in northeastern Arkansas and is over 400 km downriver from Cahokia and Crescent Quarry (Morse 1975; Morse and Morse 1990). The site has a documented Mississippian occupation with similarities to Cahokia in the form of burial practices, structure construction, ceramic tempering, and vessel morphology (Morse 1975: 214–215). Furthermore, visual analysis of chert microlithic tools indicates that they are made on Burlington chert and closely resemble raw stone resources from the Crescent Quarry (Morse and Morse 1980: 2).

Carson represents the southern extent of Burlington chert microlithic tools (Ensor 1991: 21; Johnson 1987). Other microlithic stone tool industries exist, at places like Bottle Creek (Brown 2003), Lubbub Creek near Moundville (Ensor 1991), and Cemochechobee in southwestern Georgia (Schnell et al. 1981: 222); however, these industries are not produced on Burlington chert but rather on locally available resources—one might conclude because of the significant distances between Burlington chert outcrops and these other large Mississippian sites. Studies by Johnson (1987, 1993) describe the relationship of the microlithic industry to Cahokia, delineate the reduction sequence from cores to microlithic drills, and demonstrate the extent to which trade and exchange are tied to the development of complex societies in the Yazoo Basin. Brown's (1978: 5–12) earlier survey also identified the significant extent to which Burlington chert can be identified around Carson; he claimed that Carson was "undoubtedly the major protohistoric Mississippi period center in Coahoma County, and for that reason, it deserves particular attention in future research." As has been demonstrated at other large mound centers, such as Wickliffe, there was an extensive network of trade in Burlington chert, from quarries controlled by Cahokia to sites that were not near the resource (Koldehoff 1987; Koldehoff and Brennan 2010: 148; Koldehoff and Carr 2001). Given Carson's importance as a monumental political center, much like Wickliffe, we might propose that the nature of peer polity interaction between Carson and Cahokia was similar to that between Wickliffe and Cahokia (Koldehoff and Brenann 2010: 148), especially since Burlington chert does not geologically outcrop near Carson and is not found at other nearby archaeological sites.

Charting the relationship among Carson, Cahokia, and the many Mississippian centers in between permits an understanding of what cultural features constitute "Mississippian," the historical and tangible relationships between real people who lived many hundreds of miles apart from one another, and the significance that was given to using the Mississippi River and its tributaries for the trade and exchange of ideas and goods (Anderson and Sassaman 2012: 163, 173). This chapter evaluates the trade and exchange of Burlington chert at Carson using previous interpretations of lithic exchange among other Mississippian centers across the Midwest and greater Southeast.

MATERIALS AND METHODS

Burlington chert samples used in this study were collected during the Carson Mounds Archaeological Project (CMAP) excavations in 2014 by the

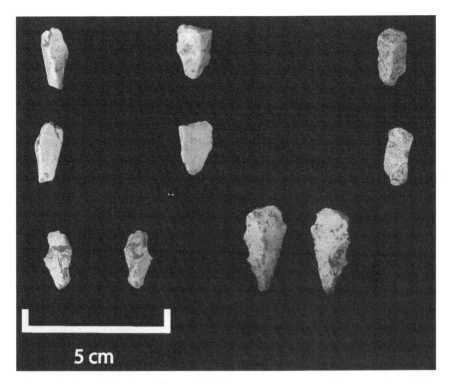

FIGURE 8.3. *Microlithic Burlington chert drills from Structure 1 at Carson*

lead author and between 2008 and 2015 by excavations at the site directed by John Connaway, archaeologist for the Mississippi Department of Archives and History; Grant McCall collected geological samples from the Ozark Mountains near Jasper, Arkansas, in the Buffalo River drainage and the Crescent Quarry source near St. Louis, Missouri, and the Mississippi River. The Crescent Quarry was sampled because it is the closest Burlington chert quarry to Cahokia, and the Buffalo River source in the Ozark Mountains was sampled through opportunistic sampling. A total of ninety-three archaeological samples from Carson Mounds were processed for this study, including flakes, cores, drills, and blades (table 8.1; figure 8.3). The archaeological samples came from excavated household contexts (figure 8.4), surface collections around the village at Carson, and a summit structure on Mound D. One hundred total geological samples were processed; fifty originated from sources in the Ozark Mountains and fifty from Crescent Quarry sources (figure 8.1; table 8.1). Our samples allow us to evaluate whether Burlington chert came

TABLE 8.1. Counts of archaeological samples and geological samples used in the study

Archaeological	N = 93
Geological	N = 100
Ouachita sources	N = 50
Crescent Quarry	N = 50

from Crescent Quarry, from the Buffalo River drainage near Jasper, Arkansas, or both. Alternatively, if none of the archaeological samples align with either geological sample, we must then presume that the Carson community was obtaining its Burlington chert from elsewhere. All of the samples were analyzed at Tulane University in the Center for Archaeology or at the University of Iowa lab using an Olympus InnovaX Delta portable X-ray fluorescence (pXRF) instrument.

We scanned each cleaned source sample and artifact for 90 seconds at three different X-ray beam energy levels to cover thirty-nine different elements, from phosphorous (P) to uranium (U). The raw spectral data were processed using the Olympus Soils software package pre-loaded with the instrument and calibrated with inductively coupled plasma mass spectrometry (ICP-MS) at the University of Iowa's Department of Earth and Environmental Sciences. The proprietary Olympus software is designed to produce quantitative trace element data on high-silica geological materials, including cherts. It also automatically corrects for matrix effects and minimizes the influence of Compton and Rayleigh scatter. The resulting elemental concentration data are quantitative, replicable, and robust.

While a variety of issues troubled earlier generations of pXRF machines for archaeological applications, more recent advances have made the machines more reliable and better suited to geological sourcing studies (Frahm 2012a, 2012b, 2013; Frahm and Doonan 2013; Frahm et al. 2014; Gauthier et al. 2012; Kahn et al. 2013; Newlander et al. 2015; Ortega et al. 2013; Phillips and Speakman 2009; Shackley 2011). Cherts can be challenging to evaluate quantitatively compared to obsidian, which tends to contain a broad spectrum of elements; most cherts are composed principally of silicon and oxygen, making them geochemically difficult to isolate (Barton 1918; Gauthier et al. 2012: 2436; Speer 2014). As Gauthier and colleagues (2012) delineate clearly, chert tends to be quite heterogeneous; pXRF meters are the ideal tool for studying the chemical composition of chert because they can sample a large area, cover a broad range of elements with precision and sensitivity and with low detection limits, and do this work quickly (see also Luedtke 1979).

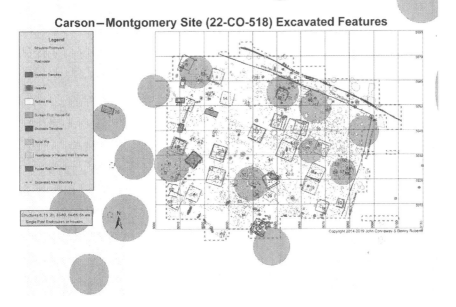

FIGURE 8.4. *Archaeological features inside the excavation area inside the village at Carson. Visible are square houses, pits, and several palisade lines (image courtesy of Benny Roberts and John Connaway).*

RESULTS

Geochemical data in the form of minor and trace element counts from the archaeological cherts and geological Burlington chert samples were analyzed statistically using Statistical Package for Social Sciences v. 13. We first conducted an exploratory principal components analysis on the element concentration data from both the geological and archaeological samples and found that iron (Fe) concentration was the principal factor explaining variability across the dataset, accounting for slightly over 69 percent of the total variation. A second principal component, represented by sulfur, calcium, and potassium, explained a further 17 percent of the remaining variability in the total dataset. This suggests that patterned variability exists in the underlying geochemistry of the Burlington chert formation that may be useful for distinguishing sources.

We used the elemental concentrations from the Ozark and Crescent Quarry source areas as training data to generate a discriminant function analysis to predict the possible sources of the unknown artifacts from Carson Mounds.

TABLE 8.2. Results of the discriminant function analysis. Eighty percent of original grouped cases were correctly classified, and 78 percent of cross-validated grouped cases were correctly classified.

		Source	Ozark	Crescent Hills	Total
Original	Count	Ozark	33	17	50
		Crescent Hills	3	47	50
		Carson	84	9	93
	Percent	Ozark	66	34	100
		Crescent Hills	6	94	100
		Carson	90.3	9.7	100
Cross-validated	Count	Ozark	31	19	50
		Crescent Hills	3	47	50
	Percent	Ozark	62	38	100
		Crescent Hills	6	94	100

This analysis (table 8.2) demonstrates that only a very small percentage of the Burlington chert discovered at the Carson site (n = 9; 9.7%) is geochemically similar to Burlington chert from the Crescent Quarry source.

Elemental iron (Fe) best discriminated group membership and was used to classify archaeological chert according to geological source; n = 84 samples (90.3%) were defined as falling within the Ozark category. While this classification functionally matches some of the Ozark materials best, there was a significant amount of variation in the sample set that is best indicative of broader regional variations in chert geochemistry. Namely, the sample set matches our "Ozark" category but categorically exhibits more variation than the Ozark materials. There was a statistically significant difference between Carson Burlington chert and Ozark and Crescent Quarry Burlington chert based on concentrations of iron [(Fe in ppm), $F(8) = 46.9, p < 0.0005$; Wilks's $\Lambda = 0.607$ (table 8.3; figure 8.4)]. Given these data, we must presume that much of the Carson sample came from a geologic source outside of the Crescent Quarry but not from the Buffalo River drainage in the Ozarks. Consequently, our original hypothesis that Carson's Burlington chert originated from Crescent Quarry is not supported. The range of variation in iron (Fe) in the archaeological assemblage is significantly greater than in the Ozark or Crescent Quarry sources (figure 8.5); thus the Carson chert was obtained from another source and may have come from a broad variety of different places, not simply from one of two places.

TABLE 8.3. Wilks's Lambda from the discriminant function analysis

Test of Functions	Wilks's Lambda	Chi-square	df	Significance
1	0.607	46.956	8	< 0.000

DISCUSSION

The Lower Mississippi Valley is an excellent case study for the procurement and use of non-local lithic resources. In and around Carson and the Yazoo Basin, no geologic outcrops of usable lithic materials are present; only stream-floated lithic resources are available. Consequently, if a particular lithic resource was desired, it had to be actively procured through interaction with groups upriver or traders working downriver. An evaluation of the trade and exchange of Burlington chert allows a fascinating inquiry into the social and economic relationships of Mississippian people and societies that, across a broad region, had roughly similar cultural practices, such as maize agriculture, platform mound construction, and shell-tempered pottery. Despite these shared cultural features, they nevertheless had their own individual histories. Documents from the sixteenth-century Hernando de Soto expedition contain descriptions of broadly diverse Native towns and provinces (see Clayton et al. 1993; Hudson 1997). We learn from the de Soto documents that caciques[1] developed patron-client relationships with other chiefs spread across the greater Southeast (see DePratter 1989; Hudson et al. 1985: 732 for a description of the Coosa chiefdom and its relationship to other chiefdoms). In the vicinity of the northern Yazoo Basin (and perhaps at Carson itself), the chief of the province of Quiz Quiz maintained a political alliance with the chiefdom of Pacaha, whose principal towns and territories were found on the opposite side of the Mississippi River (Hudson 1997: 278). These alliances were likely built on numerous social, economic, and political factors (see Galloway 2002; King 1999); for example, between the Coosa and Lake Jackson chiefdoms, long-distance trade in copper and shell reinforced political alliances (Hudson et al. 1985). Examples of the importance of trade and exchange during the Mississippian Era abound (see Brown et al. 1990), most notably of shell, copper galena, ceramics, and lithics.[2] In light of the documentary record and studies of Mississippian exchange, as well as the presence of non-local lithics at Carson, we must presume that networks of long- and short-term trade existed in the greater Mississippi River Valley during the Mississippi period. This study clarifies the nature of trade and exchange and determined that the chert at Carson was not from the Crescent Quarry but instead had multiple points of origin.

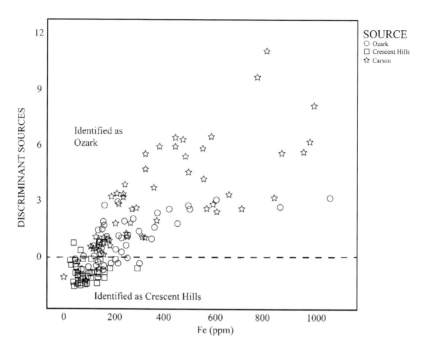

FIGURE 8.5. *In this image, ★ represents Carson samples, circles represent Arkansas Ozark material, and squares represent Crescent Quarry material. The results of the discriminant function analysis against Fe (ppm) demonstrate clustering of a small percentage of the sample into the Crescent Quarry geological group; otherwise, much of the archaeological sample lies outside the range of variation for Ozark material as well.*

Earlier studies used the visual features of Burlington chert, primarily its coloration (generally whitish and translucent) and graining (striations and patterning in inclusions), to determine the origins of archaeological samples. Our study relied on pXRF to source archaeological samples to their geologic origins. Published studies of white-colored lithics at Carson postulated that based on visual appearance they must have originated from Cahokian-controlled sources (Johnson 1987, 1993). If networks of trade and exchange were singularly controlled, then a single geologic source would represent the source of lithics at Carson. However, our pXRF data do not corroborate previous assessments based on visual comparison. Rather, our data seem to indicate that while some Burlington chert at Carson did come from Cahokia (9.7%), most of the Burlington chert in the sample seems to have originated from other sources. At least one of those geologic sources may have been the source we sampled in the Buffalo River drainage; however, given the variation in Fe in the sample, many other geologic sources must also be represented (see figure 8.5). Therefore, we propose that multi-agent, multi-source networks of trade and exchange in Burlington chert existed at Carson in the time period before Hernando de Soto (1540 CE). This means that given the geochemical variation in the sample set, Burlington chert at Carson arrived by way of many different pathways, not through a network controlled exclusively by a single agent. This study is a first step in evaluating the trade in Burlington chert, and there are several potential challenges to our interpretation; nevertheless, the data are compelling enough to suggest a multi-agent network and to pursue additional research controlling for both chronology of occupation at Carson and the sampling of additional geologic sources of Burlington chert.

One principal concern for future analysis is the sampling of geologic chert sources. Our analysis compares archaeological material to two sources and investigates the relationship between Carson and the Crescent Quarry. Our study demonstrates that most of the Burlington chert at Carson did not come from Crescent Quarry; however, it also did not come exclusively from the Ozark source. Consequently, we propose that multiple geologic sources must also have been involved in the trade and exchange of Burlington chert. Identifying these other sources and other potential sources of geochemical variation in the lithic material will require extensive survey and sampling across an extensive geologic formation (see figure 8.1). One way we could subvert this sampling issue is to sample Burlington chert from archaeological contexts in and around the Lower Mississippi Valley; presuming that proximity plays a role in lithic procurement (see Binford 1982; Nelson 1991: 60; Parry and Kelly 1987) and following Koldehoff and Brennan's (2010) proposition that large Mississippian villages controlled specific lithic outcrops, it might be possible to sample and analyze Burlington chert from a variety of Mississippian villages and to determine Carson's other potential trading partners from archaeological contexts. This would not help us identify the geologic sources, but since the sourcing is primarily directed toward understanding the social contexts of exchanging lithic materials, this strategy might show promise in the future.

CONCLUSION

This study uses pXRF and the geochemical analysis of lithic resources to evaluate the nature of trade and exchange of Burlington chert in the Lower

Mississippi Valley. Lithic resources located upriver of Carson could have arrived at the site through a variety of mechanisms, including direct trade with one or several societies upriver and through the selective harvesting of Burlington chert river cobbles that occasionally floated downriver through natural processes. Both natural and anthropogenic processes likely brought Burlington chert to Carson; given the significant quantities of the material there, trade and exchange are the likely mechanisms. Until this study, however, it was unclear whether single or multiple agents were responsible for bringing the material to the site.

Our study successfully uses pXRF geochemistry to suggest that Cahokia did not control Carson's ability to acquire Burlington chert. Rather, the geochemical variation in our Carson assemblage shows that Burlington chert likely came from many different places. Some did come from Cahokia, and future work should identify and differentiate these specific contexts. The most likely scenario, based on our data, is that many different agents were active in providing Carson's communities with Burlington chert for various purposes. Moving forward, we anticipate continuing this work by sampling additional geologic and archaeological contexts and historicizing our study by elaborating the complex network of trade and exchange in the Lower Mississippi Valley during late prehistory.

NOTES

1. A term for Mississippian chiefs coined by the Spanish (see Beck et al. 2006: 66).
2. In previous cultural periods, like the Poverty Point period (1730–1350 BCE), extensive and far-reaching networks of trade and exchange brought exotic goods to central Louisiana and the Lower Mississippi Valley (Jackson 1991).

REFERENCES

Anderson, David G., and Kenneth E. Sassaman. 2012. *Recent Developments in Southeastern Archaeology: From Colonization to Complexity*. Washington, DC: Society for American Archaeology Press.

Barton, Donald C. 1918. "Notes on the Mississippian Chert of the St. Louis Area." *Journal of Geology* 26 (4): 361–374.

Beck, Robin A., David G. Moore, and Christopher B. Rodning. 2006. "Identifying Fort San Juan: A Sixteenth-Century Spanish Occupation at the Berry Site, North Carolina." *Southeastern Archaeology* 25 (1): 65–77.

Binford, Lewis R. 1982. "The Archaeology of Place." *Journal of Anthropological Archaeology* 1 (1): 5–31.

Brown, Calvin S. 1926. *Archaeology of Mississippi*. Oxford: University Press of Mississippi.

Brown, Ian W. 1978. "An Archaeological Survey of Mississippi Period Sites in Coahoma County, Mississippi: Final Report." Unpublished manuscript, Lower Mississippi Survey. Cambridge: Peabody Museum, Harvard University.

Brown, Ian W. 2003. *Bottle Creek: A Pensacola Culture Site in South Alabama*. Tuscaloosa: University of Alabama Press.

Brown, James A., Richard Kerber, and Howard D. Winters. 1990. "Trade and Evolution of Exchange Relations at the Beginning of the Mississippian Period." In *The Mississippian Emergence*, ed. Bruce D. Smith, 251–280. Washington, DC: Smithsonian Institution Press.

Butz, Samuel. 2015. "Excavations of Mound B: A Ridge-Top Mound at the Carson Site, a Mississippian Mound Center in the Northern Yazoo Basin." Master's thesis, University of Mississippi, Oxford.

Clayton, Lawrence A., Vernon James Knight Jr., and Edward C. Moore. 1993. *The De Soto Chronicles: The Expedition of Hernando De Soto to North America in 1539–1543*. Tuscaloosa: University of Alabama Press.

DePratter, Chester B. 1989. "Cofitachequi: Ethnohistorical and Archaeological Evidence." In *Studies in South Carolina Archaeology: Essays in Honor of Robert L. Stephenson*, ed. Albert C. Goodyear III and Glen T. Hanson, 132–156. Columbia: South Carolina Institute of Archaeology and Anthropology, University of South Carolina.

Emerson, Thomas E., and Kristin M. Hedman. 2015. "The Dangers of Diversity: The Consolidation and Dissolution of Cahokia, Native North America's First Urban Polity." In *Beyond Collapse: Archaeological Perspectives on Resilience, Revitalization, and Transformation in Complex Societies*, ed. Ronald Faulseit, 147–175. Carbondale: Southern Illinois University Press.

Ensor, H. Blaine. 1991. "The Lubbub Creek Microlithic Industry." *Southeastern Archaeology* 10 (1): 18–39.

Ethridge, Robbie. 2010. *From Chicaza to Chickasaw: The European Invasion and the Transformation of the Mississippian World, 1540–1715*. Chapel Hill: University of North Carolina Press.

Fisk, Harold N. 1944. *Geologic Investigation of the Alluvial Valley of the Lower Mississippi River*. Vicksburg: US Army Corps, Mississippi River Commission.

Fowke, Gerard. 1928. *Archaeological Investigations Part 2*. 44th Annual Report of the Bureau of American Ethnography for 1926–1927, 399–540. Washington, DC: Smithsonian Institution.

Frahm, Ellery. 2012a. "Distinguishing Nemrut Dag and Bingol A Obsidians: Geochemical and Landscape Differences and the Archaeological Implications." *Journal of Archaeological Science* 29: 1436–1444.

Frahm, Ellery. 2012b. "Evaluation of Archaeological Sourcing Techniques: Reconsidering and Re-deriving Hughes' Fourfold Assessment Scheme." *Geoarchaeology* 27: 166–174.

Frahm, Ellery. 2013. "Validity of 'Off-the-Shelf' Handheld Portable XRF for Sourcing Near Eastern Obsidian Chip Debris." *Journal of Archaeological Science* 40 (2): 1080–1092.

Frahm, Ellery, and Roger C.P. Doonan. 2013. "The Technological versus Methodological Revolution of Portable XRF in Archaeology." *Journal of Archaeological Science* 40: 1425–1434.

Frahm, Ellery, Beverly A. Schmidt, Boris Gasparyan, Benik Yeriksyan, Sergei Karapetian, Khachatur Meliksetian, and Daniel S. Adler. 2014. "Ten Seconds in the Field: Rapid Armenian Obsidian Sourcing with Portable XRF to Inform Excavations and Survey." *Journal of Archaeological Science* 41: 333–348.

Gagliano, Sherwood M., and Johannes L. van Beek. 1970. *Geologic and Geomorphic Aspects of Deltaic Processes*. Baton Rouge: Coastal Resources Unit, Center for Wetland Resources, Louisiana State University.

Galloway, Patricia Kay. 2002. "Colonial Period Transformations in the Mississippi Valley: Disintegration, Alliance, Confederation, Playoff." In *The Transformation of the Southeastern Indians, 1540–1760*, ed. Robbie Ethridge and Charles Hudson, 225–248. Jackson: University Press of Mississippi.

Gauthier, Gilles, Adrian L. Burke, and Mathieu Leclerc. 2012. "Assessing XRF for the Geochemical Characterization of Radiolarian Chert: Artifacts from Northeastern North America." *Journal of Archaeological Science* 39: 2436–2451.

Hudson, Charles C. 1997. *Knights of Spain, Warriors of the Sun: Hernando de Soto and the South's Ancient Chiefdoms*. Athens: University of Georgia Press.

Hudson, Charles, Marvin Smith, David Hally, Richard Polhemus, and Chester DePratter. 1985. "Coosa: A Chiefdom in the Sixteenth-Century Southeastern United States." *American Antiquity* 50 (4): 723–737.

Jackson, H. Edwin. 1991. "The Trade Fair in Hunter-Gatherer Interaction: The Role of Intersocietal Trade in the Evolution of Poverty Point Culture." In *Between Bands and States: Sedentism, Subsistence, and Interaction in Small-Scale Societies*, ed. Susan A. Gregg, 265–286. Occasional Paper 9, Center for Archaeological Investigations. Carbondale: Southern Illinois University.

Jackson, Paul D. 2003. "The Bottle Creek Microlithic Industry." In *Bottle Creek: A Pensacola Culture Site in South Alabama*, ed. Ian W. Brown, 168–185. Tuscaloosa: University of Alabama Press.

James, Jenna L.A. 2010. "Modeling Mortuary Behavior Based on Secondary Burial Data from Carson Mound Group, Coahoma County, Mississippi." Master's thesis, University of Mississippi, Oxford.

Johnson, Jay K. 1987. "Cahokia Core Technology in Mississippi: The View from the South." In *The Organization of Core Technology*, ed. Jay K. Johnson and Carol A. Morrow, 187–206. Boulder: Westview.

Johnson, Jay K. 1993. "Poverty Point Period Crystal Drill Bits, Microliths, and Social Organization in the Yazoo Basin, Mississippi." *Southeastern Archaeology* 12: 59–64.

Kahn, Jennifer G., John Sinton, Peter R. Mills, and Steven P. Lundblad. 2013. "X-Ray Fluorescence Analysis and Intra-Island Exchange in the Society Island Archipelago (Central Eastern Polynesia)." *Journal of Archaeological Science* 40: 1194–1202.

King, Adam. 1999. "De Soto's Itaba and the Nature of Sixteenth Century Paramount Chiefdoms." *Southeastern Archaeology* 18: 110–123.

Koldehoff, Brad. 1987. "The Cahokia Flake Tool Industry: Socioeconomic Implications for Late Prehistory in the Central Mississippi Valley." In *The Organization of Core Technology*, ed. Jay K. Johnson and Carol A. Morrow, 187–206. Boulder: Westview.

Koldehoff, Brad, and Tamira Brennan. 2010. "Exploring Mississippian Polity Interaction and Craft Specialization with Ozark Chipped-Stone Resources." *Missouri Archaeology* 71: 131–165.

Koldehoff, Brad, and Philip J. Carr. 2001. "Chipped-Stone Technology: Patterns of Procurement, Production, and Consumption." In *Excavations at Wickliffe Mounds*, ed. Kit W. Wesler, CD-ROM. Tuscaloosa: University of Alabama Press.

Lansdell, Brent. 2009. "A Chronological Assessment of the Carson Mound Group, Stovall, Mississippi." Master's thesis, University of Mississippi, Oxford.

Luedtke, Barbara E. 1979. "The Identification of Sources of Chert Artifacts." *American Antiquity* 44 (4): 744–757.

Mason, Ronald J., and Gregory Perino. 1961. "Microblades at Cahokia." *American Antiquity* 26 (4): 553–557.

McLeod, Todd Bryan. 2015. "Developing an Architectural Sequence for a Portion of the Mound A Enclosure at the Carson Mound Group, Coahoma County, Mississippi." Master's thesis, University of Mississippi, Oxford.

McNutt, Charles H. 1996. "The Central Mississippi Valley: A Summary." In *Prehistory of the Central Mississippi Valley*, ed. Charles H. McNutt, 187–257. Tuscaloosa: University of Alabama Press.

Mehta, Jayur M. 2015. "Native American Monuments and Landscape in the Lower Mississippi Valley." PhD dissertation, Tulane University, New Orleans, LA.

Mehta, Jayur M., David M. Abbott, and Charlotte D. Pevny. 2016a. "Mississippian Craft Production in the Yazoo Basin: Thin-Section Analysis of a Mississippian

Structure Floor on the Summit of Mound D at the Carson Site." *Journal of Archaeological Science: Reports* 5: 471–484.

Mehta, Jayur M., Kelsey M. Lowe, Rachel Stout-Evans, and John Connaway. 2012. "Moving Earth and Building Monuments at the Carson Mounds Site, Coahoma County, Mississippi." *Journal of Anthropology* 2012: 1–21.

Mehta, Jayur M., Grant McCall, Theodore Marks, and James Enloe. 2017. "Geochemical Source Evaluation of Archaeological Chert from the Carson Mounds Site in Northwestern Mississippi Using Portable X-Ray Fluorescence (pXRF)." *Journal of Archaeological Science Reports* 11: 381–389.

Mehta, Jayur M., Zhixiong Shen, and Rachel Stout-Evans. 2016b. "Mississippian Monumentality in the Yazoo Basin: Recent Investigations at the Carson Site (22CO505), Northwestern Mississippi." *Southeastern Archaeology* 36 (1): 14–33.

Morse, Dan F. 1975. *Report of Excavations at the Zebree Site, 1969*. Research Report 4. Fayetteville: Arkansas Archaeological Survey.

Morse, Dan F., and Phyllis A. Morse. 1980. *Excavation, Data Interpretation, and Report on the Zebree Homestead Site, Mississippi County, Arkansas*. Fayetteville: Arkansas Archaeological Survey.

Morse, Dan F., and Michael C. Sierzchula. 1977. "The Zebree Microlithic Industry." In *Excavation, Data Interpretation, and Report on the Zebree Homestead Site, Mississippi County, Arkansas*, ed. Dan F. Morse and Phyllis A. Morse, 19–33. Fayetteville: Arkansas Archaeological Survey.

Morse, Phyllis A., and Dan F. Morse. 1990. "The Zebree Site: An Emerged Early Mississippian Expression in Northeast Arkansas." In *The Mississippian Emergence*, ed. Bruce Smith, 51–66. Washington, DC: Smithsonian Institution Press.

Nelson, Margaret C. 1991. "The Study of Technological Organization." *Archaeological Method and Theory* 3: 57–100.

Newlander, Khori, Nathan Goodale, George T. Jones, and David G. Bailey. 2015. "Empirical Study of the Effect of Count Time on the Precision and Accuracy of pXRF Data." *Journal of Archaeological Science: Reports* 3: 534–548.

Ortega, David, Juan José Ibañez, Lamya Khalidi, Vicenç Méndez, Daniel Campos, and Luís Teira. 2013. "Towards a Multi-Agent-Based Modelling of Obsidian Exchange in the Neolithic Near East." *Journal of Archaeological Method and Theory* 21 (2): 461–485.

Parry, William, and Robert Kelly. 1987. "Expedient Core Technology and Sedentism." In *The Organization of Core Technology*, ed. Jay K. Johnson and Carol A. Morrow, 285–309. Boulder: Westview.

Pauketat, Timothy R. 1997. "Cahokian Political Economy." In *Cahokia: Domination and Ideology in the Mississippian World*, ed. Timothy R. Pauketat and Thomas E. Emerson, 30–51. Lincoln, University of Nebraska Press.

Pauketat, Timothy R. 2004. *Ancient Cahokia and the Mississippians*. Cambridge: Cambridge University Press.

Pauketat, Timothy R. 2007. *Chiefdoms and Other Archaeological Delusions*. Lanham, MD: Altamira.

Peregrine, Peter N., and Stephen H. Lekson. 2012. "The North American Oikoumene." In *The Oxford Handbook of North American Archaeology*, ed. Timothy R. Pauketat, 64–72. Oxford: Oxford University Press.

Phillips, Philip. 1970. *Archaeological Survey in the Lower Yazoo Basin, Mississippi, 1949–1955*. Papers of the Peabody Museum of Archaeology and Ethnology 60. Cambridge: Harvard University.

Phillips, Philip, James A. Ford, and James B. Griffin. 2003 [1951]. *Archaeological Survey in the Lower Mississippi Alluvial Valley, 1940–1947*. Tuscaloosa: University of Alabama Press.

Phillips, S. Colby, and Robert J. Speakman. 2009. "Initial Source Evaluation of Archaeological Obsidian from the Kuril Islands of the Russian Far East Using Portable XRF." *Journal of Archaeological Science* 36: 1256–1263.

Ray, Jack H. 2007. *Ozark Chipped-Stone Resources: A Guide to the Identification, Distribution, and Prehistoric Use of Cherts and Other Siliceous Raw Materials*. Special Publication 8. Springfield: Missouri Archaeological Society.

Rees, Mark A. 1997. "Coercion, Tribute, and Chiefly Authority: The Regional Development of Mississippian Political Culture." *Southeastern Archaeology* 16 (2): 113–133.

Saucier, Roger T. 1974. *Quaternary Geology of the Lower Mississippi Valley*. Arkansas Archaeological Survey Research Series 6. Fayetteville: Arkansas Archaeological Survey.

Saucier, Roger T. 1994. *Geomorphology and Quaternary Geology of the Lower Mississippi Valley*. Vicksburg, MS: Army Engineer Waterways Experiment Station.

Schnell, Frank, Vernon J. Knight, and Gail S. Schnell. 1981. *Cemochechobee: Archaeology of a Mississippian Ceremonial Center on the Chattahoochee River*. Gainesville: University of Florida Press.

Settle, Sarah E. 2012. "An Ethnobotanical Analysis of Two Late Mississippian Period Sites in the Upper Yazoo Basin." Honors thesis, University of North Carolina, Chapel Hill.

Shackley, Myra S. 2011. "X-Ray Fluorescence Spectrometry in Twenty-First Century Archaeology." In *X-Ray Fluorescence Spectrometry (XRF) in Geoarchaeology*, ed. Myra S. Shackley, 1–6. New York: Springer.

Smith, Bruce D. 1984. "Mississippian Expansion: Tracing the Historical Development of an Explanatory Model." *Southeastern Archaeology* 3 (1): 13–32.

Smith, Bruce D. 1990. "Introduction: Research on the Origins of Mississippian Chiefdoms in Eastern North America." In *The Mississippian Emergence*, ed. Bruce D. Smith, 1–8. Washington, DC: Smithsonian Institution Press.

Speer, Charles A. 2014. "LA-ICP-MS Analysis of Clovis Period Projectile Points from the Gault Site." *Journal of Archaeological Science* 52: 1–11.

Steponaitis, Vincas. 1991. "Contrasting Patterns of Mississippian Development." In *Chiefdoms: Power, Economy, and Ideology*, ed. Timothy K. Earle, 193–228. Cambridge: Cambridge University Press.

Stuckey, Sarah D., and Juliet E. Morrow. 2013. "Sourcing Burlington Formation Chert: Implications for Long Distance Procurement and Exchange." *Quarry* 10: 20–29.

Thomas, Cyrus. 1891. *Catalog of Prehistoric Works East of the Rocky Mountains*. 12th Annual Bulletin of the Bureau of American Ethnology. Washington, DC: Smithsonian Institution.

Thomas, Cyrus. 1894. *Report on the Mound Explorations of the Bureau of Ethnology for the Years 1890–1891*. 12th Annual Report to the Bureau of American Ethnology. Washington, DC: Smithsonian Institution.

Trubitt, Mary Beth. 2000. "Mound Building and Prestige Goods Exchange: Changing Strategies in the Cahokia Chiefdom." *American Antiquity* 65 (4): 669–690.

Trubitt, Mary Beth. 2003. "The Production and Exchange of Marine Shell Prestige Goods." *Journal of Archaeological Research* 11 (3): 1–34.

Yerkes, Richard W. 1983. "Microwear, Microdrills, and Mississippian Craft Specialization." *American Antiquity* 48: 499–518.

Yerkes, Richard W. 1987. *Prehistoric Life on the Mississippi Floodplain: Stone Tool Use, Settlement Organization, and Subsistence Practices at the Labras Lake Site, Illinois*. Chicago: University of Chicago Press.

Yerkes, Richard W. 1989. "Mississippian Craft Specialization on the American Bottom." *Southeastern Archaeology* 8 (2): 93–106.

Yerkes, Richard W. 1991. "Specialization in Shell Artifact Production at Cahokia." In *New Perspectives on Cahokia: Views from the Periphery*, ed. James B. Stoltman, 49–64. Madison, WI: Prehistory Press.

9

Stone Age Economics

Efficiency, Blades, Specialization, and Obsolescence

John C. Whittaker

This chapter began as comments on the symposium papers included in this volume, where a diversity of approaches, geographic locations, and tool types led me to consider common themes in light of some issues that had been rattling around in my head for a long time. Accordingly, my thanks to the organizers and participants.

Petraphilic lithic archaeologists like us bemoan the disdain some others show for stone tools and complain about the "lithic blindness" of some colleagues. Like Horowitz and Arakawa in this volume, we may feel that others see the formal tools such as Maya axes or Southwestern projectile points as the only part of lithic assemblages that could possibly be of interest, or, as Davis suggests, they may fail to recognize stone tools at all, either lacking the training to do so or believing that because they work in periods where metal tools are common, stone tools must have become extinct. As Horowitz and McCall argue in the introduction, scholars interested in current themes like practice and identity may feel that stone tools are too utilitarian and simple to be invested with much social or symbolic meaning.

Stone tools are as suitable for symbolic communication as any other artifacts, from paper clips to crucifixes, but because most are intended as utilitarian artifacts, produced by a technology that perhaps allows less variability for carrying symbolic content, economic understandings usually have the most to offer and are by far

DOI: 10.5876/9781607328926.c009

the most common theoretical underpinnings of lithic analyses. In particular, concepts of efficiency explain many things in lithic assemblages, from raw material consumption and exploitation, tool form and use, learning and trading, discard patterns and recycling to specialization and political and social organization (Ahler and Geib 2002; Bergman et al. 1999; Clark 1986; Dockall and Shafer 1993; Feder 1981; Ferguson 2008; Hester and Shafer 1984; Johnson and Morrow 1987; McAnany 1988; Shafer and Hester 1991; Sheets 1978; Torres 2000). Thus I see economic analysis of stone tools in terms of their efficiency as a theme common to almost all of the chapters in this volume, and it does not usually require very elaborate economic theorizing.

In their introduction, Horowitz and McCall discuss the sometimes baffling coexistence in sedentary societies of simple, informal, expedient stone technologies alongside complex formal tools made by specialists. As they note, the latter generally require complex systems to move raw materials and organize production and distribution. The "expedient" manufacture and use of "informal" stone tools is almost universally considered the result of economic principles of efficiency (Arakawa; Manclossi and Rosen, this volume). Perhaps no other technology is so efficient. If the material is at hand (and in many places tool stone is abundant and immediately available), a sharp cutting edge can be made literally in seconds by most members of society, with very little training. Only a little more work to shape a flake produces a "scraper" with a more robust edge suitable for a variety of cutting and scraping tasks. You can choose to spend an hour making a fine, shapely projectile point to display your status, demonstrate skill, honor the dead, or use as a really effective tool if this is culturally appropriate; but often the choice is to expend only a few minutes on a simple but perfectly usable form. Finer tools for finer purposes can be left to experts.

In many later complex sedentary societies, the formal, specialized lithic industries that overshadow the informal tools are often blade industries. To my mind, these industries represent the most ubiquitous demonstration of the efficiency principles of stone tool manufacture. The systematic production of flakes with long straight edges occurs in many cultures widely spread over the globe and through the millennia. They appear in the Indus and at Harappa (Davis, this volume) and in the Mediterranean (Manclossi and Rosen, this volume). Blades are an important component of many lithic industries in Mesoamerica as well (McCall et al. and Paling, this volume; Edens 1999; Hartenberger et al. 2000; Hirth 2003; Hirth and Andrews 2002; Johnson and Morrow 1987; Pelegrin 2006; Rosen 2013). They occur less frequently in North America but are present in some areas at Cahokia and some Hopewell sites in later prehistory (Hofman

1987; Morrow 1987) and are associated with the Clovis manifestation in very early times (Collins 1999). They are characteristic of European industries from the Upper Paleolithic through the Neolithic and beyond (Ihuel 2004). In more complexly organized societies of late prehistoric and recent times, they are often the dominant "platform" or lithic technology, serving a wide range of purposes. Always, they are accompanied by simpler "expedient" technologies.

I want to use two examples of very late blade industries to illustrate how they embody the economic principles of efficiency and related issues. These two blade industries are the production of flint blades for agricultural sickles and threshing sledges all around the Mediterranean from ancient times until recently and the historic European gunflint industries.

THE MEDITERRANEAN THRESHING SLEDGE INDUSTRY

Among the various methods of threshing to separate grain from chaff, the threshing sledge, or *tribulum*, was favored all around the dry parts of the Mediterranean (Whittaker 2000). The typical form was a heavy wooden sledge made of one or several boards, the undersides of which were studded with flint blades hammered into sockets (figures 9.1, 9.2). The threshing sledge was dragged by animals over the harvested grain on a prepared surface, breaking the chaff into small bits and separating it from the grain so the grain could be sorted out by winnowing. There is evidence that some form of threshing sledge was in use by the Bronze Age, and a widespread specialist industry in the Middle East produced large, broad "Canaanean blades" for threshing sledges and other purposes (Anderson et al. 2004; Rosen 2013; Rosen et al. 2014). Threshing sledges were always accompanied by sickles, which also had a cutting edge of stone blades. Once metal became common, metal sickles eventually replaced stone ones, but the industries producing flint blades and threshing sledges lasted into modern times. In Turkey and Cyprus, both Nick Kardulias and I have studied what was left of the industry, and the older work of Jacques Bordaz is well-known.

In Cyprus, the knappers collected flint from drainages in the south. The knappers were often but not always the same craftsmen who made the sledges, residing in the north where wood supplies were better. In more recent times, especially after the partition of Cyprus in 1976, the last sledge flintknappers in southern Cyprus no longer made the wood sledges. They continued to exploit the southern flint sources and traveled around making blades and inserting them in existing sledges of farmers all across Cyprus (Kardulias and Yerkes 1996; Whittaker 1996, 2014a).

FIGURE 9.1. *Underside of a typical old threshing sledge* (döven) *in Kastamonu, Turkey, 2009*

In Turkey, the industry was a bit different. Flint was mined in deep shafts much like the well-known Neolithic mines at Grimes Graves in England and those supplying the later Brandon gunflint knappers. At least a few Turkish villages made mining and knapping a profitable specialty. The blades they produced were sold all over the region and worked by others into the threshing sledges many local carpenters made. Jacques Bordaz (1965, 1969) documented this industry at a village called Çakmak in the 1960s. *Çakmak* means flint, gunflint, fire starter, and threshing sledge blade (figure 9.3). We went back and talked to retired knappers at Çakmak in 2008 (figure 9.4; Whittaker et al. 2009) and also found another village in a different region but with an industry that used similar tools and techniques to make similar blades for a wide regional market (Whittaker 2014a).

FIGURE 9.2. *Closer view of the flint blades inset into the underside of the threshing sledge. The sockets were cut with a special chisel.*

In both Turkey and Cyprus, every farmer had a sledge or two, and every sledge had 100 to several hundred flints, so the production of threshing sledges and their flint inserts there and elsewhere around the Mediterranean was once an enormous and important industry. The various crafts involved in producing *tribula* could be organized in a number of ways, sometimes the domain of specialists, sometimes home products. The knappers, for instance, sometimes also made the sledges but as often just the flints. Products of some of the knapping industries were widely distributed; others had a more limited range. They probably often produced strike-a-light flints and gunflints, but these became obsolete much before the sledges, and ethnographic informants in recent times have not provided information on these products. We have no information on the use of expedient flint tools in these regions, but it must have existed for a while at least.

EUROPEAN GUNFLINTS

Flintlock guns (figure 9.5) came into use in the early 1600s and were superseded in the mid-1800s by percussion and cartridge firearms but continued to

FIGURE 9.3. *Waste cores from blade making, Çakmak, Turkey, 2007*

see some use into the present. Gunflints and strike-a-lights for fire starting were important in many regions that did not use threshing sledges. There were knapping industries all over Europe, for instance, although the best-known ones were in England and France. Brandon, England, is the most famous of the world's gunflint centers, and studying the production of gunflints there influenced early archaeological knowledge of stone tools and contributed the word *knapping* to our vocabulary.

Gunflint knapping had been a cottage industry in Great Britain since the late 1600s. The knapping at Brandon was in place by the late 1700s. Some early gunflints were merely crude trimmed flakes, and in some cases, soldiers were expected to be able to make their own. However, as guns and governments became more standardized, British gunflint makers began producing regularized "spall" gunflints from flakes struck off regular cores. Sometime shortly before 1800, the British knappers learned a much more efficient process of segmenting long straight blades into quadrilateral gunflints. Reputedly, they got this process from the French (Ballin 2012; de Lotbiniere 1984; Hamilton 1987 [1980]).

FIGURE 9.4. *Retired knapper Nihat Yilmaz demonstrates flaking, Harmancik, Turkey, 2007. The hammers used by the Turkish knappers were strikingly parallel to those used by the British knappers.*

At Brandon, fine black flint was mined from deep shafts in the chalk, not far from the much older mines at Grimes Graves. The miners were generally not knappers, and both types of specialists had their own set of customs, specialized tools, and odd vocabulary. The Brandon mining, at least in later years, was an individual enterprise (Skertchly 1984 [1879]), in contrast to the teams that mined flint in the Turkish villages we visited.

As in Turkey, the knappers usually worked in small collectives, with someone who organized marketing and logistics. Knapping was done in small shops behind village houses or, famously, behind the pub in Brandon. There

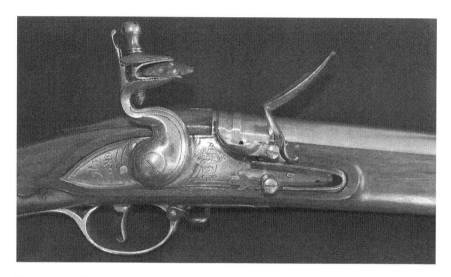

Figure 9.5. *Flintlock mechanism. The hammer holding the flint is cocked. When the trigger is pulled, it falls forward, striking sparks off the frizzen and knocking it open (as shown), exposing priming powder in the pan, which ignites, exploding the main charge in the barrel through the touchhole visible above the pan.*

was a highly standardized *chaîne opératoire* of different steps in the process of making gunflints, often performed by different craftsmen (Gould 1981; Karklins 1984; Skertchly 1984 [1879]). The large blocks of flint were first "quartered" with a heavy hammer, then shaped into cores and "flaked" to make blades, which was considered the most difficult part of the process. The flakes then passed to the knapper, who segmented them with a specialized hammer on an iron stake, producing distinctive markings on the flints as he turned out gunflints in a suite of well-defined sizes and qualities (figure 9.6). According to Sydney Skertchly (1984 [1879]), the best of the nineteenth-century reporters, a skilled flaker could produce 10,000 blades a day, while a knapper could produce about 4,000 finished gunflints in the same time. The French, who made smaller blades that could only be knapped into a single finished flint per blade, were reputedly less efficient (Hamilton 1987 [1980]; Karklins 1991). Brandon probably became the primary gunflint center in England because it was near a top-quality source of flint that came in large pieces, allowing the most efficient production of high-quality gunflints.

British and French gunflints were sold all over the world. Gunflints were a critical military resource but were only good for a certain number of shots. As

FIGURE 9.6. *British gunflint blades (upper left and right) are segmented to produce characteristic waste bits (center) and finished rectangular gunflints (bottom left and right).*

the major nations of Europe were almost continually at war throughout the eighteenth and early nineteenth centuries, both at home and in their colonies, the demand was continuous. Remember also that flints were produced not just at the better-known French and British centers but in many smaller operations and in many other countries as well, although these industries have been little studied. The total output of flints is incalculable.

BLADES REPRESENT EFFICIENCY

The knot that ties all stone industries together is the principle of efficiency, and it is best exemplified in these recent Stone Age survivals into modern

STONE AGE ECONOMICS 237

times. Blades like these are the dominant "platform," or basic technology, of stone tools in complex societies.

It is often suggested that blades are the most efficient way to use material because making blades allows the production of more length of cutting edge per stone than any other technique (Sheets and Muto 1972). Although this can be contested, there is another efficiency principle that I consider much more important: blades are the fastest way to make *standardized* tools, whether household cutting gear, prehistoric harvest and threshing tools, or, in my examples, the few stone tools that survived into the Industrial Age.

Efficiency for standardization and relatively low cost explain the case of threshing sledges. Their teeth could be made of metal, and in fact they sometimes were—especially as sledges began to be replaced by modern mechanical technology and became scarcer and the knapping industries that supported them died out. However, a knapper can produce dozens, if not hundreds, of flint blades in the time it takes a smith to make a metal one—the stone blades are cheaper and do the job as well as or better than metal. Similarly, flint-blade sickles were only replaced by bronze when that metal became more common and less expensive (Rosen 1997).

In the case of gunflints, for over two centuries these blade segments were by far the most effective way to fire a gun or start a fire. Flint and steel constituted necessary military and household technology everywhere until supplanted by matches and percussion firearms in the middle of the nineteenth century. Only by knapping blades could small industries produce the staggering number of flints necessary to fire the world's guns and ignite its tobacco pipes and household fires. The shift from simpler flake-based gunflints to segmented blades in both France and England reflects a technological innovation responding to the need for increased production efficiency in growing industries.

We should consider other ways the efficiency of blade making allows useful standardization. For instance, it is handy if little blades for micro-drills and for the cutting edges of compound projectile points can be easily replaced in their haftings with minimal modification. Craftsmen always have tool forms they favor as well as individualized tools. Blades that are similar in shape and size are easier to use and more efficiently "changed out" as they wear without disrupting the more complex, expensive, and individually shaped non-lithic parts. Standardization improves ease of packing and transport. In the case of the ubiquitous obsidian blades of Mesoamerica, which were at least sometimes exchanged in strongly formalized systems controlled by elites, a highly standardized product was more easily treated as a countable unit or an even measure of exchange.

SOCIAL ENTANGLEMENTS

Another feature of modern lithic studies is an emphasis on the wider social and economic implications of stone tools. As any technology changes, so, too, do the social institutions that are intertwined with the production and use of every technology. The increased efficiency of production by blades in the threshing sledge and gunflint industries drives a couple of directions in the productive systems: toward expansion of the system and toward exclusivity in specialization. Efficiency or related concepts are often used to explain the rise of specialized crafts and political functionaries. Many things are made more effectively by a skilled specialist who is supported by exchanging what he or she makes with others. However, in many cases, specialists are only needed and can only be supported by complex systems, especially where, as with stone tools, simple items can often be made by anyone (Clark 1987; Horowitz and McCall, this volume).

Specialization also implies exclusion. Only a certain number of specialists in any field can be supported, and there is often competition. In the case of gunflints, the blade technique was a trade secret so important that the French government was involved in protecting it (Hamilton 1987 [1980]). Naturally, government officials did not want to allow their frequent opponent, Great Britain, to learn a better way of making military goods. Both countries also exported flints all over the world (and not just to allies), so there was commercial competition as well.

The development of specialized trades also led to expansion of those trades in early industrial markets, especially in the case of British gunflints, and the expansion of industries affects a lot of people. The stone tool industries in complex societies everywhere in the world, prehistoric to modern, do more than support specialist craftsmen or the elites who may or may not control them. They also support communities. Brandon was only one of a number of villages where knapping was a profitable specialty. The Turkish villages with flint sources and a knapping industry, like Çakmak and Gölcüğez, felt that they were relatively prosperous as a result of their specialist craft (Whittaker et al. 2009).

The specialists in any craft are intimately connected, or to use current jargon, entangled with craftsmen of other technologies, those who make the tools to make the stone tools—such as the iron hammers and their wooden handles—or who make the sledges or the guns in which the flints are used. The raw materials for all these tools, in turn, come from other specialists in mining, quarrying, smelting, woodcutting—supported *ad infinitum* by a further panorama of crafts receding into the distance. And the artisans of any trade are supported by social institutions—families, villages, guilds, temples, markets. Their products are moved by others—merchants, lords, middlemen, shopkeepers, government contractors—through different systems of exchange that may be patron-client relationships, capitalistic markets, or other forms.

One reason for the longevity of some stone tools is that so many people depend on them both socially and economically. When stone tools are replaced, these people are displaced, and the institutions surrounding the manufacture, distribution, and use of the tools refocus on other enterprises or wither away. Replacement and obsolescence can usually be explained by efficiency principles as well. Flintlocks were rapidly replaced by more reliable percussion ignition systems in the early to mid-1800s. Britain's military, for instance, began the transition to percussion muskets in the 1830s. Flintlocks continued to hang on where they were cheaper or more obtainable than newer guns or their ammunition, as in Africa and India (Cranmer 2004; Harding 1999; Warnier 1980; White 1971). In Cyprus in the 1950s and after economic liberalization in Turkey in 1980, threshing machines driven by gasoline-powered tractors began to replace threshing sledges. They were faster but more expensive, so not everyone had access. A few farmers preferred threshing sledges and their animals for aesthetic reasons, and sledge threshing produced a somewhat different quality of chopped chaff, which was important as animal fodder and for temper in mud bricks (Whittaker 2014b).

Knappers everywhere responded to changing circumstances. Our Cypriot informant restricted his movements and trade to more local consumers and eventually abandoned knapping and took up other businesses. The Turkish knappers also gave up for the most part, although at least one continued to use his knapping skills in making flint blocks for ball mills that ground clay for a very different industry: fine ceramics. The British gunflint industry shriveled through the late 1800s and into the next century, supporting itself by supplying flintlock users in Africa and elsewhere and making specimens of the old craft for museums and collectors (Whittaker 2001). The last of the Brandon knappers who was trained in the traditional context maintained his knapping as a sideline until he died in 1996 (Gould 1981; Ruhe 1997; Whittaker 2001). A few new knappers continue to supply flintlock shooters and hunters, mostly in America, but both the range of products and the number of knappers making them are merely a vestige of the large industry of the 1800s. As the knapping industry faded, all of the subsidiaries that supported it also dried up, and the villages that had made their living from gunflints moved on to other pursuits.

Stone tool industries, like any other pursuit, can be assigned symbolic meanings and values by the changing society around them. At Brandon today, the archaeological imprint of blades and lithic specialization remains in the form of cottages built of flint blocks, knapping debris in every exposed patch of ground, and some pride in the local heritage expressed in the museum and the Flintknappers Pub with a colorful sign. In Turkey, many traditions are devalued as "old-fashioned" in a modernizing nation, and the ancient knapping industry is little known beyond local memory and the curiosity of archaeologists.

REFERENCES

Ahler, Stanley A., and Phil R. Geib. 2002. "Why the Folsom Point Was Fluted: Implications from a Particular Technofunctional Explanation." In *Folsom Technology and Lifeways*, ed. John E. Clark and Michael B. Collins, 371–390. Lithic Technology, Special Publication 4. Walnut Creek, CA: Left Coast Press.

Anderson, Patricia C., Jacques Chabot, and Annelou van Gijn. 2004. "The Functional Riddle of 'Glossy' Canaanean Blades and the Near Eastern Threshing Sledge." *Journal of Mediterranean Archaeology* 17 (1): 87–129.

Ballin, Torben Bjarke. 2012. "'State of the Art' of British Gunflint Research, with Special Focus on the Early Gunflint Workshop at Dun Eistean, Lewis." *Post-Medieval Archaeology* 46 (1): 116–142.

Bergman, Mary Jane, April K. Sievert, and Thomas R. Whyte. 1999. "Form and Function of Bipolar Lithic Artifacts from the Three Dog Site, San Salvador, Bahamas." *Latin American Antiquity* 10 (4): 415–432.

Bordaz, Jacques. 1965. "The Threshing Sledge." *Natural History* 74 (4): 26–29.

Bordaz, Jacques. 1969. "Flint Flaking in Turkey." *Natural History* 78 (2): 73–77.

Clark, John E. 1986. "From Mountains to Molehills: A Critical Review of Teotihuacan's Obsidian Industry." *Research in Economic Anthropology*, Supplement 2: 23–74. Greenwich, CT: JAI Press.

Clark, John E. 1987. "Politics, Prismatic Blades, and Mesoamerican Civilization." In *The Organization of Core Technology*, ed. Jay K. Johnson and Carol A. Morrow, 259–284. Boulder: Westview.

Collins, Michael B. 1999. *Clovis Blade Technology: A Comparative Study of the Keven Davis Cache, Texas*. Austin: University of Texas Press.

Cranmer, Christian. 2004. *Treasure Is Where You Find It: The Thirty-Year Quest to Save the Royal Armory of Nepal*. Godstone, UK: Tharston.

de Lotbiniere, Seymour. 1984. "Introduction: Updating Skertchly." In *On the Manufacture of Gun-Flints, the Methods of Excavating for Flint, the Age of Palaeolithic Man, and the Connexion between Neolithic Art and the Gun-Flint Trade*, ed. Sydney B.J. Skertchly, v–viii. Bloomsfield, ON: Museum Restoration Service. First published 1879 by Memoirs of the Geological Society of England and Wales, London.

Dockall, John E., and Harry J. Shafer. 1993. "Testing the Producer-Consumer Model for Santa Rita Corozal, Belize." *Latin American Antiquity* 4 (2): 158–179.

Edens, Christopher. 1999. "The Chipped Stone Industry at Hacinebi: Technological Styles and Social Identity." *Paléorient* 25 (1): 23–33.

Feder, Kenneth L. 1981. "Waste Not, Want Not—Differential Lithic Utilization and Efficiency of Use." *North American Archaeologist* 2 (3): 193–205.

Ferguson, Jeffrey R. 2008. "The When, Where, and How of Novices in Craft Production." *Journal of Archeological Method and Theory* 15: 51–57.

Gould, Richard A. 1981. "Brandon Revisited: A New Look at an Old Technology." In *Modern Material Culture: The Archaeology of Us*, ed. Richard A. Gould and Michael Schiffer, 269–282. New York: Academic.

Hamilton, Theodore M. 1987 [1980]. "The Gunflint in North America." In *Colonial Frontier Guns*, ed. Theodore M. Hamilton, 138–147. Chadron: Fur Press. Reprint, Union City, TN: Pioneer Press.

Harding, David F. 1999. *Smallarms of the East India Company 1600–1856*, vol. 3: *Ammunition and Performance*. London: Foresight Books.

Hartenberger, Britt, Steven Rosen, and Timothy Matney. 2000. "The Early Bronze Age Blade Workshops at Titris Hoyuk: Lithic Specialization in an Urban Context." *Near Eastern Archaeology* 63 (1): 51–58.

Hester, Thomas R., and Harry J. Shafer. 1984. "Exploitation of Chert Resources by the Ancient Maya of Northern Belize, Central America." *World Archaeology* 16 (2): 157–173.

Hirth, Kenneth G., ed. 2003. *Mesoamerican Lithic Technology: Experimentation and Interpretation*. Salt Lake City: University of Utah Press.

Hirth, Kenneth G., and Bradford Andrews, eds. 2002. *Pathways to Prismatic Blades: A Study in Mesoamerican Obsidian Core-Blade Technology*. Monograph 45. Los Angeles: Cotsen Institute of Archaeology, University of California.

Hofman, Jack L. 1987. "Hopewell Blades from Twenhafel: Distinguishing Local and Foreign Core Technology." In *The Organization of Core Technology*, ed. Jay K. Johnson and Carol A. Morrow, 87–118. Boulder: Westview.

Ihuel, Ewen. 2004. *La Diffusion du Silex du Grand-Pressigny dans le Massif Armoricain au Néolithique*. Bulletin de l'Association des Amis du Musée du Grand-Pressigny Supplement 2. Indre-et-Loire: Comité des Travaux Historiques et Scientifiques.

Johnson, Jay K., and Carol A. Morrow, eds. 1987. *The Organization of Core Technology*. Boulder: Westview.

Kardulias, P. Nick, and Richard W. Yerkes. 1996. "Microwear and Metric Analysis of Threshing Sledge Flints from Greece and Cyprus." *Journal of Archaeological Science* 23: 657–666.

Karklins, Karlis. 1984. "The Gunflint Industry at Brandon." *Canadian Journal of Arms Collecting* 22 (2): 51–59.

Karklins, Karlis. 1991. "French Gunflint Manufacture and the New Edinburgh Encyclopedia (First American Edition)." *Arms Collecting* 29 (1): 17–19.

McAnany, Patricia. 1988. "The Effects of Lithic Procurement Strategies on Tool Curation and Recycling." *Lithic Technology* 17 (1): 3–11.

Morrow, Carol A. 1987. "Blades and Cobden Chert: A Technological Argument for Their Role as Markers of Regional Identification during the Hopewell Period in Illinois." In *The Organization of Core Technology*, ed. Jay K. Johnson and Carol A. Morrow, 119–150. Boulder: Westview.

Pelegrin, Jacques. 2006. "Long Blade Technology in the Old World: An Experimental Approach and Some Archaeological Results." In *Skilled Production and Social Reproduction*, ed. Jan Apel and Kjel Knutsson, 37–68. Uppsala, Sweden: Societas Archaeologica Upsaliensis.

Rosen, Steven A. 1997. *Lithics after the Stone Age: A Handbook of Stone Tools from the Levant*. Walnut Creek, CA: Altamira.

Rosen, Steven A. 2013. "Arrowheads, Axes, Ad Hoc, and Sickles: An Introduction to Aspects of Lithic Variability across the Near East in the Bronze and Iron Ages." *Lithic Technology* 38 (3): 141–149.

Rosen, Steven A, Aaron Shugar, and Jacob Vardi. 2014. "Function and Value in Sickle Segment Analysis: Odellian Perspectives." In *Contemporary Perspectives on Lithic Analysis*, ed. Michael J. Shott, 116–130. Salt Lake City: University of Utah Press.

Ruhe, Ben. 1997. "Obituary: Last Brandon Gunflint Knapper Dies." *Lithics* 17–18: 2.

Shafer, Harry J., and Thomas R. Hester. 1991. "Lithic Craft Specialization and Product Distribution at the Maya Site of Colha, Belize." *World Archaeology* 23 (1): 79–97.

Sheets, Payson. 1978. "From Craftsman to Cog: Quantitative Views of Mesoamerican Lithic Technology." In *Papers on the Economy and Architecture of the Ancient Maya*, ed. Raymond V. Sidrys, 40–71. Monograph 8. Los Angeles: Institute of Archaeology, University of California.

Sheets, Payson D., and Guy R. Muto. 1972. "Pressure Blades and Total Cutting Edge: An Experiment in Lithic Technology." *Science* 175: 632–634.

Skertchly, Sydney B.J. 1984 [1879]. *On the Manufacture of Gun-Flints, the Methods of Excavating for Flint, the Age of Palaeolithic Man, and the Connexion between Neolithic Art and the Gun-Flint Trade*. Bloomsfield, ON: Museum Restoration Service. First published 1879 by Memoirs of the Geological Society of England and Wales, London. Reprint, Bloomsfield, ON: Museum Restoration Service.

Torres, John A. 2000. "Changing Lithic Technology during the Basketmaker-Pueblo Transition." In *Foundations of Anasazi Culture: The Basketmaker-Pueblo Transition*, ed. Paul F. Reed, 221–229. Salt Lake City: University of Utah Press.

Warnier, Jean-Pierre. 1980. "Trade Guns in the Grassfields of Cameroon." *Paideuma* 26: 79–92.

White, Gavin. 1971. "Firearms in Africa: An Introduction." *Journal of African History* 12 (2): 173–184.

Whittaker, John C. 1996. "Athkiajas: A Cypriot Flintknapper and the Threshing Sledge Industry." *Lithic Technology* 21 (2): 108–119.

Whittaker, John C. 2000. "Alonia and Dhoukanes: The Ethnoarchaeology of Threshing in Cyprus." *Near Eastern Archaeology* 63 (2): 62–69.

Whittaker, John C. 2001. "'The Oldest British Industry': Continuity and Obsolescence in a Flintknapper's Sample Set." *Antiquity* 75 (288): 382–390.

Whittaker, John C. 2014a. "The Manufacture and Use of Threshing Sledges." In *Exploring and Explaining Diversity in Agricultural Technology*, vol. 2: *EARTH*, ed. Annelou van Gijn, John C. Whittaker, and Patricia C. Anderson, 143–146. Oxford: Oxbow Books.

Whittaker, John C. 2014b. "Some Principles of Technological Decline: The Case of the *Tribulum*." In *Exploring and Explaining Diversity in Agricultural Technology*, vol. 2: *EARTH*, ed. Annelou van Gijn, John C. Whittaker, and Patricia C. Anderson, 357–358. Oxford: Oxbow Books.

Whittaker, John C., Kathryn Kamp, and Emek Yilmaz. 2009. "Çakmak Revisited: Turkish Flintknappers Today." *Lithic Technology* 34 (2): 93–110.

Contributors

Fumiyasu Arakawa holds a PhD in anthropology from Washington State University and is the University Museum director and an associate professor at New Mexico State University. He specializes in southwestern archaeology, particularly the Mesa Verde and northern Rio Grande region, where he focuses on lithic analysis, GIS, and pottery temper analysis. His research interests include lithic technological organization, sociopolitical organization, and ceramics in the Mesa Verde region. He is also an associated researcher at the Crow Canyon Archaeological Center.

Mary A. Davis is a PhD candidate in the Department of Anthropology at the University of Wisconsin–Madison. Her dissertation work focused on the blade tools of Harappa, Pakistan, creating a functionally aimed classification system to examine variation in the sub-assemblages of different neighborhoods and mounds. Her research focuses on understanding social groups and interaction networks during the urbanization of northwest South Asia and the Indo-Iranian landscapes. Her other research interests include lithic technologies, technological and material culture studies, the study of urbanism, and the application of spatial and digital technologies to archaeology.

James Enloe received his PhD in anthropology from the University of New Mexico and holds the rank of professor in the Department of Anthropology at the University of Iowa. He has worked in Georgia, New Jersey, Missouri, New Mexico, Colorado, Alaska, France, Russia, and Namibia. Most of his research deals with zooarchaeological and spatial analyses of Middle and Upper Paleolithic rockshelter and open-air sites, but he is particularly skilled at excavation procedures and concerned with assessing the integrity of archaeological deposits.

Dan M. Healan received his PhD in anthropology from the University of Missouri and is Professor Emeritus in the Department of Anthropology at Tulane University. His theoretical and analytical specialties include urbanism, household organization and production, lithic technology, and quantitative methods. He has conducted prior and ongoing research at the Early Postclassic city of Tula, Hidalgo, and investigation of prehispanic settlement and obsidian exploitation in the Ucareo/Zinapécuaro region of Michoacan.

Rachel A. Horowitz holds a PhD in anthropology from Tulane University and is a lecturer in the Department of Anthropology at Appalachian State University. Her research interests include lithic technology, technological organization, economic organization, and the Maya. Her current research explores lithic production and its economic role among the Maya of western Belize. She has also performed research in the western and southeastern United States, Mexico, and Namibia. Her research has been published in several journals and edited volumes, including *American Antiquity*, *Paleoanthropology*, and the *Journal of Field Archaeology*.

Francesca Manclossi received her PhD in 2016 in a joint program from the University of Paris Ouest–Nanterre la Défense and Ben-Gurion University of the Negev. Her doctoral thesis is titled "From Stone to Metal: Dynamics of Technological Changes in the Lithic Industries in the South Levant (4th–1st Millennium BCE)." She received her AB in archaeology of the Near East at the University of Pisa (2008) and her MA in prehistory at the University of Paris (2010). She is a post-doctoral fellow at the Centre de Recherche Français in Jerusalem. Her research focuses on one of the most important technological changes in the history of mankind: the shift from stone to metal. Lithic and metallurgy are two concurrent technologies, and their comparison can clarify processes, dynamics, and modalities that explain the disappearance of flint industries and the development of metallurgy. Using a technological approach that integrates archaeology, sociology, and anthropology with material analysis of stone and metal tools, her approach aims to reconstruct historical scenarios concerning one of the key moments in technological evolution.

Theodore Marks received his PhD in anthropology from the University of Iowa and is a member of the faculty at the New Orleans Center for Creative Arts. He specializes in raw material sourcing of stone tools from Late Pleistocene archaeological sites in South Africa. He has led surveys and excavations at three sites in Namibia since 2009 and has published on this work in journals in the United States and South Africa.

Grant S. McCall received his PhD in anthropology from the University of Iowa and is executive director of the Center for Human-Environmental Research (CHER) and an associate professor in the Department of Anthropology at Tulane University. McCall's interests include stone tool technology, human evolution, rock art research, hunter-gatherer ethnology, African prehistory, and political philosophy. He is also the editor of the journal *Lithic Technology*.

Jayur Madhusudan Mehta is an assistant professor in anthropology at Florida State University. As an archaeologist, he is focused on human-environment relationships and the consequences of French and Spanish colonization in the Gulf South. He has conducted excavations in the United States and Mexico and is PI for the Carson Mounds Archaeological Project (CMAP), a long-term study of the development of hierarchical and agricultural monument-building societies in the Lower Mississippi Valley, and Resilience in the Ancient Gulf South (RAGS), an interdisciplinary investigation into delta formation, hunter-gatherer settlement dynamics, and monumentality in formerly aggrading, currently subsiding environments.

Jason S.R. Paling is a teaching lecturer in the Social Sciences Department at Plymouth State University in Plymouth, New Hampshire. His experience in Mesoamerican archaeology focuses on the impact of trade and the early development of economic hierarchies. Paling's research is informed by active field projects at the sites of Chiquilistagua in Nicaragua and Hamontún in Guatemala.

Steven A Rosen serves as vice president for external affairs at Ben-Gurion University of the Negev and holds the Canada Chair in Near Eastern archaeology. He received his AB in mathematics and anthropology from the University of California at Berkeley (1975) and his advanced degrees from the University of Chicago (AM 1978, PhD 1983). Prior to joining Ben-Gurion University in 1988, he worked as a survey team leader for the Emergency Survey of the Negev. He served as editor of the *Journal of the Israel Prehistoric Society* for seven years, is on the scientific board of *Paléorient*, and has been a member of the Archaeological Council of Israel since 1997. He is the author of six books and over 150 professional papers. Current research focuses on the archaeology of mobile pastoralists in the Negev and deserts of the southern Levant and lithic industries from the Metal Ages. Among field projects, he directed excavations at the Camel site, an Early Bronze Age encampment in the central Negev; the Neolithic cult center of Ramat Saharonim in the Ramon Crater; shepherd stations in rock shelters in the Negev; the lithic workshop at Titris Hoyuk in eastern Turkey, and other sites. His book *Lithics after the Stone Age* (Altamira 1997) won the American Schools of Oriental Research G. E. Wright publication prize (1998). His most recent book is *Revolutions in the Desert: The Rise of Mobile Pastoral Societies in the Southern Levant* (Routledge 2017).

John Whittaker teaches at Grinnell College as an anthropologist doing mostly archaeology, "specializing in old, dead, and dirty." He has worked all over the world but most frequently in the American Southwest. Prehistoric technologies like stone tools have always fascinated him, and replicative experiments are fun and cheap and tell us a lot that we need to know. Survivals of lithic technology are of particular current interest, as are atlatls and other early projectile technologies.

Index

Aggregate analysis, 182. *See also* Mass analysis
Agriculture: economy, 7, 89–90; maize, 219; production, 56, 98–99, 125, 150, 177; societies, 12–13, 184–186, 201, 208; tool, 6, 17, 95, 110, 188, 231
Ashkelon, 70, 77, 79, 83
Attribute analysis: method, 39, 54, 142, 143, 147, 156, 167–168, 181, 184, 187. *See also* Metric analysis

Bagasara, 54
Banawali, 54
Basketmaker period, 195
BBB Motor, 213
Belize, 89, 91, 95, 99–100, 139, 142, 144
Biface: expedient, 102, 111, 124; form, 102–104, 107, 112, 117, 123; formal tool, 13; oval, 90, 97, 103, 107, 110–112, 124; production, 5, 101–102, 148–151, 154, 164, 169; retouch, 5, 96; small, 104, 112; use, 90, 97, 110, 116, 185, 197
Blade: Canaanean, 10, 18–19, 70, 231–232; form, 101–102, 107; gunflints, 237–239; macroblade, 90, 95, 97, 102, 108, 115, 124; microblade, 102, 213; naviform, 17–18; prismatic, 17, 102, 105, 115; production, 3, 13–14, 17, 36, 40–45, 72, 164–165, 174, 178, 235–236; sickle, 6, 10, 17, 69, 231, 234; transport, 49–51; tribula (*see* sickle); use, 18–19, 45–47, 53–56, 116, 213, 215, 231
Bordaz, Jacques, 232
Bottle Creek, 214
Brandon, England, 232–236, 240–241
Bronze Age, 10–11, 18, 38–39, 54, 58, 69–70, 84, 232
Buenavista del Cayo (Buenavista), 142, 151–152, 154
Buenavista device, 152, 153
Bullard, William, 99
Burin, 106, 108, 113–114, 116–118
Burlington chert, 209–214, 217–222

Cahokia, 208–209, 212–215, 220, 222, 231
Çakmak, 232, 235, 240
Callar Creek Quarry (CCQ), 141, 143–144, 146–154
Cambay, 140
Canaanean blade. *See* Blade: Canaanean
Carson, 209–212, 214–221
Castle Rock Pueblo, 200
CCQ. *See* Callar Creek Quarry
Cemochechobee, 214
Central Mississippi Valley (CMV), 209, 212
Cerros, 90, 95–96, 99, 110, 116
Chaa Creek, 155
Chaco Canyon, 199
Chaîne opératoire, 5, 44, 70, 235
Chalcatzingo, 13–14, 19, 165–168, 170–172, 174, 177–182

Chalcedony, 90, 96–97, 106, 109–111, 115, 195
Chalcolithic, 40, 48, 69, 84
Chan, 154–155
Chert: access, 13, 101, 192, 209–218, 220–222; artifacts, 45, 48, 90, 93, 95–97, 102, 164–168; extraction, 41, 140–146; production, 7, 11, 14, 19, 44, 148–150, 152–156, 177–182; raw material, 3, 8, 39, 49, 51, 54–55, 109–111, 115–120, 123–124
Chiefdom, 219
Cival, 121, 125
CMV. *See* Central Mississippi Valley
Colha, 90, 95–97, 99, 102, 116–117, 124, 149–151
Contact period, 17
Coosa, 219
Copper, 36, 39, 58, 69, 219
Core: bipolar, 186; distribution, 50, 58, 191–192; formal, 17–19, 36, 41–44, 115–119, 234–235; informal, 13, 15, 22, 72–75, 78–81, 96, 105–106, 114, 147–149, 168–169; polyhedral, 74, 106, 109, 114, 115, 118–120, 124; production, 3, 5–7, 15, 45–48, 70, 101, 120–124, 143, 150, 154, 213; reduction, 14, 164, 166, 170–174, 178, 185; use, 54
Corozal (Santa Rita Corozal), 90, 95–96, 99, 110
Cortex: frequency, 47, 54, 121–122; raw material, 71–72, 145; relation with production, 45, 80–81, 97, 101–102, 185, 187
Craft, 3, 49, 58
Craft production: economy, 14; organization of, 90–91, 93–95, 98–99, 148, 150, 164, 178; study of, 15, 16, 20–21, 101, 180; types, 125, 213; workshop, 9, 19, 209
Craft specialist, 4, 6, 12, 17–18, 37, 50, 94, 232, 235, 239–240
Crescent Quarry, 209–213, 215–221
Crow Canyon, 187, 199–200
Cuello, 90, 96–97, 102, 104, 116
Curation, 12–13, 49

Debitage: production, 41, 45, 70, 95–98, 121–122, 124, 143, 145–155, 191–193; study of, 90–91, 101, 181, 184–187, 196–198, 201
Decortication, 44, 81
Depopulation, 196, 200–201
Dholavira, 54
Dolomitic, 102
Döven, 233
Drill, 117, 167, 169, 213–215, 239

Eastern Woodlands, 208
El Mirador, 90, 95
El Pedernal, 98, 101
El Pilar, 98
El Pozito, 110
Elite: individuals, 3–5, 91–94, 97, 213, 239–240; production, 17, 19, 153, 164–165, 178–179, 209
Endscraper, 56
Ethnographic, 13, 18, 50, 188–190, 233
Ethnoarchaeology, 166, 177
Expedient biface. *See* Biface: expedient
Expedient: production, 3–4, 7, 16–17, 19, 96, 173–179, 181–182, 186; technologies, 11, 12, 15, 20, 70, 84, 164–169, 230–231; tools, 56, 116, 124–125; use, 13, 101, 233
Expedient uniface. *See* Uniface

Fall-off, 193
Figurehut Tract, 213
Flake: decortication, 44, 70, 72, 97, 101; expedient, 17; production, 15, 41, 45, 47, 50, 69, 73–74, 78, 81–82, 96, 102, 121, 147, 165, 168, 172, 186, 190, 215; retouched, 56, 78, 80, 123–124, 174; tool, 82, 90, 116, 119, 123, 125, 147, 148–150, 154, 230, 234; unretouched, 13, 78, 80, 82–84, 126, 169; utilized, 12, 16, 184, 197
Flake tool. *See* Flake: tool
Flint, 69, 71–72, 74, 78, 84, 231–234, 240
Flintknapper, 50, 78, 185–186, 209, 232, 236
Flintknappers Pub, 241
Flintlock gun, 233, 237, 240–241
Formal biface. *See* Biface: formal
Formal tool: economies, 8; production, 12–13, 84, 94–98, 116, 148, 229–230; types, 70, 110, 124, 143
Formative period, 17, 165
Four Corners, 190

General Utility Biface (GUB), 103, 110, 148–149
Government Mountains, 196, 198
Greco-Roman, 9
Greenstone, 165
Grimes Graves, 232, 234
Guatemala, 17, 89, 91, 100, 144
GUB. *See* General Utility Biface
Gulf Coast, 165, 178, 182
Gunflints, 10, 231, 233–241

Hammerstone, 101, 106, 109, 114, 116, 118–120, 124, 167, 169, 191
Hamontún, 89, 91–92, 100–102, 107, 109–114, 116–118, 126
Harappa, 36–39, 45–53, 56, 58
Hard hammer, 78, 104–105
Harmancik, 236
Hernando de Soto, 211, 219, 221
Hideworker, 11
Holmul, 92, 100, 120, 124–125
Hopi, 189, 190, 196
Household: discard, 110, 120–121; economies, 165, 177, 181, 186, 189, 237, 239; production, 8, 22, 101, 111, 115–116, 123–126, 139, 142, 144–151; specialists, 90–99, 154, 213, 215
Hunter-gatherer, 4, 7, 13, 22, 143, 176

ICP-MS. *See* Inductively coupled plasma mass spectroscopy
Inductively coupled plasma mass spectroscopy (ICP-MS), 216
Indus, 36–40, 45, 48–49, 51, 54, 58
Industrial Age, 238
Industrial production, 10, 58, 240
Invasiveness, 57
Iron Age, 69–70

Jasper, 215–216
Jemez Mountains, 196–198

K'axob, 90, 95–96, 99, 102, 110, 116
K'o, 89, 91–92, 100, 109, 115, 118–123, 126
Kalibangan, 54
Kastamonu, 233
Khambhat. *See* Cambay
Kichpanha, 110, 117
Kokeal, 99
Kot Diji, 38–39, 58

Labras Lake, 213
Lacandon, 11
Lamanai, 99
Levallois, 3
Life-way, 4, 7
LMV. *See* Lower Mississippi Valley (LMV)
Lohmann, 213
Long distance, 19, 36–37, 90–91, 124, 139, 141, 178, 192, 198, 219
Lower Mississippi Valley (LMV), 209, 212
Lubbub Creek, 214

Macroblade. *See* Blade: macroblade
Malyan, 45
Mano, 114, 188
Marketplace, 51, 142, 151, 153–154
Mass analysis, 101, 185, 187. *See also* Aggregate analysis
Maya: Classic, 14, 93–94, 98–100, 139, 142, 144, 152, 155; highlands, 140; lowlands, 19, 89–90, 92–93, 95, 97, 99, 110, 125, 156; Postclassic, 141; Preclassic, 89–93, 95–101, 109–111, 115–125, 141, 144; Terminal Classic, 97, 139, 142, 144, 152
Mehrgarh, 37–38
Mesa Verde region, 184, 186–187, 190, 192–193, 196–198, 200
Metate, 188
Metric analysis, 185, 187. *See also* Attribute analysis
Mexico, 7, 17, 100, 165–166
Microblade. *See* Blade: mircroblade
Microlithic, 209, 213–214
Microwear, 54, 84
Midwest, 214
Mississippian, 208–210, 212–214, 219, 221
Mississippi River Valley, 209, 219
Mitchell, 213
Mohenjo-Daro, 42, 54, 56, 58
Mopan River, 142, 145
Mopan Valley, 141–144, 149, 152, 154
Morelos, 165
Morphology, 83, 106, 209
Morphometric, 71–72, 84
Morrison formation, 190–192, 195
Moundville, 214
Mount Taylor, 196, 198
Multicrafting, 9, 98, 124–125
Multifaceted, 58, 173
Multifunctional, 58, 148–149
Multipurpose, 57, 116

Nasharo, 54
Naviform. *See* Blade: naviform
NBCBZ. *See* Northern Belize Chert-bearing Zone
Near East, 10–11, 17–19
Neolithic, 3, 17, 37–38, 48, 184, 201, 231–232
New River, 99
Nohmul, 99, 110
Non-diagnostic, 69
Nondestructive, 196

Northern Belize Chert-bearing Zone (NBCBZ), 90–91, 97, 111, 115, 125, 142

Obsidian: production, 10–11, 14, 17–19, 140, 164–166, 180, 182, 239; raw material, 3, 12, 192, 196–201, 216; study of, 156, 178
Olmec, 17, 19, 165, 178
Ouachita, 216
Outcrop, 41, 90, 97, 101, 123, 193, 209, 210–212, 214, 219, 221
Oval biface. *See* Biface: oval
Overexploited, 119
Ozark Mountains, 210–211, 215, 217–218, 220–221

Pakistan, 36–38, 59
Paleogene, 142
Paleolithic, 41–42, 231
Peckingstone, 188, 190–192
Petén, 97, 100, 110, 124–125
Piedras Negras, 14, 93, 98
Plio-Pleistocene, 7
Polyhedral core. *See* Core: polyhedral
Portable X-Ray Florescence (pXRF), 211, 216, 220–221. *See also* X-ray florescence
Post-depositional, 49, 71–72
Practice theory, 15, 20
Pressure flaking, 40, 105, 186
Prismatic blade. *See* Blade: prismatic
Producer-consumer, 95–96
Projectile point, 3, 167, 169, 176, 185–188, 190, 192, 197, 229, 231, 239
Pseudo-glyph, 152
Pulltrouser Swamp, 90, 95–96, 99, 102, 116
Punjab, 38

Quartz, 106, 109–111, 115, 118–119, 195
Quiz Quiz, 219

Ravi phase, 38, 49, 105
Raw material: access, 5, 13–14, 17–20, 48, 58, 71–73, 156; acquisition, 97, 109–110, 139, 140–142, 164–166, 172, 174–180, 182, 208, 230; analysis, 185, 187–188; production, 153, 168, 199, 240; properties, 10–12, 15–16, 101, 115, 146–147, 149; sources, 7, 9, 36–37, 40–41, 49–52, 126, 191–194, 212
Recycling: analysis, 101; discard, 20, 230; production, 5, 16, 96–97, 104, 116, 173–174
Redistribution, 51

Reduction: core, 3, 14–16, 19–22, 41, 147, 166, 173–174, 178–179, 181–186; production, 5, 96–97, 101, 143, 201; sequence, 70–74, 76–77, 80–81, 95, 124, 149, 164, 168–169, 214; stages, 6
Regionalization era, 37–38
Resharpening, 48, 96–97, 115, 124
Retouch: production, 18, 40, 44, 47, 54, 116, 147, 177, 186; tools, 5, 13, 16, 37, 56, 78, 80–83, 164, 166–169, 172–174, 181. *See also* Flake: retouched
Rift Valley, 7
Rio Pasion, 91
Rohri Hills, 39, 41–44, 50, 58

S'reni, 49
Saktunha, 97
Salesar Formation, 49
Salt Range, 49
San Estevan, 89, 91–92, 98–100, 102, 104, 107–119, 121–126
San Francisco Peak, 196
San Jose Succotz. *See* Succotz
San Lorenzo, 141, 143, 145, 148, 150–151, 154–155
Santa Clara Pueblo, 189
Santa Rita Corozal. *See* Corozal
Shadee Shaheed Shrine, 44
Shell production, 118
Shell working, 116–118
Shields Pueblo, 200
Shikarpur, 54
Sickle blade. *See* Blade: sickle
Silica, 56, 216
Siltstone, 192
Small biface. *See* Biface: small
Sourcing, 196–200, 217–221
South Asia, 40
Southeastern United States, 208–209, 212, 214, 219
Southern Levant, 69
Southwestern United States, 8, 186, 196–197, 229
Specialized: producers, 48–49, 154, 239–240; production, 3–5, 36, 45, 70, 90, 94–95, 142, 164–166, 178–182; tool forms, 6, 11, 13, 17–22, 57, 69, 231, 235
Standardized: form, 18, 41, 45, 82, 125, 234; production, 69–70, 90, 235, 237, 239
State, 9, 38, 84, 89, 94, 98

Strike-a-light, 233
Sub-saharan Africa, 7
Succotz (San Jose Succotz), 141, 143, 146, 148, 150–151, 154

Techno-typological, 54, 71
Tel Safi, 70, 75, 77, 79, 83
Tel Yarmuth, 70, 83
Tepe Hissar, 45–46
Tewa, 188–189
Thar Desert, 42
Threshing sledge, 6, 10, 231–234, 237–240
Tibaat, 99
Tikal, 90, 95, 97–98
Tool manufacture, 3, 20, 147, 190, 192, 231
Tool stone, 5, 7, 186, 188, 190, 192–194, 196, 201, 230
Toolkit, 208, 213
Tranchet, 90, 97, 103, 110, 112, 121, 124
Tranchet bit. *See* Tranchet
Tribula. *See* Blade: sickle
Tribulum. *See* Threshing sledge
Turner, 213
Typology, 54, 101, 111, 187

Uaxactún, 95
UBRV. *See* Upper Belize River Valley
Uniface, 101–102, 105, 113, 115–117, 123
Unretouched flake. *See* Flake: unretouched
Upper Belize River valley (UBRV), 141–142, 150–152, 154

Upper Paleolithic, 231
Urban, 36–39, 41–43, 45, 48, 51, 89, 98, 165
Urban period, 37, 58
Use-life, 7–8
Use-wear, 54, 58, 102, 104–106, 116, 118, 186

Village: production, 9, 149, 221, 232, 235, 240–241; settlement, 17, 38, 58, 84, 90, 99, 184, 188–190, 192, 196–197, 211, 213, 215, 217

West Asia, 22, 36
Wickliffe, 214
Woods Canyon Pueblo, 200
Workshop: production, 18–20, 22, 36, 39, 57–58, 151, 154, 165; specialization, 41, 45, 54, 90, 95, 98, 124, 178

X-ray florescence, 196–197. *See also* Portable X-Ray Florescence
Xunantunich, 142, 145–146, 151–152

Yazoo Basin, 208, 211, 213–214, 219
Yellow Jacket Canyon, 190–191
Yellow Jacket Pueblo (YJP), 186, 188, 190–191
Yilmaz, Nihat, 236
YJP. *See* Yellow Jacket Pueblo

Zebree, 213
Zuni, 189, 190, 196